FREDERICK W. TAYLOR
The Father of Scientific Management
Myth and Reality

FREDERICK W. TAYLOR
The Father of
Scientific Management
Myth and Reality

Charles D. Wrege
Rutgers University

Ronald G. Greenwood
GMI Engineering & Management Institute

BUSINESS ONE IRWIN
Homewood, Illinois 60430

Sponsoring editor: Jeffrey A. Krames
Project editor: Jean Lou Hess
Production manager: Ann Cassady
Jacket designer: Renee Klyczek Nordstrom
Compositor: Precision Typographers
Typeface: 11/13 Century Schoolbook
Printer: The Book Press, Inc.

Library of Congress Cataloging-in-Publication Data

Wrege, Charles D.
    Frederick W. Taylor, the father of scientific management : myth and reality / Charles D. Wrege, Ronald G. Greenwood.
        p.   cm.
    ISBN 1-55623-501-1
    1. Taylor, Frederick Winslow, 1856–1915. 2. Industrial engineers––United States—Biography. I. Greenwood, Ronald G. II. Title.
T55.85.T38W74 1991
670'.92—dc20
[B]   91-8345

Printed in the United States of America
1 2 3 4 5 6 7 8 9 0 BP 8 7 6 5 4 3 2 1

The authors wish to dedicate this book
to their wives for their sacrifices
during the preparation of this volume:

Beulah M. Wrege
Regina A. Greenwood

PREFACE

Frederick W. Taylor's contributions to the early development of management thought and practice have earned him the title "Father of Scientific Management."

Acccording to Dr. Harlow Person in 1920, "Taylor lived his life, so far as posterity is concerned—made his great contribution to society—chiefly in the period 1878-89 . . . Scientific Management was developed during that period and the story of its development step by step is the story of Taylor."* After Taylor's death in 1915, Frank B. Copley was employed to prepare a biography that would not only cover the period of Taylor's life stressed by Person, but also Taylor's later years. Copley's biography represents a compromise between what Copley believed were the important features of Taylor's career, and what Mrs. Taylor and Taylor's closest associates believed should be included in any book on Taylor's life and work.

---

*Harlow Person, "Final Memorandum on Manuscript of Copley's 'Taylor,' " n.d., p.2. Morris L. Cooke Papers, Franklin D. Roosevelt Library, Box 19, Folder 140.

The present volume approaches Taylor's life from a different perspective, since the authors have gathered additional information contemporary to the various phases of Taylor's career in order to present a more complete account.

The acquisition of such primary source material was a difficult task due to the passage of more than 100 years since Taylor's pioneer work. The authors, however, managed to locate information in a variety of sources: letters and manuscripts preserved in a number of archives, city directories, official deeds and maps, wills, cemetery records, and material preserved in the private collections of individuals.

The preparation of the manuscript and the search for contemporary records was aided by a number of people whose individual contributions deserve recognition. Special thanks are due Mrs. Jane C. Hartye, Curator of Special Collections at the Stevens Institute of Technology in Hoboken, New Jersey. For over ten years Mrs. Hartye has been a continual source of information and help to the senior author.

Sakae Hata and Cynthia Jankech must be thanked for their help in preparing portions of the manuscript, as is Edouard L. Desrochers, archivist at Phillips Exeter Academy, and Matthew Ebert, current Exeter student, for searching the records of Taylor's Exeter days.

A number of the senior author's students were active in several stages of the research. Kathleen Drury Mazewski, Deborah Klein, and Yan Yan Ng researched the files of law libraries for legal records concerning the Midvale Steel Company, the Simonds Rolling Machine Company, Hathorn Manufacturing Company, the Bethlehem Steel Company, the Niles-Bement-Pond Company, the Taylor family, and the Newbold family. Further research into the Taylor and Newbold families was carried out by Anthony Krisak and Kathy Barks. The original records of the suit of the Bethlehem Steel Company versus Niles-Bement-Pond Company were reviewed by Tom Hricay, Nancy Matlaga, and William Kadar. John Palmer, Frank Hocko, Patty Rice, and Sherman Trimm studied both the Philadelphia, Pennsylvania, and the Wilmington, Delaware, city directories and newspapers. Gail

Spuler and Marylu Buono-DiLorenzo examined deeds and old city maps in Philadelphia. Records of Philadelphia cemeteries were researched by Matthew Major, Mary Alice Herrigel, and Nicole Bovillon.

We must mention the existence of a remarkable set of photographs of the Midvale Steel Company, its buildings, equipment, and employees. These photographs were taken in the 1880s and 1890s and have been in the private possession of descendants of Charles Jefferson Harrah (who purchased Midvale in 1887) for over 100 years. The present Harrah descendant holding these photographs is Mrs. William Hearne of Ridgewood, New Jersey, who has graciously allowed the authors to copy all 48 photographs that were taken between 1883 and 1889. Several of these are published for the first time in this volume.

Carmon Liversedge of GMI worked long and hard with our photographs, many of which were in poor shape and over 100 years old, to make them publishable. We are most appreciative.

The late Mr. Howard C. Myers, Jr., "Mister Midvale" of Philadelphia, was director of metallurgy of the Midvale-Heppenstall Company, successor to the Midvale Company. Mr. Myers personally salvaged the company's records when they were to be discarded in 1970. This collection of papers and photographs was made available to the authors through the kindness of Mrs. Howard C. Myers of Philadelphia, Pennsylvania, and Mr. Jean Myers of Germantown Hill, Illinois.

Regina Greenwood spent many hours reading and rereading this book. Her quest for a complete sentence now and again pushed the authors to more than one rewrite.

William J. Greenwood asked many probing questions on the manuscript, some of which were answerable.

Scotti Lucasse deciphered hand scrawls and incomplete thoughts against short deadlines to get the manuscript into a word processor. We offer her our heartfelt thanks.

Finally, the authors' wives provided encouragement and support during the preparation of the manuscript. The senior author is especially grateful to his wife Beulah Wrege. Forty years ago she presented him with a copy of Taylor's *Principles of Scientific Management* as a gift. Subsequent reading of this book initiated an interest in Taylor that continues even today as reflected in the present volume.

Charles D. Wrege

Ronald G. Greenwood

CONTENTS

PART I

THE EARLY YEARS

INTRODUCTION

Frederick Winslow Taylor (1856–1915), the "Father of Scientific Management" had an important influence on the development of management methodology and theory. Since his death, there have been numerous accounts of his contributions, many of which have been erroneous, stereotyped revisions of the same story, repeated again and again. In fact, Frank B. Copley's two-volume biography of Taylor represents a compromise. Copley (1923) originally attempted to give a detailed account of Taylor's life, but Mrs. Taylor, along with the Frederick W. Taylor Cooperators (primarily Morris L. Cooke, Harlow Person, and Sanford Thompson) desired a book that would glorify Taylor's life. Copley began working on this biography in 1916 and completed the manuscript by 1919, but the original version of this manuscript did not meet with Mrs. Taylor's or the Cooperators' approval.

The group, however, was initially unable to persuade Copley to revise his original manuscript, so plans were to have it secretly rewritten. While several possible candidates for rewriting the biography were proposed, Professor Henry Greenleaf Pearson of the Massachusetts Institute of Technology was eventually selected.[1] Pearson reviewed Copley's manuscript in the summer of 1919, and by October 1, 1919, had produced a new outline, apparently differing greatly from Copley's original.

In July 1919, when Copley was made aware of the plan to secure the aid of Pearson he complained to Edward W. Clark III, the administrator of Taylor's estate. After almost a year of negotiations, a compromise was reached between Copley and the committee, and the biography was published in 1923, in its present form. The fate of Copley's original manuscript is presently unknown.

Due to the lack of an unbiased biography and because Taylor never prepared a detailed, step-by-step account of the development of his concepts, only a careful study of Taylor's personal papers and other records will give students of management a true idea of the scope of his contributions to management theory.

Taylor's unusual career may be divided into seven distinct periods:

1. Youth (1856–74).
2. Apprentice at The Enterprise Hydraulic Works in Philadelphia, 1874–78.
3. Apprentice, gang boss, foreman, master mechanic, and chief engineer, at the Midvale Steel Company, 1878–98.
4. Manager of The Manufacturing Investment Company, 1890–93.
5. Management consultant to several companies, 1893–98.
6. Consultant to The Bethlehem Steel Company, 1898–1901.
7. Spokesman and propagandist for the scientific management movement, 1901–15.

Taylor's earliest contributions at Midvale Steel in Philadelphia, in the period 1878–90, were achieved by a combination of hard work, dedication, and creativity, plus a favored status in this company because of his family's personal connections with the owners. Likewise, in many future activities, Taylor secured advantages by purchasing stock in the companies he worked for from 1890–98. Later—in1911—he was able to introduce the Taylor system into the Tabor Company in Philadelphia after purchasing a block of stock in the company.

These personal advantages and investment in these companies enabled Taylor to introduce his unique managerial ideas under conditions that another person would have found difficult if not impossible.

GROWING UP

Taylor lived in relative luxury from birth until death. His father, Franklin, a lawyer, had inherited great wealth, and the family lived in affluent Germantown, a section of Philadelphia. The Taylor family wealth came from their ownership of a large number of farms and other properties in Bucks County, Pennsylvania, and in Philadelphia. In fact, Franklin Taylor's older brother, Caleb Newbold Taylor, a bank president, devoted his entire life to managing the family assets. At his death in 1887, Caleb owned more than 1,335 acres, 9 farms, and 30 houses, the total worth $315,617.73.[2]

The Taylor family had a cook, maid, and coachman at their house on Ross Street. Nevertheless, the system of child-rearing of Emily Winslow Taylor, Fred's mother, was based on "work, and drill, and discipline," and she believed in "definite instructions" that young Fred "readily could be trained to follow them."[3]

According to his biographer, Taylor was unhappy with anything short of "the one best way" and he had the courage to "seek and follow the one best way regardless of how it might appear to others."[4] After Taylor's death in 1915, Birge Harrison, Taylor's childhood friend, described how even the game of croquet was to Taylor as a boy:

> . . . a source of study and careful analysis with Fred, who worked out carefully the angles of the various strokes, the force of the

impact, and the advantages and disadvantages of the under-stroke, the overstroke, etc.[5]

These aspects of Taylor's personality played an important role when he entered industry.

When Taylor was 13, the family went to Europe, spending the winter of 1869–70 in Paris and of 1870–72 in Germany. In a biographic letter to his close friend, Morris L. Cooke, in 1910, Taylor wrote:

> The two years in school in France, one in Germany, and then a year and a half of travel in Italy, Switzerland, Norway, England, France, Germany, Austria, etc. (all of which I disapprove for a young boy), then a return to the healthy out-of-door life of Germantown, than which I believe there is nothing finer in the world, in which sport is the leading idea, with education a long way back, second. Then two years of really very hard study, coupled with athletics, at Exeter, and what I look back upon as perhaps the very best experience of my early life, namely, the very severe Exeter discipline, in which no excuse was taken for any delinquency what-ever, and in which everybody had to toe the mark in all respects.[6]

Before going to Europe, Taylor attended the Germantown Academy. After the family's return from Germany in 1872, Fred attended Phillips Exeter Academy, a leading prep school, at Exeter, New Hampshire. His older brother by two years, Edward, followed Fred to Exeter in 1873 and stayed only for one year. The parents wanted Fred to become a lawyer and Edward to become a physician.

At Exeter, Fred was a student in the middle class in 1872, preparing for Harvard College. He was an excellent student who achieved superior results through hard work. He was also an athlete, a gymnast, a member of the boat crew, a fancy skater, and captain of the baseball team.[7] According to Copley, Taylor was an excellent pitcher:

> In those days pitchers were supposed to deliver the ball under-hand or from below the shoulder, but he needs to deliver the ball from above his shoulder, and in consequence had frequent wrangles with umpires.[8]

From this evidence, Taylor was an early advocate of pitching the baseball overhand to attain momentum and velocity.

Taylor's experience at Exeter reveals the first indication of interest that, perhaps, led him to conceive of time study. The story is interesting and best put in Taylor's own words:

> When I was at Phillips Exeter Academy, Mr. George A. Wentworth was the professor of mathematics. I, as a student, wondered how it was possible (that right along steadily, right through from the beginning to the end of the year, as we went on from month to month) that the old bull, Wentworth, as he was called, gave us a lesson which it always took me two hours to get. For the two years I was there I always had to spend two hours getting that lesson, and finally we got on to his method. We were very slow in getting on to it, however.
>
> Mr. Wentworth would sit with his watch always hid behind a ledge on his desk, and while we knew it was there we did not know what the darn thing was for. About once a week or sometimes twice a week he went through the same kind of exercise with the class. He would give a series of problems and insisted that the first boy that got them done would raise his hand and snap his fingers. Then he would call his name. He went right through the class until just half of the class held up their hands. We always noted that he got half way through the class and the middle boy would snap his fingers. He would say, "That is enough: that will do." What he wanted was to find out just how many minutes it took the average boy in the class to do the example which he gave. Then we found that Wentworth timed himself when he first tackled those problems. He got his own time by doing those five examples, and the ratio between his time for doing the examples and the time of the middle boy of the class enabled him to fix the exact stunt for us right along. The speed of the class changed. He did not change. All he had to do was to get this ratio of change, and he could say, for instance, the average of that class will take two hours if I could do the example in 25 minutes, and in this way he was able to give the class its proper stunt right along. That was the first instance of time study of mental operation which I have ever seen.[9]

If Wentworth thought the two hours was a fair assignment to give an average student, then Wentworth could assign the proper number of problems to fill a two-hour period for that student. Naturally, better students would be able to do their homework in perhaps an hour and a half and slower students might take two and a half hours, but average students should take two hours. Therefore, if problems took 20 minutes each; he would assign six problems as homework; if they only took 10 minutes each to do, he would assign 12 problems as homework, or a combination thereof, to add up to two hours of homework.

The insight, of course, is the key, and Taylor, though not knowing at the time, would devote much of his life doing this very type of work—measuring how long it should take a certain type of individual to do a certain type of work.

Taylor never graduated from Exeter, but left in 1874 after completing the 10th and 11th grades and only the fall term of his senior year (Exeter had three terms per year), because of poor health and eye problems. Although he claimed in 1897 that he had graduated in 1874, Exeter did not have graduation until the 1880s.[10] During this period it was common for Exeter students to stay until they were accepted in college, and Taylor had passed the entrance examinations for Harvard University, but didn't enroll because his eyes began to fail him. The family feared that he might actually go blind if he were to try the rigorous studies of a Harvard education. His biographer said, "As it was, his eyes had to have a long rest from reading. And so it was that, while his brother went on to college and became a physician, Frederick W. Taylor did not become a lawyer."[11] However, despite his eye problems, Taylor decided to enter industry and to learn the trades of pattern maker and machinist.

TAYLOR AS AN APPRENTICE

Taylor's career has been described by some as remarkable.[12] In 1897, only 20 years after he had been a young apprentice machinist in Philadelphia, Taylor had the opportunity to personally outline his career. In a deposition given on October 11,

1897, in a patent suit between the Simonds Rolling Machine Company and the Hathorn Manufacturing Company, Taylor said:

> I graduated at Phillips Exeter Academy in 1874 and entered Harvard College in the same year. I started to serve my apprenticeship as a pattern maker in 1874, and during the years between 1874 and 1878 completed my apprenticeship both as a pattern maker and a machinist. In 1878 I entered the employ of the Midvale Steel Works as a laborer, and during the period between 1878 and 1884 I occupied the positions of laborer, machinist, gang boss, assistant foreman, and foreman of the machine shop in the steel works. Also master mechanic in charge of the maintenance and repairs and erection of new machinery throughout all parts of the steel works. Then chief draughtsman, in charge of the design of new machinery and buildings, which were put into the works, and finally, in 1884, I became chief engineer of the works, having all of the machinery and apparatus in the works under my charge, and having also charge of the introduction and development of all new processes, and the design and construction of new machinery and buildings, which were put in. This position I filled until 1890. The greater part of my time and study, during this time, was devoted to the study of the processes and methods of melting and casting and making steel, and to the subsequent manufacture of steel while hot into a great variety of forms, rolling mills of various sizes and styles, hammers of various kinds, presses, punches, shears and smithing tools of large variety, being in use in the works.[13]

Taylor began his apprenticeship late in 1874, he said, at the Enterprise Hydraulic Works at 2215 Race Street, Philadelphia, near William Sellers & Company. It was also called Ferrell & Jones, because it was formed by a partnership of Joseph L. Ferrell and William H. Jones.[14] Ferrell lived in Germantown on Johnson Street.[15] The Taylors, who lived on Ross Street, were friends of Ferrell.

The short history of Ferrell & Jones began on March 23, 1859, when John Greenwood, a Philadelphia machinist, sold his machine shop at 2218 and 2220 Race Street, Philadelphia, to Maneah Alden. Alden operated this machine shop until

1872, when he became ill and was declared mentally ill and committed to an asylum. Maneah Alden died in 1876.

The shop lay idle for four years until it was purchased in 1876, by Joseph L. Ferrell, a mechanical engineer, for $6,583.[16]

In 1876, Ferrell formed a partnership with Jones and established the Enterprise Hydraulic Works at the Race Street location. The name of the company was more impressive than the building, which although brick, was only 42 feet wide and 70 feet deep.

Taylor testified before the house subcommittee in 1912 that he worked there from 1874 to 1878, but because Ferrell purchased this building in October 1876, Taylor could not have worked there as early as 1874. He may have worked elsewhere, but we have no data on such employment. *Gopsill's*, the Philadelphia city directory for this period, only lists Taylor's name in 1879, and does not give his occupation.[17] Copley reported that Taylor left his apprenticeship for six months in 1876, to work at the Philadelphia Centennial Exhibition.[18] The exhibition closed in September 1876, and Taylor may then have obtained his position with Ferrell.

Taylor said that during his apprenticeship he worked for low wages and was given special opportunities:

> My father had some means, and owing to the fact that I worked during my first year of apprenticeship for nothing, and the second year for $1.50 a week and the third year $1.50 a week, and the fourth year for $3.00 a week, I was given, perhaps, special opportunities to progress from one kind of work to another; that is, I told the owners of the establishment that I wanted an opportunity to learn fast rather than earn wages, and for that reason, I think I had special good opportunities to progress. I am merely saying to explain why in four years I was able to get through with my apprenticeship as a pattern maker and as a machinist. It was a very short time, as you will realize. I may add that I do not think I was a very high order of journeyman when I started.[19]

In the period that Taylor was serving his apprenticeship, his social life continued, especially his association with a boyhood friend, Clarence M. Clark, who eventually married Taylor's sister Mary. In 1880, Taylor found it difficult to secure a job as a machinist or pattern maker and began searching for other work. He was aided in his search by Clark, who had just obtained a job as a chemist at the Midvale Steel Works in 1879. The son of Philadelphia banker Edward Clark, (the richest man in Germantown), Clarence had graduated from the University of Pennsylvania with a B.A. in May, 1878.[20]

MIDVALE STEEL COMPANY

A brief history of the Midvale Steel Works is necessary to understand Taylor's career as well as the events influencing the development of his thoughts about management.

The Midvale Steel Works was located in the northwest section of Philadelphia, known as Nicetown. The moving force behind the formation of the original steel works that grew 24 years later into the Midvale Steel Company was Philip Syng Justice, who owned the wholesale hardware firm of Philip S. Justice & Company. With the growth of railroads, the company abandoned the hardware business in 1859 and concentrated on railroad supplies. In this capacity, it was the first company to import wrought iron wheels and steel rails from England into the United States.

Philip S. Justice's father, George Middleton Justice, had purchased in 1845 a large farm (called "Riverview Farm") in the town of Yardley, in Bucks County, not far from Caleb Taylor's properties.[21] The Justice family was related to the Wright family through marriage and therefore related to the Taylor family, again through marriage. A number of Fred Taylor's cousins had the surname Wright. We do not know if the Justice family had any relationships with the Taylor family because of owning property in Bucks County, but this is a possibility.

During the Civil War, Philip S. Justice & Company manufactured guns and bayonets. The actual manufacturing was done at the Bridesburg Manufacturing Company located in the Richmond section of Philadelphia.[22] In 1863, Justice had formed the Philip S. Justice Car and Locomotive Springs Manufactory. Simultaneously, he purchased a small building at the corner of 17th Street and Coates Street (now Fairmount Avenue) close to the plant of William Sellers and Company.[23]

By 1865, however, the springs business had grown so large that the Coates Street building (only 110 by 105 feet) became inadequate.[24] In the Fall of that year, Justice wrote the Baldwin Locomotive Works (located adjacent to his springs factory) that he had entered into an agreement with William Butcher of Sheffield, England, to join him in a new company:

> It is proposed to start an Establishment in this city or neighborhood, immediately, for the manufacture of Cast Steel Tyres and heavy forgings of Cast Steel with the ultimate intention of making Cast Steel Rails as well. The superintendent for the present to be in the hands of Mr. Wm. Butcher of Sheffield who proposes to bring out a complete staff of men and machinery if necessary . . . (and who) is the first manufacturer who made a solid Cast Steel Tyre in England and has had a very large experience in them, as well as all kinds of Steel. It is only reasonable to presume therefore that none of the ordinary contingent failures of a new concern will attend the present.[25]

The "Wm. Butcher" referred to by Justice was actually William Butcher, Jr., of Sheffield, England. Nevertheless, Justice implied that the William Butcher he referred to in his letter was the owner of William and Samuel Butcher Company of Sheffield, England, one of the most famous for the manufacture of steel tools.

On September 12, 1865, Justice wrote M. W. Baldwin details about plans for a company that would utilize the Bessemer process not only to manufacture rails but also other projects. In addition, Justice said that he and Butcher were also planning a chain of rail mills:

> A company formed which undertakes to manufacture and utilize the waste which with the Bessemer process comes with it can afford to sell all the rails they make at *cost* if needed and yet make money largely on their *other products*. So that you will see that one of the elements of success is in the making of such articles as tires, asels, hinges, hasps, boiler plates, shafts, and the many articles which cast steel is daily being brought into use for in connection with the heavier article of rails.[26]

Justice continued to capitalize on his supposed connection with the famous William Butcher by forming in 1866 "Butcher's Cast Steel Works," using his office address of 14 North 5th Street, Philadelphia, as the address of the company.[27]

In July of 1866, Justice finally formed the William Butcher Steel Works.[28] The stock of the William Butcher Steel Works was finally subscribed by April 1867. The company had 5,000 shares, with Philip Justice owning 3,000 shares at $100 per share. No other subscriber had more than 800 shares. William Butcher, Jr., held only 70 shares.[29]

On November 16, 1866, William Butcher, Jr., purchased as a site for the company seven acres of land in the Nicetown section of Philadelphia from Coffin Colket of the Philadelphia and Reading Railroad. The price was $7,180.18, and Butcher "got the cash necessary . . . from Mr. Smith, president of the Philadelphia and Reading Railroad."[30]

The charter for the company was issued by Governor John W. Geary on June 18, 1867. Butcher was named president, Rollin N. Rathbun (of Rathbun & Stearn Company, coal shippers) treasurer, and Edward N. Walton (a former plant foreman) as secretary.[31]

Thomas Shaw of Philadelphia was appointed superintendent and consulting engineer. Shaw and Butcher had just obtained U.S. Patent No. 65,339 for an "Improved Machine for Shoting Metals" on June 4, 1867. One year later, on June 25, 1868, this patent was assigned to the William Butcher Steel Works.[32]

On August 20, 1867, William Butcher, Jr., and his wife, Annie, sold the seven acres of land including "the buildings thereon erected and the steam engines, boilers and machinery thereon. . . ." to the William Butcher Steel Works for $175,000, giving him an apparent profit of $167,819.82 over the 1866 purchase.[33] (The cost of erecting buildings, etc., would, of course, reduce this profit.)

The purchase of the land for the Midvale site by William Butcher, Jr., in 1866 and the 1867 patent obtained by Thomas Shaw and William Butcher, Jr., of Sheffield, England, raise a series of problems. The William Butcher of Ward S. Butcher Company of Sheffield, England, that Justice implied would be the superintendent of the new steel company, was the son of James Butcher and therefore was not the William Butcher, Jr., who purchased the land in 1866. Furthermore, James's only son supposedly died in infancy in the 1820s.[34] It is more likely that the Philadelphia William Butcher, Jr., was a nephew of William Butcher of Sheffield, England. It is also unlikely that Butcher of Ward S. Butcher Company was in Philadelphia in 1868–69. He was ill in Sheffield at this time and died there on November 8, 1870.[35] Because William Butcher, Jr., remained with the Butcher Steel Works until September 22, 1871, he is obviously not the famous steel expert William Butcher who died in Sheffield in November 1870.

Evidence concerning the individual named William Butcher who was president of the William Butcher Steel Works from 1866 to 1869 can be found in *Gopsill's Philadelphia City Directory* for the years 1867 to 1870, under the names "William Butcher" and "William Butcher Steel Works" (we must note that the material for each *Gopsill's* was compiled by Isaac Costa for James Gopsill, the publisher, the year prior to publication: the 1867 material was gathered in 1866, the 1868 material in 1867, etc.). William Butcher's name as superintendent in 1870 is found in *Gopsill's* for 1871, under the names "William Butcher" and "William Butcher Steel Works."

Records of the Midvale company indicate that William Butcher, Jr., resigned as president of the company on January 10, 1870, and as superintendent on September 22, 1871.[36]

After 1870, the name "William Butcher" appears in *Gopsill's* for 1872 and 1873. In 1871 this "William Butcher" has no business address (but was living at the Continental Hotel). In 1872 he was associated with the William Butcher and Company dealing in steel, with an office address at 218 South 4th Street, and still living at the Continental Hotel. The eventual fate of this "William Butcher" is a mystery since he disappears from *Gopsill's* after 1872. A complete list of the "William Butcher" individuals associated with the steel industry in Philadelphia appears in Tble I–1.

In 1868, the company found need for a steam hammer to forge tires and purchased one (known as Hammer Number One)

TABLE I–1

List of "William Butcher" Names Associated with Steel in
Gopsill's Philadelphia City Directory, **1866–1872**

Year Data Gathered for Gopsill's	Data, Date Published, and Page Numbers	Remarks
1866	William Butcher (steel manufacturing); office, 14 North 5th Street; home, Continental Hotel (*Gopsill's*, 1867, p.277, p.1594)	Butcher's Cast Steel Works, formed by Philip Justice
1867	William Butcher, President; office, 203 Walnut Street; home, Continental Hotel (*Gopsill's*, 1868, p.314)	William Butcher Steel Works formed in July 1866
1868	William Butcher, President; office, Nicetown Lane near 22nd Street; home, Contintental Hotel (*Gopsill's*, 1869, p.209)	William Butcher Steel Works in operation
1869	William Butcher, President; office, Nicetown Lane near 22nd Street; home, 406 Walnut Street (*Gopsill's*, 1870, p.306)	William Butcher Steel Works in operation
1870	William Butcher, Superintendent; office, 407 Walnut Street; home, Continental Hotel (*Gopsill's*, 1871, p.301)	William Butcher Steel Works reorganized. Samuel Huston now president
1871	William Butcher; home, Continental Hotel (*Gopsill's*, 1872, p.286)	W. F. Durfee now superintendent of William Butcher Steel Works
1872	William Butcher (William Butcher and Company); home Continental Hotel. William Butcher and Company (William Butcher), steel; office, 218 South 4th Street (*Gopsill's*, 1873, p.281)	This William Butcher is unknown

from William Sellers and Company of Philadelphia. Because "the price of this hammer and some other equipment was paid for partly in stock," William Sellers became a stockholder in the company.[37] It is strange that the company purchased a hammer from Sellers because Thomas Shaw had patented a steam hammer on February 22, 1866, that could have been manufactured for use by the company. In 1868, Rathbun became president; Walton, secretary; and Butcher, superintendent, replacing Thomas Shaw.[38]

In 1869, the company began the relatively new process of manufacturing steel in open hearth furnaces. The many difficulties involved in this new method resulted in large financial losses. New capital was obtained by Philip Justice through Edward W. Clark & Company, a Philadelphia bank. The bulk of the funds ($80,000) came from Samuel Huston, a Philadelphia lawyer and brewer; $60,000 more came from William Sellers, John Sellers, Jr., and Edward W. Clark.[39]

Samuel Huston's first association with Butcher's began as an investment of earnings from both his law practice and his business, the brewing firm of Massey, Huston and Company.[40] The company was owned by William Massey and Samuel Huston. Massey lived in Montgomery County, Pennsylvania, close to John S. Newbold, a relative of F. W. Taylor.[41] Huston lived at 722 Pine Street in Philadelphia, but had a country home in Haverford, Lower Merion Township, Montgomery County, Pennsylvania. On April 1, 1869, he and his wife Wilhelmina, sold property in Norristown, Pennsylvania, to partially provide the funds for the reorganization of Butcher's.[42] As a brewer, Huston was a member of the United States Brewers Association. He served as a member of the Agitation Committee in 1868, where his law experience was utilized to agitate before the Secretary of the Treasury (Hugh McCulloch) and the Commissioner of Internal Revenue (E. A. Rollins) to "refund all erroneously paid taxes on malt liquors, brewed prior to September 1, 1862."[43]

The William Butcher Steel Works faced new financial difficulties during 1869, and was reorganized on January 10, 1870, with Samuel Huston as president, Henry Rutter (secretary and treasurer of the Preston Coal Importers) as treasurer, and William Butcher as superintendent.[44]

Influence of E. W. Clark

Along with the reorganization of the company in 1870, the first evidence of the influence of the Philadelphia banking house of E. W. Clark on the activities of the William Butcher Steel Works occurs. This influence appears with the construction of a large railroad bridge over the Mississippi at St. Louis, Missouri.

The bridge was designed by James Eads and was built for the Saint Louis and Illinois Bridge Company by the Keystone Bridge Company of Pittsburgh. Some of the key investors in Keystone were J. Edgar Thompson, president, and Thomas A. Scott, vice president, of the Pennsylvania Railroad; and Andrew Carnegie, who was the vice president of the Keystone Company.

In 1870, the Saint Louis and Illinois Bridge Company desperately needed a loan of $250,000, which Carnegie secured from the E. W. Clark Company. The Clarks, however, through Samuel Huston and William Sellers, had an interest in Butcher's and told Carnegie that they would only back the loan if Keystone contracted with Butcher for the 2,000 tons of chromium steel required. On March 7, 1870, Carnegie telegraphed the Clarks that Keystone would give the contract to Butcher but that this agreement would have to be a secret from the directors of the Saint Louis and Illinois Bridge Company.[45] The Butcher Steel Works signed a contract with the Keystone Bridge Company on October 24, 1870, to supply 8,800 tons of steel for the Eads bridge.[46]

The influence of the Clarks at this early stage is indicative of their power in both Butcher and Midvale Steel for more than 16 years. Since Taylor's family was friends with Clark's (Fred's sister married E. W. Clark's son Clarence on November 13, 1884), the pathway to employment for Fred and Clarence, at Midvale, was a relatively easy one.

In 1871, Thomas Shaw was again offered his old position

of superintendent but turned it down because he was already busy forming a company to manufacture his own inventions. As a result of Shaw's not accepting the position, William F. Durfee (former superintendent of the Kelly Process Company) became superintendent.[47]

The appointment of Durfee was a necessary step to enable the company to fulfill the Eads bridge contract. Because Eads' specifications called for the use of chromium in the steel, Butcher's paid the Chrome Steel Company of New York a lump sum for the right to use chromium under their patents. The original plan called for the production of the steel from open-hearth steel, but this method resulted in failure and the agreement with the Chrome Steel Company was terminated.

In 1871, efforts were once again made to produce the steel by the open-hearth method with the help of the Richmond, Potts, and Loring Company of Boston:

> . . . The contract for the Eads Bridge steel was signed in October 1870. Three months later, January 21, 1871, the first open-hearth heat was tapped under the supervision of a Mr. Dodds of the firm of Richmond, Potts, and Loring of Boston—agents in this country for the Siemens patents on regenerative heating. Dodds ran 79 heats and then Butcher took over and ran the final 13 heats of a 92-heat campaign ending September 9, 1871.[48]

All these efforts again resulted in failure, and after Durfee became superintendent he did not run the open hearth furnace for over a year. The failure was primarily due to mistakes in the furnace construction by Richmond, Potts, and Loring in 1870.[49] Durfee, instead, turned to the crucible method and produced 8,092,704 pounds of crucible steel in 1872, compared to the 665,333 pounds of Dodds-Butcher open-hearth furnace effort.[50]

On September 16, 1872, the William Butcher Steel Works was renamed the Midvale Steel Works. This name was given by William Sellers who was owner and president of the Edgemoor Iron Works in Delaware. He had chosen the name "Edgemoor" because the plant was close to the "moors" of the Delaware River and it occurred to him that the Nicetown plant was "midway between the Delaware and Schuykill Rivers. Hence, he decided upon 'Midvale'."[51]

Charles A. Brinley's Contributions

The problems associated with the manufacture of the chromium steel for the Eads bridge continued. The company still hoped to manufacture the steel by the open-hearth method and toward this end Charles A. Brinley was hired in 1873. Brinley was a young Yale chemist whose job was to place the manufacture of steel at Midvale on a scientific footing.

Brinley arrived at Midvale in July 1873. Durfee resigned in August and was replaced by Samuel Middleton, who was a relative of Philip Justice. Brinley's appointment at Midvale may have been obtained through some family relationship, since Middleton was a friend of Brinley's mother.

Our knowledge of Brinley's work at Midvale is derived from a biography of Russell Davenport, which Brinley wrote in 1905, and copies of some original Brinley letters found in the Howard Myers, Jr., papers. Brinley established a small laboratory and hired a fellow Yale chemist, Russell Davenport, to help him with the open-hearth work.[52] In July 1874, Middleton became ill and died in November 1874. By November 24, 1874, Brinley had been appointed superintendent and at this time wrote a letter to a close college friend, which gives us insight into his efforts:

> I would almost rather see you get on rapidly than do so myself. I hope we may meet in two or three years at least, each of us successful and affluent. When you come to Philadelphia I shall be able to show you a great steel works, I hope, risen from the mire under my care. But it will not do to anticipate or count the unhatched chickens.
>
> Imagine my life for a moment, and if success were assured and wealth in hand you would hardly like to change places with me. I have breakfast at 6 O. C. and from that time until 6 in the evening am in a constant whirl of business, and business that can never be done, organization improvement, even invention sometimes. I take my meals alone in my office except dinner

when Mr. Smyth and I discuss matters we have not time for during the rest of the day. In the evening I am generally off for a few hours. I come back, make the tour of the works, and go to bed with the probability of being called up again during the night. I never get away from one absorbing interest, and the result is perhaps not worth an hour of one's own hearth.[53]

Though Brinley succeeded in introducing chemistry into steel-making, financial problems continued. In January 1873, Samuel Huston, in poor health and unable to provide more money, sought aid from Clark and Sellers. This led to the issue of additional stock, first-mortgage bonds, and a note on the company, with Sellers and Clark as active managers. Even with these changes the company continued to decline, was almost bankrupt, and Huston's health continued to deteriorate.

William Sellers (1824–1905) became president of Midvale in 1873, a title he held until 1887. He was simultaneously president of Edgemoor Iron Company (which he formed in 1868). He had attended a private school, built and maintained by his father and two relations, for the education of their children. At age 14 he was apprenticed to the machinists' trade with his uncle, John Poule, and in 1845, at age 21, was foreman for Fairbanks, Bancroft & Company of Providence, Rhode Island. In 1848, he began the manufacture of machinists' tools and mill gearing in Philadelphia and then joined Edward Bancroft to form Bancroft & Sellers. His brother John Sellers, Jr., joined the firm, and in 1856, with the death of Bancroft, the firm became William Sellers & Co. Sellers was president of the Franklin Institute from 1864 to 1867.[54]

On May 13, 1873, an agreement designed to save the Midvale company was signed between Huston, Clark, and Sellers. Under this agreement, Huston was relieved of all responsibility for the debts of the corporation, and his bonds and note of Midvale were pledged, along with funds provided by Clark and Sellers, to a "guaranty fund for paying the debts of said works. . . ."[55] Under this fund, Huston was to receive a reimbursement for the money he had invested in the company. But he never received this money and eventually took Sellers and Clark to court.

In an effort to improve the debt situation of the company, Midvale solicited orders for guns for the U.S. government. On March 18, 1875, Midvale received the first order from the Bureau of Ordnance of the United States Navy to an American company for the manufacture of steel guns. These forgings were for small three-inch howitzers to be used by the United States Life-Saving Service. Midvale lacked the personnel for these howitzer forgings and hired George Roxborough, an experienced hammerman, to complete the work. Despite these efforts, the order was not completed until 1876. Midvale continued taking government contracts and by 1905 was the nation's largest defense contractor.[56]

In 1875–76, Brinley made a significant step forward by establishing a piecework system. Nalle says this occurred in the rolling mill and open-hearth furnaces in 1875:

> In 1875, Brinley introduced piecework, with most beneficial results. Previous to that time, the maximum number of tires rolled in 10 hours was 18, and the usual number 16. Under the piecework system, an agreement was made with each man in the rolling gang that he should be paid so much per tire rolled, according to the weight. Under this plan, with no changes in the machinery employed, except a simple device for keeping the roll necks cool, the production grew to from 28 to 40 tires in 10 hours, according to size. Taking 30 as an average, the increase in production was about 90 percent.
>
> There was also a marked increase in the outputs of the open-hearth furnaces. Average output of the 5-ton open-hearth in 1873 and 1874 was 8,582 pounds of good ingots per heat, and 261,059 pounds of good ingots per month; whereas in 1880 the respective outputs per heat and per month were 12,095 and 475,714 pounds. This represented an increase in output *per heat* of 41 percent, and *per month* of 83 percent.[57]

Guillemeau Aertsen joined Midvale in 1876, after graduating from the University of Pennsylvania. Because of the need for supervisory help at Midvale and because of family connections, Aertsen soon assumed executive status. Aertsen's rapid rise may be partially explained because his father, James Aertsen, was a former partner of William H. Newbold, who was related to the Taylor, Wright, and Clark families through marriage.[58] Except for a short period from 1887 to 1890, he remained at Midvale until 1924. From 1876 to 1882, he worked closely with Brinley, who informed his relatives in 1878, that "Aertsen has proved an excellent man in the hammer shop."[59]

Aertsen, in 1915 and 1917, mentioned that Brinley had developed the "Differential" Piece Rate System and that Taylor had found Brinley's piece-rate systems in use in 1881, and applied them to machine shop operations:

> He found, when he came to Midvale, piecework systems established by Brinley and cooperated in extending and elaborating these, particularly as applied to operations in the machine shops. Brinley inaugurated the "differential" piece-rate system under which a rate was based upon what was considered fair output. When this output increased, the rate for each unit was also increased so that the workman's increased earnings were more than proportionate to the increased production.
>
> Taylor did admirable work in developing and perfecting this whole system by careful and exact time studies.[60]

We may never know why Brinley refused to take credit for the development of the differential piece rate. His father had died in 1875, leaving Brinley well off financially, and therefore he may have had little interest in getting credit for either the piece-rate system or differential rate system.

Brinley's development of the differential piece-rate system in 1875 was remarkable. His idea of paying workmen higher wages for increased output was entirely the opposite of the discussions on the value of low wages found in the literature devoted to the iron and steel industry.

The Iron Age for December 21, 1876, argued that production in some cases had increased 20 percent since 1871. They attributed this increase to the fact that "wages are lower and employment difficult to find, and much steadier working is the result."[61]

In April 1879, the trustees of the East River Bridge (now known as the Brooklyn Bridge) decided to substitute steel for iron in the suspended superstructure of the new bridge. They called for bids for 10,728,000 pounds of steel and 34,000 pounds of iron. William Sellers, seeking additional business for Midvale, bid on this contract through his own iron company, the Edgemoor Iron Company, Edgemoor, Delaware. Edgemoor secured the contract on July 10, 1879, with steel eyebolt bars for the bridge to be manufactured at Midvale.

The steel order for the bridge began with the Cambria Iron Company in Johnstown, Pennsylvania, manufacturing the basic steel bars. The bars were then shipped to Midvale where the angles, I-beams, and channels for the bridge were to be rolled from rectangular steel billets. The original contract called for delivery of 5,500 tons of the steel bars in nine months, but this was changed so only 500 tons had to be delivered in 1879. Because detailed drawings were not delivered by the bridge engineers until February 1880, work did not start until March 1880.[62]

Meanwhile, Midvale continued to operate at a loss and in the spring of 1880 the interest of the first-mortgage bonds of Midvale were in arrears. At this time, Clarence H. Clark, who held some of the bonds as collateral for loans to his brother, Edward W. Clark, brought suit against Midvale. Later:

> upon a decree of the court of common pleas No. 3 of Philadelphia, the works were sold on October 30, 1880, to William Sellers for $450,000, and a new corporation, the Midvale Steel Company, was formed on December 11, 1880.[63]

The new company principals consisted of William Sellers, John Sellers, Edward W. Clark, Clarence H. Clark (brother of E. W. Clark), James Brooks, and James A. Wright. James A. Wright was Frederick W. Taylor's uncle whose ancestor was John Scholey (who married Frances Taylor). Their daughter Mary Taylor married Samuel Wright, who was related through marriage to the Justice family.[64]

In January 1881, shortly after the incorporation of Midvale, William Sellers sold the company about eight acres of land in Nicetown for $45,000. This land was north of the original plant and was used in 1883 as the site for a new melting furnace and molding shop.[65]

When the work for the bridge contract began at Midvale

the rolling of the steel became a serious problem. The company had an old rolling mill which was under the supervision of Joseph Binney, but more knowledge was needed about rolling-mill methods:

> It was necessary, in order to start the mill, to bring into the works at this time nearly 100 new laborers—gathered from any-where. A certain amount of work had to be turned out daily to escape a serious loss. The new rolling-mill hands thought half this quantity enough; when pressed, they struck to a man, and were paid off. Another lot of men had to be found, and the problem of lack of adequate production continued.[66]

When these events actually occurred is unknown, but Brinley's letters show that Midvale had a "fine rolling mill in operation" by July 16, 1880.[67] The success of this mill operation enabled Sellers to deliver 14 tons of steel to the storage yard in Brooklyn.[68] Problems with the mill continued until 1882, when, as *The New York Times* observed "some-body was really anxious to know when one of the great mys-teries of the 19th century—the completion of the bridge—would no longer be a mystery."[69] This somebody was Mayor Seth Low, of Brooklyn, who became a member of the Board of Trustees of the East River Bridge. As the paper observed, Low discovered that "Col. William Sellers, . . . was the per-son mainly responsible for the delay in providing the steel required," and he had arranged for Sellers to appear before the trustees on June 21, 1882, to explain the delay.[70] Sellers' testimony, however, was heard behind closed doors and not revealed, However, on June 25, 1882, Sellers announced that the steel would be delivered by October 1882.[71] Coincidental with Sellers' announcement came Brinley's departure from Midvale to assume the position of manager of the Franklin Sugar Refineries in Philadelphia in July 1882. Russell W. Davenport was now appointed superintendent.

Copley did not include a discussion of Midvale and the Brooklyn Bridge contract in his chapter on Midvale. He may have deliberately excluded this material because it did not fit his view of Sellers as a highly successful engineer-businessman. On the other hand, the methods Brinley used to overcome these problems may have actually foreshadowed Taylor's early work. This fact is something Copley certainly did not want to introduce into a biography on Taylor. Even if he had done so, Mrs. Taylor and the Taylor Cooperators would have censored such data.

CONTEMPORARY RECORDS ON TAYLOR'S OCCUPATION: 1878-1890

The panic of 1873 had a long-lasting effect on the economy of the United States. It was one of the two major depressions in this country's history before the Great Depression of the 1930s. By 1878, the country had slowly begun to pull itself out of the depths of the panic. Midvale was attempting to improve its operations and, although its wages were low, was hiring new employees. Taylor was hired through the efforts of Clarence M. Clark. In an effort to secure contemporary evidence of Taylor's career in the period 1878–90, a study was made of Taylor's name and occupation in *Gopsill's Philadelphia City Directory* for the years 1878–90.

Taylor's name does not appear in *Gopsill's* prior to the 1879 issue. In the 1879 *Gopsill's* (assembled in 1878), Taylor is listed as living on "Ross N. Penn, GTn," (Ross Street near Penn Street, Germantown), but no occupation is given.[72] This would imply that Taylor was still an apprentice at the Enterprise Hydraulic Works and not working at Midvale. His name does not appear in the 1880 (gathered in 1879), or 1881 *Gopsill's* (gathered in 1880), although his father's name appears in the 1881 issue.[73]

This gap in *Gopsill's* listing is important because in 1906, Taylor said he was "the newly appointed foreman" of the Midvale machine shop in 1880.[74] If Taylor had been appointed foreman in 1880, then it had to have been after June 8, 1880, since the Taylor family was surveyed during the United States Official Census of 1880 on that date and Frederick W. Taylor is listed as being 26 years old and his occupation as "N. Engineer" (novice engineer). He is not listed as "foreman" or even as "machinist." The term "novice engineer" would seem to imply that he had already been accepted at Stevens Institute of Technology.

In the period 1881–84, *Gopsill's* lists Taylor as a "machinist" still living at Ross Street in Germantown.[75] For the years 1886-89, Taylor is listed as a "mechanical engineer," and since he was now married, he no longer lived in his father's home on Ross Street, but on Locust Street.[76]

Gopsill's recorded Taylor as "machinist" in 1882 for the 1883 issue, in 1883 for the 1884 issue, and 1884 for the 1885 issue; so Taylor was a "machinist" for 1881–84, and "superintendent" in 1884. Finally, he was listed as a "mechanical engineer" by Costa in 1885, 1886, 1887, and 1888. Taylor, however, was probably more proud to be a machinist than a foreman, since he never informed Costa's surveyors that he was a "foreman" or "superintendent." The *Germantown Independent* for June 2, 1883, said he was the "foreman" of the machine shop at Midvale, but not "superintendent."[77]

Information from a "Personnel Chronologies," prepared at the Midvale Company in the 1930s (likely 1937, from internal evidence), reveals that Taylor became "Superintendent of the Machine Shops" in 1881.[78] If the promotion practices at Midvale at this time followed earlier procedures, then Taylor was most likely hired in the late Summer or Fall of 1880, after the preparation of the Census on June 8, 1880. An analysis of the earlier procedures at Midvale reveals that individuals were promoted rapidly, usually a year after being hired. Russell Davenport was hired in 1874, and placed in charge of the open-hearth furnace in 1875. Guillemeau Aertsen was hired in 1876, and placed in charge of the forge in 1877. Finally, Clarence M. Clark was hired in 1878 and put in charge of the forge in 1879.[79]

While the above data point to Taylor being hired after June 8, 1880, another record from Midvale implies that the date was 1878. About 1925 (according to internal evidence), Midvale prepared a two-page document titled "Comments on Frederick W. Taylor." In these notes, Guillemeau Aertsen is quoted as stating in 1915, that: "Not long after Mr. Petre's arrival, Mr.

F. W. Taylor, afterwards famous as an 'Efficiency Engineer,' entered Midvale's employ." In a note to this statement, it is added that: "In 1877, Axel Petre entered the service of the company."[80]

The "Personnel Chronologies," however, show that Axel Petre was placed in charge of the rolling mill in 1881. If Petre's promotion followed the previous pattern we have mentioned, then he may have been hired in 1880, and Aertsen may have a faulty memory. He may have been hired in the Spring of 1880, and Taylor in the Fall of 1880. This would account for Aertsen's comment that Taylor was hired "not long after Mr. Petre's arrival."

Rapid promotions were common at Midvale and the promotions of Aertsen, Brinley, Davenport, etc., are cases in point. The *Germantown Independent* for October 8, 1886, listed Guillemeau Aertsen as assistant superintendent at Midvale. This was only nine years after he began working there as a clerk in 1876.[81] The Midvale records show he was placed in charge of the forge in 1877 and was replaced by Clarence M. Clark in 1879. In 1879, two years later, he is listed as a "machinist."[82] For 1880 and 1881, he is listed as a "foreman."[83] In short, Aertsen was hired in 1876, placed in charge of the forge in 1877, and became a foreman by 1879, and assistant superintendent six years later. Aertsen's rapid rise parallels that of Taylor and can be explained, in part, as we have previously noted, because of family connections. From Brinley's letters we discussed earlier, we can see that every effort was made to improve the plant, so promotions came quickly.

While we cannot accurately ascertain the exact date when Taylor joined Midvale, we must remember that this does not vitiate Taylor's accomplishments. In fact, if he possibly achieved them in a short span of possibly 10 years (1880–89), this would make them even more remarkable than if he achieved them in 12 years (1878–89), as has been often asserted.

Considering the data available, it appears that after he joined Midvale, Taylor worked only a short time as a laborer. Because of his machinist training and family connections with the Clarks, Taylor was almost immediately assigned to the machine shop by Brinley, certainly not the usual procedure in the case of a new employee, especially a laborer. Shortly after Taylor was hired, the tool clerk of the machine shop was dismissed under suspicious circumstances. Because of his education, Brinley assigned Taylor to the tool clerk's job. In giving Taylor this job, Brinley told him his "duty was to keep the time records and watch the work of the men."[84]

Taylor, true to his personality, did exactly what Brinley told him to do. He watched the work of the men, both from the viewpoint of the machine time and the handling time. He observed what he had learned as an apprentice, namely, that the men "soldiered" or "loafed," that is, they only did one-third of the work that could be accomplished.

Copley said Taylor found the clerical work distasteful and trained a new man for the job. He then asked Brinley for a job as a machinist and because of his earlier training and performance in carrying out his job as clerk he was given this position. Taylor was never quite sure how long he worked as a machine operator. In his prepared statement for his 1912 testimony, Taylor said he had "worked for *some time* with the lathe gang."[85] However, when answering the questions of Chairman Wilson, he said he had only worked for two months as a machinist.[86]

NOTES

1. Winthrop Scudder to Morris L. Cooke, July 14, 1919.
2. Inventory of the Estate of Caleb N. Taylor, Charles E. Scott, Bucks County, Pennsylvania, November 10, 1888, Bucks County Historical Society.
3. Copley, I, pp. 52, 55.
4. Copley, I, p. 56.
5. Copley, I, p. 57.
6. Copley, I, pp. 67–68.
7. Copley, I, pp. 71–72.
8. Copley, I, p. 72.
9. House Resolution, 1912, pp. 1494–95.

10. *Simonds* v. *Hathorn*, Testimony 1898, p. 386.
11. Copley, I. p. 75.
12. Person, 1945.
13. *Simonds* v. *Hathorn*, Deposition 1898, p. 386.
14. *Gopsill's Philadelphia City Directory*, 1876, pp. 507, 796.
15. *Gopsill's*, 1876, p. 507.
16. Sarah Alden to Joseph L. Ferrell, Philadelphia Department of Records, Deed Book File D.H.L., No. 52, page 86.
17. *Gopsill's*, 1879, p. 1586.
18. Copley, I, p. 78.
19. House Resolution, 1912, p. 1427.
20. "Clarence Munroe Clark," *National Cyclopaedia of American Biography*, Vol. 34, p. 502.
21. Cyrus Caldwellader to George M. Justice, March 7, 1845, Bucks County Deed Records, Deed Book FY120788, No. FX146375A.
22. E. Hexamer Fire Insurance Maps, Philadelphia, 1866, p. 75.
23. Wistar Morris to Philip S. Justice, Philadelphia Department of Records, Deed Book PSJ, No. 108, p. 327; *Gopsill's*, 1867, p. 474.
24. E. Hexamer Fire Insurance Maps, Philadelphia, 1866, p. 12.
25. Tweesdale, 1986, p. 113.
26. Phillip S. Justice to M. W. Baldwin, September 12, 1865, *Baldwin Papers*, Historical Society of Pennsylvania.
27. *Gopsill's*, 1867, B.
28. *Germantown Telegraph*, September 1, 1880, p. 3.
29. B. F. Fulky to Charles M. Parker, July 15, 1948, p. 3; Howard C. Myers papers.
30. Philadelphia Department of Records, Deed Book JTO, No. 2, p. 345, and Charles T. Harrah to Florence Harrah Wood, November 22, 1922, Courtesy of Mrs. William Hearne.
31. *Gopsill's*, 1868, p. 1645.
32. Assignment by William Butcher, Jr., and Thomas Shaw, Howard C. Myers, Jr., papers.
33. Philadelphia, Department of Records, Deed Book JTO, No. 146, p. 305.
34. Tweesdale, 1986, p. 28.
35. Tweesdale, 1986, pp. 27–28.
36. F. B. Fulky to Charles M. Parker, July 15, 1948, p. 2; Howard C. Myers, Jr., papers.
37. Midvale, 1971, p. 1.
38. *Gopsill's*, 1869, p. 1809, 1588.

39. Charles A. Brinley letter of January 1, 1878, Howard C. Myers, Jr., papers.
40. *Gopsill's*, 1867, p. 575.
41. *Atlas of the County of Montgomery*, State of Pennsylvania, 1871.
42. Samuel Huston to Reverend William McCombs, Montgomery County, Deed Book 166, April 1, 1869, pp. 112–14.
43. U.S. Brewers, 1868, p. 13.
44. *Gopsill's*, 1870, p. 1699, and F. B. Fulky to Charles M. Parker, July 15, 1948, p. 2; Howard C. Myers, Jr., papers.
45. Kouwenhoven, 1982, p. 560.
46. F. B. Fulky to Charles M. Parker, July 15, 1948, p. 1; Howard C. Myers, Jr., papers.
47. *Gopsill's*, 1872, p. 1471; *Appleton's Cyclopedia of American Biography*, 1892, Vol. 2, p. 271.
48. F. B. Fulky to Charles M. Parker, July 15, 1948, p. 2; Howard C. Myers, Jr., papers.
49. Samuel Huston to Richmond, Potts, and Loring, June 24, 1871; July 26, 1871; November 27, 1871; and February 20, 1872. Howard C. Myers, Jr., papers.
50. F. B. Fulky to Charles M. Parker, July 15, 1948, p. 2; Howard C. Myers, Jr., papers.
51. "William Sellers Gave Us This Name," *Midvale Safety Bulletin*, April 1938, Vol. 26, Nos. 3 and 4.
52. Charles A. Brinley letters, 1873–80, Howard C. Myers, Jr., papers.
53. Charles A. Brinley letters, 1873–80, Howard C. Myers, Jr., papers.
54. Sellers, 1905.
55. *Atlantic Reporter,* 1892, Vol. 22, p. 422.
56. Scranton and Licht, 1986, p. 199.
57. Nalle, *Midvale*, 1948, p. 14.
58. *Gopsill's*, 1869, p. 135; 1870, p. 135; 1871, p. 135; 1872, p. 135; 1873, p. 135; 1874, p. 102.
59. Brinley letters, January 1, 1878, Howard C. Myers, Jr., papers.
60. Comments on Frederick W. Taylor, Midvale Company (1925); Howard C. Myers, Jr., papers, and *Midvale*, 1917, p. 26.
61. *The Iron Age*, December 21, 1876, p. 13.
62. *The Iron Age*, June 19, 1882, p. 14.
63. *Atlantic Reporter*, 1893, Vol. 23, p. 423, and Appeal of Samuel Huston, 1894, p. 9.

64. Francis B. Lea, *Genealogical and Memorial History of New Jersey*, Vol. IV, 1923, p. 1201.
65. *Germantown Independent*, January 17, 1881, p. 3.
66. Brinley, 1905, p. 45.
67. Brinley letter, July 16, 1880, Howard C. Myers, Jr., papers.
68. *The Iron Age*, June 29, 1882, p. 14.
69. *New York Times*, June 22, 1882, p. 4.
70. *New York Times*, June 22, 1882, p. 4.
71. *New York Times*, June 25, 1882, p. 6.
72. *Gopsill's*, 1879, p. 1586.
73. *Gopsill's*, 1881, p. 1605.
74. Taylor, 1907, p. 33.
75. *Gopsill's*, 1882, p. 1607; 1883, p. 1571; 1884, p. 1561.
76. *Gopsill's*, 1886, p. 1698; 1887, p. 1693; 1888, p. 1703; and 1889, p. 1753.
77. *Germantown Independent*, June 2, 1883, p. 2.
78. Personnel Chronologies, Midvale Company (1937?). Howard C. Myers, Jr., papers.
79. Personnel Chronologies, Midvale Company (1937?). Howard C. Myers, Jr., papers.
80. Comments on Frederick W. Taylor, Midvale Company (1925). Howard C. Myers, Jr., papers.
81. *Gopsill's*, 1877, p. 92.
82. *Gopsill's*, 1879, p. 88.
83. *Gopsill's*, 1880, p. 88; *Gopsill's*, 1881, p. 88.
84. Copley, I, p. 157.
85. House Resolution, 1912, p. 1411.
86. House Resolution, 1912, p. 1427.

PART II

THE MIDVALE DAYS

TAYLOR AS SUPERINTENDENT OF THE MACHINE SHOPS

In 1912, Taylor said that after he had worked for some time with the lathe gang, Brinley made him "gang boss"; why he did not say "superintendent," which was his official title, is unknown. In the brief story of Taylor's life preceding his paper "On the Art of Cutting Metals," we are told that he was promoted rapidly. When he was promoted to superintendent of the machine shops, we can imagine Taylor's problems since his former fellow machinists probably resented the appointment of a 23-year-old young man (with "influence" in the company) to this job. This situation possibly added to Taylor's difficulties with his men. The resistance offered by the men when he demanded more work gave young Taylor his first problem as an executive and in this role he reverted to the characteristics engendered in him by his mother. Just as his mother demanded work and discipline, Taylor demanded work from his men, disciplining them if he believed they did not work to their full capacity.

Taylor at this point in his life exhibited an unusual driving personality which epitomized his character. As an example, his work day was like this: He usually worked from 6:30 in the morning to 5:15 in the afternoon, volunteering frequently for overtime and Sunday work. As Taylor advised Sanford Thompson in 1893:

> . . . be sure and find out what scheme the owners are after most and work to accomplish that ahead of anything else. . . . I would warn you about the Sunday side of the matter. You will certainly, for a good while to come, have to subordinate your own inclination and religious tendencies to the interests of the mill, that is, if you place success as your goal.[1]

Taylor traveled to work on the Reading Railroad, using the "workingmen's" train which left Germantown (Main Street) at 6 A.M., stopping at Wingohocking (now Wistar) Station (near Taylor's house at Ross Street) at 6:04 A.M., arriving at Nicetown six minutes later, at 6:10 A.M. (The "workingmen's train consisted of old, dilapidated coaches not assigned to the regular Germantown runs, but considered suitable for workmen.)[2]

Taylor could have taken the 5:28 P.M. train from Nicetown to reach home, but he chose to walk the one and three-quarter miles back along the tracks to Wingohocking Station. In fact, Taylor continued to walk this lonely route even when threatened by the Midvale workmen.

Although Taylor's exact whereabouts in 1879–80 cannot be accurately ascertained from the data in *Gopsill's*, we do know that he and Clarence M. Clark played in the first tournament of the United States Lawn Tennis Association at Newport, Rhode Island, in 1881. Whether the absence of Taylor's name from *Gopsill's* for 1880–81 means that he was not in Philadelphia, but elsewhere in 1879 and 1880, we do not know.

Developments in the formation of an official tennis association in 1880–81 are interesting. In 1880, the Young American Tennis Club of Philadelphia played a tennis tournament with a club from Staten Island, New York. Immediately, the lack of standardization in the game of tennis became evident. The net used by the Young American Club was at a different height and the tennis balls of a different size and weight than they were at the Staten Island Club.

This lack of standardization caused three clubs in New

York, Philadelphia, and Boston to invite other clubs to a meeting in New York City to discuss the problem. At this meeting, held May 21, 1881, the United States Lawn Tennis Association was formed, and it was decided to have a championship tournament at Newport, Rhode Island, from August 31 to September 3, 1881. Clarence M. Clark was elected Secretary-Treasurer of the Association.

At the August tournament, 25 players participated in the singles and 13 pairs in the doubles. Among the 13 double pairs were Clarence M. Clark and Frederick W. Taylor. The peculiar situation of the doubles section of the tournament on September 2 and 3, 1881, was described in 1931, by Richard D. Sears, who said that he and Dr. James Dwight lost to the team of Clark and Taylor:

> All of the players entered came from the East, and most of the doubles teams were made up on the spur of the moment, with the result that there was little teamwork and the partners were constantly interfering with each other. The ultimate winners of the pairs showed much better team play than anyone else, with the result they won without much difficulty. These winners, Clarence Clark and Fred Taylor of Philadelphia, played one man close to the net with the other in the back court. Lobbing had not come in at this time and when this pair met (Dr.) Dwight (who also volleyed) and myself, they won fairly handily.[3]

The results of the tournament as reported in *The New York Times* for September 2 and September 3, 1881, were different. On September 2, 1881, the results were: "Sears and Dwight of the Beacon Park Club beat Prince and Coggeswell of Albany.... Clark and Taylor of the Young American Club, beat Smith and Nightingale of Providence...."[4] On the closing day of the tournament, September 3, 1881, the final doubles match was held between two teams of the Young American Club of Philadelphia, not between Clark and Taylor of the Young American Club and Sears and Dwight of the Beacon Park Club. The results were: "Messrs. Clark and Taylor and Messrs. Van Rensselaer and Newbold. The former won on three straight heats, Clark and Taylor winning the first prize and Newbold and Van Rensselaer the second."[5] From this data we know

Taylor was not in Philadelphia on August 31–September 3, 1881, but on "vacation" in Rhode Island. Vacations were not common for laborers in the 1880s.

TAYLOR EARNS M.E. DEGREE

It was poor health and particularly eye problems which forced Taylor to forgo a Harvard education, yet he spent much of his spare time studying and playing tennis. He eventually did pursue and receive a Mechanical Engineering degree from Stevens Institute of Technology in Hoboken, New Jersey. The actual circumstances surrounding Taylor's degree are unclear. In an autobiographic letter to Morris Cooke in 1910, Taylor wrote:

> Throughout my early days at Midvale I found myself very much short of scientific education, and began by taking a home study course in mathematics and physics, which was given by the scientific professors at Harvard University. After getting all that I could by correspondence in the way, I then went to the professors at Stevens Institute, and asked them for proper textbooks, etc., and this started my home study course at Stevens.
>
> About two years and a half after this time, namely, in June, 1883, I graduated as M.E. from Stevens, without however, having been there except for the purpose of pursuing all of the entrance examinations and finally one after another of the examinations required throughout the course.[6]

Taylor tells us that he studied at least three hours every night, including Sunday. At one point he tried to study in the early hours. He would set his alarm clock for two in the morning, rise, bathe, dress and study till five. He would then lie down for about half an hour. At 5:30 A.M. the cook would have breakfast ready and Taylor would eat. Usually it appears that he studied from 9 P.M. until about midnight, at which hour he would prepare himself for sleep by going out for a half hour run; he was an early jogger.

Taylor once told his son, Robert, that he needed an engineering degree in order to be promoted. Whatever the reason,

Taylor's pursuit of a degree at Stevens was unusual. The president of Stevens, Henry Morton, was a personal friend of William Sellers, which most likely affected Taylor's choice of schools. Robert also reports that because of Taylor's eye problems, his mother Emily Taylor often read his textbooks to him.

Although his name does not appear on any of the official class lists at Stevens of the period 1881–83, there is, according to Stevens' Professor Myron Johnson, a notation in the faculty minutes reporting Taylor having passed physics. Johnson believes that "it seems highly probable that he never attended a single class!"[7] While Taylor apparently never attended or infrequently attended class, he did belong to the Theta Xi, Gamma Chapter, fraternity. It was a small fraternity, however, with only 11 members in 1883, including Taylor and his relation Ernest Wright.[8] Searching the Stevens graduation lists, Johnson found that "Taylor clearly caught the faculty by surprise when he presented himself for a degree. The faculty minutes show that the 1883 graduation list had already been printed when, in pencil, someone inserted the name of Frederick W. Taylor. The official published list of the graduates for the year 1883 was published in the Stevens' publication *The Bolt*. It does not contain Taylor's name, although his relative Ernest Wright is listed.[9] Taylor presented not one but two theses for his degree.[10]

CAMPAIGN AGAINST SOLDIERING

Taylor, according to his own account, said he began a one-man campaign to eliminate "soldiering" at the Midvale Machine Shop:

> As soon as I became gang boss, the men who were working under me and who, of course, knew that I was onto the whole game of soldiering or deliberately restricting output, came to me at once and said "Now Fred, you are not going to be a damn piece-work hog are you?" I said, "If you fellows mean you are afraid I'm going to try to get a larger amount from these lathes," I said, "Yes, I do propose to get more out." I said, "You must

remember I have been square with you fellows up to now and worked with you. I have not broken a single rate; I have been on your side of the fence. But now I have accepted a job under the management of this company and I am on the other side of the fence, and I will tell you perfectly frankly that I am going to try to get a bigger output from those lathes."

They answered, "Then, you are going to be a damn hog."

I said, "Well, if you fellows put it that way, all right." They said, "We warn you, Fred, if you try to bust any of these rates we will have you over the fence in six weeks." I said, "That is all right; I will tell you fellows again frankly that I propose to try to get a bigger output off of these machines."

Now that was the beginning of a piecework fight which lasted for nearly three years, as I remember it—two or three years in which I was doing everything in my power to increase the output of the shop, while the men were absolutely determined that output should not be increased.[11]

Taylor first introduced the story of this fight with his workmen when he testified before a Special Committee of the House of Representatives in 1912. He had never mentioned this fight in any of his earlier publications.

The machinists at Midvale were paid low wages (according to Brinley) on a daily or an hourly rate; in brief, if the men were there, they were paid. Output was not taken into consideration except if the workmen fell below some set standard, and then they would be discharged (Brinley letters, July 31, 1874, Howard C. Myers, Jr., papers). Whether they produced slightly above that standard, twice that standard, three times that standard, or whatever, they were still paid the daily rate. This, of course, added to "soldiering," as Taylor used the word, because once you met your daily standard, you had no encouragement to work beyond that point. Taylor first tried verbally to encourage his men to produce more, but output did not increase. From time to time he would show a man how to do his job better. He said:

I got on the lathe myself and showed them that it could be done, (to increase output). In spite of this, he, the worker, went ahead and turned out exactly the same output and refused to adopt better methods or to work quicker so finally I laid them off or got another man in his place.[12]

Actually Taylor said he couldn't blame these men, for under the circumstances, why should they produce more? They weren't paid to produce more. After becoming chief engineer of the machine shops in 1881, he began a new effort to increase the output. Through a friend in Germantown, Joseph B. King— Taylor's assistant who was to replace Taylor in the machine shops in 1890—he found especially bright laborers who had never had the opportunity to learn a trade. He personally taught these men how to run a lathe, how to work fast, how to work correctly, and each of these laborers promised Taylor, "now if you will teach me the machinist trade, when I learn how to run a lathe I will do a fair day's work."[13] But after Taylor had taught these men how to run a lathe, one after another would join the rest of their fellows in "soldiering." Taylor was disappointed. After he had taught them they did not work any faster than the previous workers, even though they had promised that they would. Taylor told these men:

> I know that very heavy social pressure has been put upon you outside the works to keep from carrying out your agreement with me, and it is very difficult for you to stand out against this pressure, but you ought not to have made your bargain with me if you did not intend to keep your end of it. Now, I am going to cut your rate in two tomorrow and you are going to work for half price from now on. But all you have to do is to turn out a fair day's work and you can earn better wages than you have been earning.[14]

The men as it turns out, went straight to management to protest. They said:

> I was a tyrant, and nigger driver, and for a long time they stood right by the rest of the men in the shop and refused to increase their output one particle. Finally, they all of a sudden gave right in and did a fair day's work.[15]

But the workers weren't through, for as soon as Taylor was successful in forcing the men to do what he thought was a fair day's work, "they played what is usually the winning card."[16] Taylor said he knew what was going to come:

> Every time I broke a rate or forced one new man which I had trained to work at a reasonable and proper speed, some one of the machinists would deliberately break some part of his machine as an object lesson to demonstrate to the management that a fool foreman was driving the men to overload the machines until they broke. Almost every day ingenious accidents were planned, and these happened to machines in different parts of the shop, and were, of course, always laid to the fool foreman which were driving the men and machines beyond their limit.[17]

But Taylor retaliated and said:

> All right, from this time on, any accident that happens in the shop, every time you break any part of the machine, you will have to pay part of the cost of repairing it or else quit. I don't care if the roof falls in and breaks your machine, you will pay all the same.[18]

Taylor's version of the "soldiering" problem at Midvale concentrated entirely upon the machine shop where he worked, and he never mentioned that the problem probably existed throughout Midvale in 1880–83, primarily the result of the Brooklyn Bridge contract (discussed earlier.) As we mentioned, 100 extra men were hired to fulfill this contract, increasing the work force to 600. Efforts were made throughout the plant to double production, but the new men believed that only one-half of the new production goals was a suitable day's labor and "soldiered."[19]

It is possible that Taylor's machine-shop crew included some of these new men and that this was the primary cause of his "soldiering" problem. The existence of the Brooklyn Bridge contract may also have influenced plant superintendent Davenport's backing of Taylor's efforts to increase output. In addition, Davenport was also a "rigid disciplinarian," who would support Taylor's rigid rules. This coupled with the bridge contract problems allowed Davenport to back Taylor's work to a degree not possible under normal conditions.[20]

Because Davenport backed Taylor instead of the workers, the fines were paid, and the opposition seemed to stop. Machine breakdown ceased and the workers began producing a fair day's work as determined by Taylor.

It was through this type of work experience that Taylor came to the conclusion that no one had exact knowledge on how long it should take the workmen to do a fair day's work. It was his belief that if the workers were paid a fair price they would respond with equivalently increased work output.

The problem was that no one knew what a fair day's work was. Therefore, management, although it knew that labor could produce more, had not placed a value on the output that could be produced by labor. Labor was afraid to produce more because it believed that management would continue to expect more and more to a point beyond labor's endurance, and even if management paid more initially, it would soon cut rates.

TAYLOR AND THE "DIFFERENTIAL PIECE RATE"

In examining the reasons for "soldiering," Taylor determined that not only was the employer ignorant of what constituted a day's work, but the fact that employees worked in large groups destroyed individual incentive. More important, the methods that employers used to remedy the situation, namely substituting piece rates for day rates, caused new problems. When the piece rates increased daily earnings, the rates were reduced. At this point the workmen "become imbued with a grim determination to have no more cuts if soldiering can prevent it."[21]

Taylor's solution to the problem (which required many years to implement) involved two steps:

1. To give each workman each day in advance a definite task, with detailed written instructions, and an exact time allowance for each element of the work.

2. To pay extraordinary high wages to those who perform their tasks in the allotted time, and ordinary wages to those who take more than their time allowance.[22]

Taylor's first important writing was his December 1893 paper presented to the American Society of Mechanical Engineers (ASME) "Notes on Belting," which established Taylor as an engineer.[23] His second presentation to the ASME established him as a management scholar. At the June 1895 meeting in Detroit, Taylor read his "A Piece-Rate System," subtitled, "A Step Toward Partial Solution of the Labor Problem." Although the piece-rate system is intermingled with time study, we will discuss the system first and take up the time study separately.

Taylor called his piece-rate payment system "The Differential Rate System of Piece-work," and it was different. Taylor's paper was in response to two other payment plans offered to the ASME: the Henry R. Towne "Gain-Sharing Plan" (1888), and the F. A. Halsey "Premium Plan" (1891). Taylor believed that the Towne plan was:

> subject to the serious, and I think fatal, defect that it does not recognize the personal merit of each workman; the tendency being rather to herd men together and promote trades-unionism, than to develop each man's individuality.[24]

Although the Halsey plan overcame this problem, it suffered from, according to Taylor, the "temptation for the workman to 'soldier' or hold back while on day-work" and from the fact that the rates were not scientifically set.[25]

Taylor based his system on time study and incentive pay. He said:

> In 1883, while foreman of the machine shop of the Midvale Steel Company of Philadelphia, it occurred to the writer that it was simpler to time each of the elements of the various kinds of work done in the place, and then find the quickest time in which each job could be done, by summing up the total times of its component parts, than it was to search through the records of former jobs, and guess at the proper price. After practising this method of rate-fixing himself for about a year, . . . the writer then established the rate-fixing department, which has given out piecework prices . . . ever since.[26]

Once the time to perform a task is known and the amount of output which can be produced in a day is determined, then the matter turns to getting the worker to produce at that level and not to "soldier." "This," claims Taylor, "consists briefly in paying a higher price per piece, or per unit, or per job, if the work is done in the shortest possible time, and without imperfections, than is paid if the work takes a longer time or is imperfectly done."[27] This concept is best demonstrated using Taylor's own illustration:

> Suppose 20 units or pieces to be the largest amount of work of a certain kind that can be done in a day. Under the differential rate system, if a workman finishes 20 pieces per day, and all of these pieces are perfect, he receives, say, 15 cents per piece, making his pay for the day 15 × 20 = $3. If, however, he works too slowly and turns out, say, only 19 pieces, then, instead of receiving 15 cents per piece he gets only 12 cents per piece, making his pay for the day 12 × 19 = $2.28, instead of $3 per day.
>
> If he succeeds in finishing 20 pieces, some of which are imperfect, then he should receive a still lower rate of pay, say, 10 cents or 5 cents per piece, according to circumstances, making his pay for the day $2, or only $1, instead of $3.[28]

There was much discussion of Taylor's paper, both pro and con. Halsey attacked it for being too complex, suitable for large gun-forging machines and not smaller machines, and for paying the workers too much. Halsey did commend Taylor for his efforts in determining the maximum output of the machine shop. W. S. Rogers, another attendee, even claimed to have invented an "identical plan of a differential piece-rate . . . ." Rogers then claimed it didn't work well because there were times when through no fault of the workers, machines breaking, raw materials not arriving, etc., that workers could not make the rate and were paid very low wages.[29] Taylor pointed out that Rogers did not use the system as Taylor had described it—he had failed to use elementary rate-fixing (elementary time study). Henry Gantt, from the audience, was very enthusiastic. But then, he had worked with Taylor on this system at Midvale. Gantt said Taylor's paper:

> is really a system by which the employer attempts to do justice to the employee, and in return requires the employee to be hon-

est. His method of fixing rates by elements eliminates, as nearly as possible, all chance of error, and his differential rates go a long way toward harmonizing interests of employer and employee.[30]

Gantt was to later find fault with this system and develop his own, known as "Task Work with a Bonus System," which in essence is a combination of a day and piece-rate system and is based on the Taylor time-study system.[31]

Taylor did claim that "the system of differential rates was first applied by the writer . . . in . . . the Midvale Steel Company, in 1884."[32] We will discuss shortly Taylor's difficulty in pinning down the year in which "time study" was first tried by him. But from our earlier discussion of Brinley's work, we know that Taylor's claim that he was first to try the "differential rates" is incorrect.

TAYLOR'S METAL-CUTTING EXPERIMENTS

Taylor linked his metal-cutting experiments to the problems he had with the machinists, and in 1906, he gave the starting date on metal cutting as 1880 (he was probably a year off) in the machine shop at Midvale when he claimed to be foreman:

> In the fall of 1880, the machinists in the small machine shop of the Midvale Steel Company, Philadelphia, most of whom were working on piecework in machining locomotive tires, car axles, and miscellaneous forgings, had combined to do only a certain number of pieces per day on each type of work. The writer, who was the newly appointed foreman of the shop, realized that it was possible for the men to do in all cases much more work per day than they were accomplishing. He found, however, that his efforts to get them to increase their output were blocked by the fact that his knowledge of just what combination of depth of cut, feed, and cutting speed would in each case do the work in the shortest time, was much less accurate than that of the machinists who were combined against him. His conviction that the men were not doing half as much as they should do, however, was so strong that he obtained the permission of the manage-

ment to make a series of experiments to investigate the laws of cutting metals with a view to obtaining a knowledge at least equal to that of the combined machinists who were under him. He expected that these experiments would last not longer than six months.[33]

When Taylor presented his paper on the metal-cutting experiments in 1906, he admitted that many of the discoveries during this period "have been and are well known to other engineers, and we do not record them with any certainty that we were the first to discover or formulate them . . . ."[34]

One of the findings, apparently discovered 12 years before Taylor at William Sellers & Company in 1869, was the value of the round-nosed over the diamond-point tool when cutting forgings. J. Sellers Bancroft reported:

In 1869, I made a number of experiments at the works of William Sellers and Company, where I was then shop foreman, and demonstrated that the round-nosed tool would take a cut having a feed from 25 percent to 33 percent coarser than the diamond-point tool would take in the same material and the same depth of cut. . . .[35]

Taylor claimed that he first discovered the value of such a tool shape in 1881. He remarked that "a round-nosed tool could be run at a much higher cutting speed and turn out more work than the old-fashioned diamond-pointed tool."[36] Whether or not Taylor was aware of Sellers Bancroft's earlier experiments when he made his own, is virtually impossible to determine today. It seems plausible, however, that Taylor may have heard something about these earlier discoveries when we consider the close link between Midvale and William Sellers & Company.

Of other earlier work discoveries similar to those by Taylor, there was one in England about seven years before Taylor's. According to Daniel Adamson of the Joseph Adamson & Company of Hyde, England, starting in 1876 heavy streams of water were used to cool tools, but the increased amount of work was never 40 percent (as claimed by Taylor later) but only 15 percent.[37]

Taylor said that in the year 1883, he discovered "that a heavy stream of water poured directly upon the chip at the point where it is being removed from the steel forging by the tool, would permit an increase in cutting speed, and therefore the amount of work done of from 30 to 40 percent."[38] We do not know if Taylor was aware of Adamson's work in England. British engineering publications certainly were readily available in Philadelphia, but we do not know if Taylor read them. We do know that Davenport made a lengthy trip to England in 1882 to learn more about British forging methods. Whether he learned of the use of water to cool machine tools during this trip and transmitted this information to Taylor is another mystery that awaits solution.

Certainly by 1884, Taylor frequently utilized water to cool the tools in the new machine shop at Midvale. Here water (supersaturated with carbonate of soda to prevent rusting) "was thrown in a heavy stream upon the tool for the purpose of cooling it."[39]

The fact that Taylor's metal-cutting experiments were "almost exclusively" confined to " 'roughing work'; i,e., the preparation of the forgings on castings for the final finishing cut . . ." is a fact commonly ignored by scholars.[40] The fact that his work was focused on this area of machine-shop activities was not only because of the manufacture of locomotive wheels at Midvale but also because of the manufacture of experimental rifled cannon, starting at Midvale in 1881.

Because the forging of rifled cannon was an important part of the work performed in Taylor's machine shop, a brief review of the development of rifled cannon is necessary for greater understanding of Taylor's activities at Midvale from 1881 to 1889.

RIFLED CANNON AND TAYLOR'S METAL-CUTTING EXPERIMENTS AT MIDVALE

On October 11, 1897, when Taylor testified in a patent suit between the Simonds Rolling Machine Company and the Hathorn Manufacturing Company, Taylor revealed his experience with the forging of modern cannon:

> I am familiar with the manufacture of all forgings used in producing modern cannon. The Midvale Steel Works, of which I was mechanical engineer for several years, were the first company in the United States who succeeded in producing successful forgings for making modern highpower cannon, such as are used on our modern warships and in coast defence. I was actively engaged in experimenting and producing these forgings for a number of years.[41]

This statement reveals a side of Taylor unknown to management scholars. It necessitated a careful study of Midvale's contribution to the production of modern Army and Navy cannon, along with a reassessment of Taylor's work.

The authors, however, upon studying the development of modern rifled cannon in America, discovered that Taylor could hardly have avoided becoming familiar with the manufacture of forgings for modern cannon. Midvale produced many of the forgings for the experimental cannons made for the Army and Navy from 1881 to 1889, and Taylor played a significant role in this production. In fact, it appears that Taylor's metal-cutting experiments were primarily made to improve the production of these cannons and not to secure more control over the activities of the Midvale machinists. A discussion of the development of rifled cannon during 1881–89 is required if we are to understand Taylor's high-speed experiments.

Before 1850 all cannon had smooth bores, but in 1854 a Briton, William Armstrong, proposed a rifled, breech-loading field gun having spiral grooves, which gave rotation to the explosive shell, sending it a longer distance and giving it greater force when hitting the target.

Armstrong's guns were "built-up" rifled artillery, which from 1854 to 1890 became the almost universal rifled cannon constructed. Although this construction varied somewhat:

> essentially the method of "building up" the gun has been the same—the shrinking upon an inner coil of wrought iron or tube of steel forming the bore of hollow cylinders of wrought iron,

varying in numbers with the size of the piece. In guns of latest construction, steel only is employed.[42]

Army Built-Up Guns at Midvale

On March 3, 1881, Congress authorized a Board on Heavy Ordnance and Projectiles (the Getty Board) to examine and report on all plans for the fabrication of heavy guns and projectiles.

In September 1881, the Bureau of Ordnance of the Navy Department invited steelmakers to manufacture solid steel forgings for rifled cannon. In December 1881, Midvale informed the Navy it could manufacture such cannon. However, actual work on making such cannon did not begin until September 19, 1882, when Russell Davenport, as new superintendent at Midvale, wrote the Navy that "We are now ready to begin forging on the first of the two 6-inch rifled guns for which we hold orders."[43] Davenport, however, did not commit Midvale to this project until he had visited steel works in Europe to study heavy forging methods.

In 1883, upon the recommendation of the Getty Board, it was decided to authorize the construction of the first steel built-up breech-loading gun of 8-inch caliber. The forgings for the tube and jacket of this gun were ordered from Whitworth and Company of England, and the hoops from Midvale.[44] The complete gun was assembled and finished at the West Point Foundry in New York, and turned over to the government for trial in 1886.

Naval Guns at Midvale

The United States began to modernize the Navy with the Naval Appropriation bill of August 5, 1882, authorizing the building of four new cruisers with modern guns. These ships were the famous A, B, C, D ships: The *Atlanta, Boston, Chicago,* and *Dolphin.*[45] The designers included 5-, 6-, and 8-inch, breech-loading rifles, and later, guns of 10-, 12-, and 16-inch caliber. The first 6-inch gun was finished and turned over for trial in 1884, and the first 8-inch naval gun was finished in 1886.

Because the facilities of the Washington Navy Yard were limited, the rough forgings for the guns were procured from private foundries such as Midvale.[46] Midvale's work in this area was reported in the *Germantown Telegraph* on May 21, 1884:

> Eight six-inch and two five-inch breech-loading steel rifled guns are being manufactured at Midvale Steel Works, Nicetown, for the new naval cruiser *Chicago*, in course of construction at Chester. The larger of the guns will be sixteen feet and one inch in length, and will carry a projectile weighing 100 pounds.[47]

On October 1, 1886, Secretary of the Navy William C. Whitney invited all steel manufacturers in the United States to submit bids for steel gun forgings. These forgings were to be used on a number of new navy ships: The Newark, Charleston, Yorktown, Petrel, New York, Olympia, Cincinnati, and Raleigh.[48] Whitney's advertisement required that all these forgings were to be delivered rough-bored and turned in the following schedule from the closing of the contract:

> For 6-inch guns, 28 in one year, and the remainder within 18 months.
>
> For 8-inch guns, within two years.
>
> For 10-inch and larger guns, within 2½ years.[49]

Midvale successfully bid on the contract for the 6-inch guns, and in his annual report, dated December 6, 1887, Whitney reported that Midvale was the contractor for 32 guns. He said:

> The Midvale forgings are now beginning to come in, and will be taken in hand at once in the shops at the Washington Navy Yard, the contract requiring that the whole number shall be delivered by February, 1889.[50]

Although the bids for the 6-inch guns were submitted in 1886, the actual forgings were made after the Harrahs gained control of Midvale in 1887. Midvale also was working on the manufacture of forgings for 8-inch and 10-inch guns.

Because of the manufacturing problems incurred in the manufacture of 8-inch guns, Russell Davenport was very receptive to Taylor's suggestions concerning experiments to improve metal cutting. Although Taylor said that he received the approval of Sellers to conduct these experiments, it is more likely that the approval came from Davenport.

There are many strange circumstances surrounding the metal-cutting experiments. Although the improvement of metal cutting was a necessity to produce the guns for the Army and Navy, Taylor chose to maintain complete silence for this aspect of his experiments, stressing in his metal-cutting paper only the work on large locomotive tires.[51] Despite the great importance of these experiments to the development of management, the details (aside from Taylor's published account in 1906) of them are strangely missing. Their loss came to light in 1933, when Carl Barth (Taylor's most devoted associate) was asked to help prepare an exhibition concerned with the 50th anniversary of Taylor's graduation from Stevens Institute of Technology. In the process of gathering material at Taylor's home, Barth discovered that the early records of Taylor's metal-cutting experiments at Midvale had mysteriously disappeared.[52] In fact, except for Taylor's description of the experiments we have no other collaborating evidence. In 1906, Taylor said that since 1880 he had succeeded in keeping almost all the information on the results of his metal-cutting experiments a secret, saying he had never sold any information on these experiments, but: "we have given to one company after another all of the data and conclusions arrived at through our experiments in consideration for the opportunity of still further continuing our work."[53] Further, said Taylor, during these 20 years all of the companies receiving this information and the men conducting the experiments, "were bound by promises to the writer not to give any of this information away or allow it to be published."[54]

In the 84 years since Taylor made these statements, not one shred of evidence has been discovered concerning these early experiments, the companies who participated, or all the men who conducted them, although Taylor does credit G. M. Sinclair, Henry Gantt, Maunsel White, and Carl Barth as the major researchers and others, including Dwight Merrick and Sidney Newbold, as having assisted. He cites Midvale Steel, Cramp's Ship-building Co., Wm. Sellers & Co., Link-Belt Engineering, Dodge & Day, and Bethlehem Steel as being some of the participating organizations.[55] Extensive research by the authors has failed to uncover a single record of the experiments.

TAYLOR, STEAM HAMMERS, AND THE MANUFACTURE OF GUN FORGINGS

The steam hammers used at Midvale were essential to the forging of the guns manufactured during Taylor's day. The importance of steam hammers was stressed by C. Chomienne in his 1888 "Notes on Steam Hammers" in *The Railroad and Engineering Journal*:

> Without this tool it would have been impossible to . . . forge in one piece the wrought-iron wheels used on locomotives and cars; to make the armor plates of iron and steel which protect our warships, or the steel guns, the dimensions of which are every day increased.[56]

The Midvale hammers were operated by men commonly called "hammermen."[57] Chomienne, however, also described them as "machinists."[58]

Although the hammermen at Midvale were skilled machinists, the Sellers hammers, while powerful enough to forge Army hoops, were inadequate for forging 6-inch naval guns. In addition, the design of these hammers with their rigid supporting legs, eventually resulted in their destruction.[59]

After Charles Harrah acquired Midvale in 1887, it was decided to manufacture tubes and jackets for 5-, 6-, and 8-inch guns. Because such tubes and jackets had not been manufactured in the United States before this time, the Harrahs assigned the task to Taylor who accomplished it with the aid of C. Firth (who was in actual charge of the erection of Number 10 hammer) and the Morgan Engineering Company:

> Chief Engineer Taylor . . . cooperating with the Morgan Engineering Company in 1887, designed a 25-ton double-acting ham-

mer with 50 tons of top steam; which was built by the following year, and with this tool complete sets of forgings for pieces of 8″ to 13″ were made for the Navy.[60]

Taylor described this hammer in a patent application filed March 8, 1890:

> The object of my present invention is to remedy the above-mentioned defects and to attain greater efficiency and durability by taking up and distributing throughout the several members of the frame in the least-destructive manner and with the best effect the great shocks, strains, and vibrations incident to the work power-hammers are called upon to perform.[61]

The novel aspect of this hammer was that it was designed to maintain its alignment through the elasticity of its parts, which were of an unusual design:

> Taylor insuring this elasticity by designing and supplying with great initial tension an arrangement resembling great spider legs, which consisted of oil-tempered steel bolts four inches in diameter and twenty feet long.[62]

This hammer represented Taylor's last great work at Midvale. It was used experimentally in 1889, and went into regular use after Taylor had left in 1890. When it was in use, Mr. Edwin Lipp of Midvale said, "its tremendous thump nearly shook Tioga off the map" (Tioga was a 20-block-square area southeast of Midvale).[63]

During his metal-cutting experiments, Taylor said the measurement of the power required to feed a round-nosed tool with varying depths of cut and the discovery that a very dull tool required as much pressure to feed it as to drive the cut, "was one of the most important discoveries made by us."[64] He considered this discovery so important that all machines for cutting steel purchased for Midvale after 1883 were supplied with a feeding power equal to their driving power.

Taylor's metal-cutting discoveries, and his graduation from Stevens Institute of Technology in 1883, gave him increased status at Midvale. This status came at an opportune moment, because the new rifled-gun orders made the old machine shop obsolete because it was too small for the large experimental gun forgings.

In 1883, as superintendent of the machine shops, Taylor was given the assignment by Davenport to design a new and larger machine shop, based in part on what Davenport had learned during his trip to England in 1882. In fact, the *Germantown Independent* of August 11, 1883, said Midvale was "making preparations for building one of the largest machine shops in the United States."[65] In order to move large guns easily around the shop, William Sellers & Company designed the world's first overhead crane. Construction of this crane began at Midvale in August 1883 and was completed in the Spring of 1884.

In the new shop, Taylor said "about half the belts in the shop were designed according to the ordinary rules and the other half were made about two and one-half times as heavy as the usual standard."[66] He adopted this procedure after discovering during metal-cutting experiments that he had difficulty in maintaining tension of the belt driving the boring mill. Investigating the cause of this difficulty, Taylor concluded:

1. That belting rules in common use furnished belts entirely too light for economy.

2. That the proper way to take care of belting was to have each belt in a shop tightened at regular intervals with belt clamps especially fitted with spring balances . . . which permitted each belt to be retightened each time to exactly the same tension.[67]

This work led to further use of belt-tightening procedures by Taylor when he was a consultant at other factories, and to his famous 1893 paper to the ASME, "Notes on Belting."[68]

TAYLOR'S POSSIBLE DEBT
TO WILLIAM SELLERS & COMPANY

We learned earlier that J. Sellers Bancroft in 1869, at William Sellers & Company, made experiments on cutting metal with a round-nosed tool, similar to those made by Taylor in 1883.

There may have been other developments at the Sellers Company that could have influenced Taylor's later work. Unfortunately, there are only fragmentary accounts of the management methods utilized in this company.

One of the four contemporary sources of such information was a report prepared by Captain Henry Metcalfe, Officer in Charge of Manufacturing at the Frankford Arsenal in Philadelphia, on November 11, 1880. Because Metcalfe's primary interest was controlling costs at Frankford, his report was concerned with this topic. One of Metcalfe's models of cost control duplicated methods followed at William Sellers & Company.

Metcalfe discovered that at Sellers the foreman's role was not to be a clerk, but "to drive and lead men to actual results."[69] If this were true, then Taylor could have derived his model of behavior in dealing with his men both from his mother and from Sellers. Metcalfe advocated use of "competent time—and storekeeper exclusively for work in the shops, and in those capacities only."[70] This was an early form of functional activity which Metcalfe said he had developed at Frankford. Yet, he commented that its validity was supported by consultations with William Sellers & Company, where such a specialist had "done so much to give their establishment the reputation it has for good management as well as for good work."[71] This data seems to show that William Sellers & Company followed practices that would have proved useful to Taylor.

THE ORIGINS OF TIME STUDY

Long before Taylor began his work, many men had recognized the immense advantage management would have in determining suitable piece-rate schemes if it only possessed a method of accurately determining output. We do not know if Brinley had created such a system in 1876, and passed this knowledge on to Taylor as suggested by Guillemeau Aertsen in 1915 and 1917.

Taylor's biographer said that while the main work in Taylor's machine shop consisted of the repetitive machining of locomotive tires and car axles, there also was the special work on rifled cannon. In these cases there were usually accurate estimates made concerning the material needed, but it was difficult to accurately estimate the time required to complete the work; such data was desperately needed. To obtain this time, the foreman would use records he had of the total time required to do similar jobs as the basis of an estimate. However, said Copley, "estimates based on such statistics represented guesswork pure and simple."[72]

We should mention that in 1884, Benjamin Reece, chief engineer of the Lake Shore and Michigan Southern Railway, presented a paper on the "Management of Forces Engaged in Railway Track Repairs" before the American Society of Civil Engineers.[73] In his paper, Reece outlined methods of training and observing the work of track gangs. One method employed by Reece to secure more information on the work performed by such gangs, was to have the foreman fill out a form each week describing the work performed each day. Reece used the data provided in this form as a basis for further study of the work being done by the gangs:

> A recapitulation of the week's work on each section is returned to me for examination and comparison. If the amount of work done exceeds the recorded average, one of two conditions will be found to exist: either the amount of work required at the point in course of repair is less than an average of the section, or else the work is being less thoroughly done, which can be determined by the personal inspection of the road master or the engineer. If, on the other hand, the track completed shows to be less than the average, either the amount of work to be done is greater than the average, or the time and labor of the men have not been fully utilized or have been misdirected by the foreman. Again, an examination by the road master will reveal the fact, and the want of thoroughness in the one case, or the dereliction of duty in the other, will be discovered, and can be remedied at once.[74]

At present, we do not know the extent of Reece's analysis of the work of the laborers in the track gangs. He may, or may not, have used an embryonic form of time study.

Reece's methods to secure information on the work being

completed on the railroad is important because it demonstrates that, in 1884, others besides Taylor were searching for a way to secure useful information on the work being performed by workmen.

If we recall Birge Harrison's account of Taylor's study of the game of croquet, we can see that the idea of "guessing" about the time required to perform a job was against Taylor's basic outlook. He began to search for a method to arrive at this time more scientifically and probably recalling his experiences at Phillips Exeter, he began to use a stopwatch to record overall times.

The exact date when Taylor began to make time studies is unknown. In 1912, he said:

> time study was begun in the machine shop at the Midvale Steel Company in 1881, and was used during the next two years sufficiently to prove its success. In 1883, Mr. Emlen Hare Miller was employed to devote his whole time to "time study," and he worked steadily at this job for two years, using blanks similar to that shown in Para. 374 of "Shop Management."[75]

We must note that the blank shown in Para. 367 is one designed by Sanford Thompson for Taylor in 1896, so we do not know what Miller's blanks may have looked like.

However, in 1903, Taylor said he began using a stopwatch in 1883, while a foreman at Midvale, and "after practicing this method of time study himself for about a year (or to 1884), as well as circumstances would permit, it became evident that the system was a success."[76] These remarks indicate that Taylor probably began his initial time study experiments in 1883, and in 1884 he decided it was a valuable idea. To comprehend exactly what Taylor did at this time, we must turn to testimony by Carl Barth (Taylor's mathematical assistant from 1899 to 1915) given in 1920. Barth said Taylor's first efforts at Midvale to determine the amount of time required to complete a task were made in the machine shop. The first studies were made to discover "What the machine would do, and then what the men would do."[77] The operations were not divided into individual elements, since only overall times were recorded.

When Taylor turned to the study of individual workers, Barth said he performed the analysis secretly: "The stopwatch was concealed and this was the mere beginning of time. Time to remove the metal on the lathe was the big problem."[78] Taylor was to repeat this concealed time study in 1896, and at that time he had Sanford Thompson develop sophisticated methods of concealing the stopwatch during time studies. At this time, Taylor acknowledged to Thompson that at Midvale it had been "difficult to analyze the job into what constitutes really its essential elements and then put these together properly after making the analysis."[79]

With the construction and opening of the new machine shop in 1884, Taylor wanted to ensure that the new shop would be successful. Furthermore, he also continued his metal-cutting experiments and wanted to link them to the further development of time study.

To ensure that his new system of rate setting by time study would be given a fair trial, Taylor recruited two men he probably considered as "first-class workers." Taylor spoke with his assistant, Joseph B. King of Germantown, who found two suitable individuals, William Fannon and Charles Shartle. In June 1884, Taylor, Fannon, and Shartle met at King's home. At this meeting, Taylor outlined his plans for a new system of management, a system so novel that Fannon recalled it clearly 32 years later:

> Mr. Taylor's scientific system of getting data, before establishing a rate per diem, looked good to us; and, added to this, was his idea of not only one rate per diem but several rates per diem, which might be called accumulative rates.[80]

Shartle and Fannon began working at Midvale on July 1, 1884. They were employed on two special projects, Shartle on the erection of new machinery and repair work, and Fannon operating a slotting machine cutting out test bars. This project was the idea of Taylor, since he believed there was a future in selling ordnance to the government and wanted accurate data on the cutting of ordnance steel. To ensure the success of this project, he hired Emlen Hare Miller as a time-study engineer to study Shartle and Fannon in order to obtain the facts concerning the cutting of ordnance steel. William Fannon reports:

> he was very anxious to get data that was based on facts and actual practice; and I and others assisted in obtaining this data under a stop-watch, which was in constant possession and used by a man who was then known in his official capacity as an observer.[81]

THE FIRST STEPS TOWARD FUNCTIONAL FOREMANSHIP

In conjunction with his metal-cutting experiments, Taylor sought to install what he considered important methods of controlling the activities of his workmen. As he learned more about the elements important to proper use of machine tools in 1883 and 1884, Taylor began to believe that only by careful preparation and careful inspection of the completed work of workers and keeping track of the time spent on each task could he gather evidence related to the total cost of his metal-cutting experiments.

Taylor recognized these activities were actually logical extensions of his job as shop foreman and he identified them as such in 1883 and developed positions (which he later termed "functional foremen") to administer each of the activities. Taylor as foreman had "subforemen" to handle the inspection and time-tracking to directly supervise the workers and not go through Taylor himself. Taylor, by 1883, claims to have had five of these "subforemen": (1) instruction card man, (2) time man, (3) inspector, (4) gang boss, and (5) shop disciplinarian. According to Taylor, "each of these functional foremen dealt directly with the workmen instead of giving their (sic) orders through the gang boss."[82]

At first, the instruction card man and the time man only came into contact with the workmen by written notes, while Taylor performed the role of the shop disciplinarian (a role he had followed in the struggle with his men in 1881–83). However, in reviewing the individual responsibilities of these "foremen," it is discovered that the instruction card clerk prepared instruction cards which would be one of the jobs previously performed by the gang boss. The time man kept track of every minute of every employee's time. The gang boss was assigned the task of setting up the work and its preparation according to the instruction card, and to show the men how to set the work in the machines. Taylor, as shop disciplinarian, maintained records of each workman's virtues and defects and the readjusting of the wages of the workmen. Finally, because of the necessity of inspecting the work of the men under the piece-rate system, Taylor introduced the inspector who would directly inspect the work of the men without going through the gang boss. With the introduction of the inspector, Taylor said he first realized the desirability of functional foremanship as a management principle.[83]

Barth acknowledged in 1920 that, although Taylor had developed functional foremanship at Midvale, he did so "secretly because of the natural opposition of the management to so radical a change" and that "Even at Bethlehem they were very circumspect in referring to this."[84]

The fact that Taylor chose to keep functional foremanship a secret at Midvale (and Bethlehem) would imply that he developed the concept in the years 1887–90, after the company was purchased by Charles J. Harrah. If he had developed the idea when Sellers, Clark and Taylor's relatives controlled the company, he probably would have openly employed it at Midvale.

A number of years later, Taylor subdivided the work of the old gang boss in the shop into four functions: speed boss, repair boss, inspector, and gang boss. He also installed four separate bosses in a separate planning department. Three of these were the instruction card clerk, the time and cost clerk, and the disciplinarian (three of the original functional foremen of 1881–83), but he also added a new functional foreman: the order-of-work clerk.

The functional foreman idea was eventually developed into the planning department concept at the Bethlehem Steel Company in 1900. Peter Drucker has observed that the planning department concept was one of the greatest insights of Taylor:

> to have discovered that planning is different from doing was one of Taylor's most valuable insights. To emphasize that the work will become the easier, more effective, more productive, the more we plan before we do, was a greater contribution to American industrial rise than stop watch or motion and time study. On it rests the entire structure of modern management.[85]

The functional foreman concept was a major break with the traditional organization structure, whereby a single foreman had dictatorial control over the workers. The single foreman would assign work, train and discipline workers, inspect work, push workers for high production, etc. It eventually became Taylor's belief that a foreman's job was so large and complicated that one foreman could not possibly do justice to all the parts of the job and, therefore, the job must be divided into eight separate jobs with eight separate foremen. Therefore, the workers would report to each of the eight foremen for various aspects of the work. When they needed to learn how to do a job they could go to the instruction clerk; when there was a question on how fast the machine should run, how fast the cutting edge should be moving, they could go to the speed boss. It may sound very confusing, but each functional foreman had only a limited sphere in which he could give orders. The key was that the foreman who had the knowledge was to give the orders. So there wasn't as much confusion as might be expected. There was really only one master, namely knowledge.[86] Frank Gilbreth became a strong advocate of the functional foreman concept and implemented it often when consulting and in his writings.

Richard Whiting has discovered that in 1884 John Richards, owner and manager of the San Francisco Tool Company, had also developed, apparently independent of Taylor, the functional foreman concept.[87] Richards, unable to find foremen capable of carrying out all the duties required, created five separate functional areas in his shop with one man in charge of each area. We do not know, however, if Taylor was aware of Richards' work.

CHARLES HARRAH, SR., AND MIDVALE

The Midvale Steel Company changed hands in 1887, so Taylor's friends and family were no longer in financial control of the company. The Harrah family took control of Midvale, and Taylor eventually left to pursue other interests.

Charles J. Harrah, Sr., was born in Philadelphia on January 1, 1817. In 1832, he began working in the Frankford Shipyard, and on April 14, 1839, he married Anna Margaret Riehl of Philadelphia. In 1843, Harrah went to Brazil to build a shipyard. In 1857, he saw the need for railroads in Brazil and he returned to the United States to make a study of railroads.

Harrah returned to Brazil in 1858, and accepted the task of building the mountainous portion of the Dom Pedro II railroad. Although he completed this line by 1864, he was ruined financially. He regained his fortune by engaging in the mercantile business with F. M. Brandon under the name of Brandon & Harrah.

Through the completion of the Don Pedro II railroad, Harrah had gained the Emperor Don Pedro's confidence and in 1865, he was sent to the United States to purchase gunboats and arms for Brazil, but the United States government refused to supply either. It is possible that this project gave Harrah an interest in arms and armor for armies and navies.[88]

In 1868, Harrah and several other Americans organized the Botanical Garden Railroad Company, the first street railway in Brazil. In 1874, he decided to return to Philadelphia to retire and turned the operation of his Brazil business interests to his son Charles Harrah, Jr.

Returning to Philadelphia, Harrah and his wife purchased a large home at 858 North Broad Street. In 1878, his son also returned from Brazil and secured a position with H. L. Gregg & Company, a brokerage house in Philadelphia.

Although Harrah had planned to retire from all business

activities, the virtual failure of the Peoples Passenger Railway in 1883 influenced his return to business. Harrah and his son held a large block of stock in the company and had to act to preserve their investment.

The Peoples Passenger Railway of Philadelphia (awarded a charter on April 15, 1873) had George F. Work, a Philadelphia stockbroker, as president, and Thomas S. Harris as treasurer. The Peoples Passenger Railway, however, did not have any lines or equipment of its own but leased the lines and equipment of the Germantown Passenger Railway (formed April 21, 1858) and the Green and Coates Passenger Railway (formed also on April 21, 1858). The Germantown Passenger Railway operated street car lines to Germantown and Mount Airy sections of Philadelphia, while the Green and Coates line operated to Fairmount Park via Green and Coates (now Fairmount Avenue).[89]

By 1883, the Peoples Passenger Railway was virtually bankrupt. On April 26, 1883, George F. Work was arrested for the mismanagement of the company's finances. At this point the stock of the company, which formerly was selling at $35 a share, fell to $25 a share. A group of stockholders appealed to Charles Harrah, Sr., for help. Therefore, Charles J. Harrah and his son pooled their resources to purchase the bulk of the stock of the company.[90]

In April 1883, Charles Harrah, Sr., became president of the Peoples Passenger Railway, appointed his son vice president of the company, and retained Thomas Harris as treasurer. Almost immediately, the Harrahs began reorganizing and improving the company. The cars were painted distinctive colors, schedules were improved, and corrupt employees were dismissed.[91]

Charles Harrah, Sr., also initiated a regular schedule of inspection trips over the lines of the Peoples Passenger Railway Company to ensure that his improvements were being carried out. These inspection trips brought Harrah close to Midvale whose buildings dominated the area. Perhaps because of his earlier experience in arms and gunboats, Harrah became interested in Midvale's ordnance work. Upon discovering that the company was heavily mortgaged and Sellers and Clark were attempting to sell the company because of the Huston suit, Harrah decided to purchase the company.

Due to the efforts of the Harrahs, Peoples Passenger Railway was financially sound by December 1885, with the stock worth $55 a share. Eager to gain control of Midvale, the Harrahs sold their stock in the company and began negotiations to purchase Midvale.

Charles Harrah, Sr., found it was difficult to secure control of Midvale. Although Edward Clark was willing to sell his shares, Sellers and his brother were not willing to sell their shares. It was necessary that Harrah purchase the shares held by Taylor's uncle, James A. Wright, in order to gain control. It was not until February 1887 that Harrah was able to purchase Wright's shares and, as a result, on February 4, 1887, finally gained control of Midvale.

TAYLOR LEAVES MIDVALE

As President of Midvale Steel, Charles J. Harrah, Sr., appointed his son vice president and the Harrahs made plans to reorganize and improve the company's operations. By 1888, the managers selected by William Sellers when he was president, were replaced. In protest, Sellers withdrew from active participation in Midvale's day-to-day operations. Clarence Clark, Guillemeau Aertsen, William Fannon, and Charles Shartle all left, In August 1888, Russell Davenport left for the Bethlehem Iron Company's new armor-forging plant which was to be built at government expense, and young Harrah became the manager of Midvale, In 1888, because of failing health, Charles J. Harrah, Sr., withdrew from active participation in Midvale. He died two years later on February 18, 1890, and Charles J. Harrah, Jr., became president.

In 1889, Taylor, apparently convinced that his future at Midvale was limited began to search for new opportunities. Fortunately, he was contacted by the Simonds Rolling Machine Company of Fitchburg, Massachusetts, about a project to manufacture armor-piercing projectiles for rifled cannon. Taylor became a consultant to Simonds. This project was destined to prove important in Simonds later employing Taylor as an engineer.

Taylor left Midvale in 1890 and his fame was to develop thereafter, especially from his papers on "Belting," "Metal Cutting," and "Shop Management," written about his Midvale work, but published post 1890. Business historians Philip Scranton and Walter Licht wrote:

> Ironically, in his absence, the implementation of time studies at Midvale had become haphazard rather than systemic. As late as 1918, although women clutching clipboards still attempted to clock and record certain complex or slow-moving sections of war production, Taylor's comprehensive work-measurement program had been discarded as being cumbersome, productive of constant conflict, and inefficient due to the time-consuming paperwork it demanded.[92]

NOTES

1. Taylor to Thompson, August 3, 1893.
2. Philadelphia & Reading Railroad timetable, 1885.
3. Sears, 1931, p. 22.
4. *New York Times*, September 3, 1881, p. 1:5.
5. *New York Times*, September 5, 1881, p. 5:4.
6. Taylor to Cooke, December 2, 1910.
7. Johnson, 1980. p. 5.
8. *The Eccentric,* Stevens Institute of Technology, 1883, p. 33.
9. "Class of '83," *The Bolt*, Stevens Institute of Technology, 1883, p. 26.
10. Johnson, 1980, p. 6.
11. House Resolution, 1912, pp. 1411–12.
12. House Resolution, 1912, p. 1412.
13. House Resolution, 1912, p. 1413.
14. House Resolution, 1912, p. 1413.
15. House Resolution, 1912, p. 1413.
16. House Resolution, 1912, p. 1413.
17. House Resolution, 1912, pp. 1413–14.
18. House Resolution, 1912, p. 1414.

19. Brinley, 1905, p. 45.
20. Brinley, 1905, p. 50.
21. Taylor, *Principles*, 1911, p. 23.
22. Copley, I, p. 261–62.
23. Taylor, 1893.
24. Taylor, 1895, p. 865.
25. Taylor, 1895, p. 865.
26. Taylor, 1895, p. 869.
27. Taylor, 1895, p. 872.
28. Taylor, 1895, p. 872.
29. Taylor, 1895, pp. 889–90.
30. Taylor, 1895, p. 883.
31. Gantt, 1916.
32. Taylor, 1895, p. 876.
33. Taylor, 1906, p. 33.
34. Taylor, 1907, p. 36.
35. J. Sellers Bancroft in Taylor, 1907, p. 286.
36. Taylor, 1907, p. 37.
37. Daniel Adamson in Taylor, 1907, p. 316.
38. Taylor, 1907, p. 37.
39. Taylor, 1907, p. 37.
40. Taylor, 1907, p. 31.
41. *Simonds* v. *Hathorn*, Testimony 1897, pp. 419–20.
42. Califf, 1889, p. 208.
43. Brinley, 1905, pp. 41–42.
44. Califf, 1889, p. 321.
45. Bennett, *Steam Navy*, pp. 771–806.
46. Califf, 1889, p. 360.
47. *Germantown Telegraph*, May 21, 1884, p. 3.
48. Bennett, *Steam Navy*, pp. 809–14.
49. *New York Times*, October 1, 1886, p. 3.
50. *Annual Report*, 1887, p. xxix.
51. Taylor, 1906, p. 34.
52. Barth to Thompson, 1933.
53. Taylor, 1906, p. 248.
54. Taylor, 1906, p. 36.
55. Taylor, 1906, p. 35.
56. Chomienne, 1888, p. 254.
57. *Germantown Independent*, October 8, 1886.
58. Chomienne, 1888, p. 405.
59. Taylor, U.S. Patent No. 424–939, 1890, p. 1.

60. Nalle, 1948, p. 17.
61. Taylor, U.S. Patent No. 424–939, 1890, p. 1.
62. Copley, I, p. 197.
63. *Midvale Safety Bulletin*, January, 1927, p. 7.
64. Taylor, 1906, p. 38.
65. *Germantown Independent*, August 11, 1883, p. 3.
66. Taylor, 1906, para. 112.
67. Copley, I, p. 243.
68. Taylor, 1893.
69. Metcalfe, 1880, p. 12.
70. Metcalfe, 1880, pp. 15–16.
71. Metcalfe, 1880, pp. 16–17.
72. Copley, I, p. 229.
73. Reece, 1884.
74. Reece, 1884, pp. 404, 406.
75. *Present State*, 1912, p. 1198.
76. Taylor, *Shop Management*, 1911, p. 148.
77. Thompson, 1920, p. 1.
78. Thompson, 1920, p. 1.
79. Taylor to Thompson, October 16, 1896.
80. Fannon to Mitchell, April 21, 1916, p. 2.
81. Fannon to Mitchell, April 21, 1916, p. 3.
82. *Shop Management*, 1911, p. 107.
83. *Shop Management*, 1911, p. 107.
84. Thompson, 1920, p. 2.
85. Drucker, 1954, p. 284.
86. Copley, I, p. 291.
87. Whiting, 1964.
88. *Dictionary of American Biography*, p. 294.
89. *Gopsill's*, 1882, p. 1744.
90. *Philadelphia Inquirer*, April 23, 1883, p. 1.
91. *Philadelphia Inquirer*, April 27, 1883, p. 1.
92. Scranton and Licht, 1986, p. 202.

PART III

THE SYSTEM
EVOLVES

TAYLOR AND THE MANUFACTURING
INVESTMENT COMPANY

Taylor's interest in the projectile business was deferred temporarily because of other events which were to create important changes in his career and in the development of the field of management. These changes came about through the influence of William C. Whitney, a man who was to have a mysterious relationship with Taylor for the next 15 years, until Whitney's death in 1904.

William Collins Whitney was a New York lawyer who was active in New York politics. He became New York City's Corporation Counsel and in this position he became familiar with the city's transit franchises. In 1884, Whitney formed the Broadway Railway Company which initially was in competition with the New York Cable Railway controlled by Thomas F. Ryan. In 1885, Whitney and Ryan joined forces against Jacob Sharp who also was interested in a "Broadway Line." By 1889, Whitney and Ryan secured control of the line from Jacob Sharp.

In 1884, Whitney supported Grover Cleveland in his campaign for the presidency, and Cleveland (considering Whitney's railway management experience) appointed him Secretary of the Navy. When he assumed that office in 1885, Whitney began correcting what he saw as inefficiency in the Navy, primarily by improving the ordnance in the form of new guns and by installing a new accounting system. To accomplish the latter he hired William J. Calhoun, a New York City accountant. By October 7, 1885, Calhoun developed for Whitney a new system of accounting for the Navy, saying it covered:

> The establishment of a set of books to show at a glance the cost and all of the particulars of each vessel . . . and of another which shall show at the close of business each day the balance of each appropriation on hand . . . (and) . . . the establishment of rigid property accounts.[1]

Whitney, in 1886, gained control of the New York and Northern Railroad, planning it as part of a line to Boston.[2] After two years of modernization, he decided to make Calhoun auditor, but Calhoun died suddenly in 1889. Whitney then selected William D. Basley, an accountant he knew from the New York City law courts, now the Auditor of the New York, Providence and Boston Railroad, to replace Calhoun. In selecting Basley, Whitney unconsciously provided the individual to help Taylor when he became a management consultant four years later. Copley stated that in 1893, when Taylor wanted to learn something about accounting, he decided to learn "What at the time was the best thought and practice. In this he had the assistance of a professional accountant named William D. Basley. . . ."[3]

Whitney was always in search of new financial opportunities, and in 1887, he believed he had the chance of making considerable money in the wood pulp business. In 1887, Don Dickinson, a lumberman who was appointed by President Cleveland to be Postmaster General of Detroit, negotiated to purchase the American rights to Alexander Mitscherlich's patented "indirect cook" system of manufacturing sulphite pulp. In 1887, Dickinson formed the International Sulphite Fibre and Paper Company of Michigan to lease the Mitscherlich process of converting scrap lumber into pulp for paper manufacturing:

having in mind principally the utilization of the slabs, edgings, sawdust, and bark that were then being produced in the manufacture of lumber from saw logs and the accumulation was such that there were endless conveyors conveying this material, which material was considered waste material, into large burners and burning this material without getting any returns.[4]

Dickinson soon convinced Daniel Lamont (Cleveland's secretary) and Whitney of the idea of creating the Manufacturing Investment Company (MIC), formed in New Jersey on October 18, 1889, to build a chain of pulp mills using the Mitscherlich process and also sell leases to use the process. These leases would be purchased from the International Sulphite Fibre and Paper Company by MIC, who would then sell them to other companies desiring to use the Mitscherlich system.

The MIC planned two mills, one in Appleton, Wisconsin (rebuilt from the former Fletcher Paper Company Mill), and an entirely new mill in Madison, Maine. Whitney secured a leave of absence for Navy men Captain Robley O. Evans and Commander Casper F. Goodrich. Evans was to rebuild the Appleton Mill and Goodrich to build the new Madison mill which was designed by Maine Papermill Builders.

How Taylor actually became associated with MIC is still a mystery. Goodrich, in 1915, said that in 1885 Whitney (while Secretary of the Navy) had assigned Goodrich the task of locating a new superintendent of the Naval Ordnance Foundry in Washington, D.C. Goodrich, after a search, suggested Taylor. Taylor was offered the position, but he rejected the job.[5]

Contemporary evidence reveals that on September 30, 1886, Whitney signed an order changing the Washington Navy Yard into an ordnance foundry.[6] Under this order, 200 employees were discharged on October 1, but one civil engineer was retained. Whether Taylor may have been considered as superintendent of this new yard is unknown.

Taylor's role in the successful completion of the contracts for the 6- and 8-inch naval guns may have played an important role in Whitney's decision to offer Taylor a job at MIC. The importance of the gun forgings contract was indicated by Fannon in 1916.

Fannon in 1916, did not repeat the Goodrich story; instead he said that Taylor's changes in the Midvale Machine Shop, especially as they improved the manufacture of naval gun forgings, interested Whitney. As a result: "Whitney, became interested in Mr. Taylor's unique and unconventional progress and he asked Mr. Taylor to come to Washington for a conference."[7] At this conference Whitney offered Taylor the position of general manager of the MIC mill at a much larger salary than he made at Midvale. Taylor accepted Whitney's offer, with agreement that it would cover a three-year period, October 1, 1890, to October 1, 1893, and submitted his formal resignation to Midvale on June 28, 1890.[8] As a result of this agreement, Taylor reduced his interest in Simonds' projectile project, but did not discontinue his association with Simonds although the contract with Whitney said Taylor would devote his entire time to MIC after October 1, 1890.

Meanwhile, in November of 1889, MIC had started to construct the new mill at Madison, Maine, and to convert the Fletcher mill at Appleton, Wisconsin, to the Mitscherlich process. The location, purchased from a friend of Whitney, and the design of the Madison mill was an error. The land was too small for the building, the building too narrow, and the water supply inadequate. Consequently, when Taylor arrived in Madison he had to direct his attention to redesigning and rebuilding the mill.

Because he was preoccupied with the rebuilding process, Taylor had to rely on assistants to reach the production goals envisioned by Whitney and his associates. One of these was Sanford Thompson, an M.I.T. graduate. Thompson's main efforts were devoted to the development of methods to screen out knots and twigs from the pulp and studying methods of shoveling. Taylor, meanwhile, constructed an auxiliary power plant and supplemental overhead shafts to eliminate delays in the production of pulp.

Despite the rebuilding of the mills, the primary problem facing MIC was the Mitscherlich process itself. MIC had "anticipated that all other companies that wished to cook wood in a digester would have to pay MIC a royalty for the use of the lining of the digester."[9] However, the process proved faulty and the huge profits from leasing did not materialize. Because of the excessive price paid for the patents, and the financial expenses resulting from rebuilding the mills, MIC wanted to produce as much pulp as possible. Due to faulty mill-site selection, original inaccurate building, and problems with the process, output was poor. The owners partially blamed Taylor for their problems and he was given the task of increasing production.

Problems at Appleton roughly paralleled those in Madison. In reconstructing the former Fletcher mill many errors were made. Due to government control of the river, the water supply was inadequate for the new process and Taylor suggested that the company bribe the watchman to make alterations in the dam to solve this problem. The saws in the sawmill did not operate properly due to inadequate overhead belting. The labor supply was inadequate, and Taylor had the managers, A. L. Smith and William Fannon, who had followed Taylor from Midvale, force the men to produce a record amount of pulp. The men struck for higher pay, and in 1892, Taylor decided to install a piecework system to meet the workers' demand for higher wages.

Taylor relied on the differential piece rate he had used at Midvale, but without any change in the manufacturing equipment or supervision as he had tried at Midvale:

> After the digesters had been run for some time and by trying different methods of placing men . . . the most economical method was decided upon . . . and . . . a large number of observations were taken and reported . . . .These figures were taken by the foreman while the men were under his direct supervision, and the work was done steadily and with no interruption.[10]

Taylor was pleased with the piecework results, despite the inadequate methods used to initiate it, and when he was seeking some consulting work in May 1893, he wrote George Hammond:

> repairs . . . every operation in the mill done on the differential rate system from the time our materials arrive in the yard until they are shipped. For example, all the coal, wood, sulfur and

limestone, . . . are unloaded . . . and piled on piecework. They are then transported . . . on piecework . . . wood . . . is sawed on piecework.[11]

The final and production results were likewise important:

> We have reduced the cost of manufacture from $75–$85 per ton to $35 per ton. . . .We have increased the product from 20 tons per day to 36 tons per day. . . some days we have made as high as 46 tons. The cost of labor, including superintendence, was reduced between $30 and $40 per ton to about $8 per ton, . . .[12]

In the Spring of 1893, Taylor introduced piecework at Madison, but these efforts were doomed to failure due to other problems facing MIC. To finance the huge reconstruction at Madison, in November 1891 Whitney secured a $500,000 mortgage for MIC.[13] But in 1893, new problems surfaced when the Maine Supreme Court rescinded a 10-year abatement of taxes that MIC had secured in 1890. Faced with all these problems, Whitney and his associates decided to terminate all operations at Madison. Taylor resigned on May 18, 1893, and the mill closed in June 1893. Although Copley said Taylor did not continue his association with Whitney after he left MIC, there are some coincidental relationships between the companies for which Taylor acted as a consultant, from 1893 to 1904, and Whitney's activities.

The poor financial situation of MIC and Taylor's expensive life style in Madison caused financial reverses for Taylor by July of 1893. Copley said Whitney attempted to keep Taylor at MIC and suggested "it would be to Taylor's interests to remain in touch with him . . . (and) that he could promise to make Taylor a millionaire within a few years."[14] Copley claimed, however, that Taylor declined all of Whitney's offers.

Exploring some of the actions of Whitney may indicate whether or not Copley's story could possibly be true. We should remember that Whitney and Lamont were deeply interested in street railways. Whitney and his associates incorporated the Metropolitan Traction Company of New Jersey on February 18, 1886.[15] This company was designed to operate street railways in New York City. Whitney is not listed as an incorporator, but was represented by his brother-in-law, Colonel Oliver Payne, who was also an officer in the Manufacturing Investment Company and the New York and Northern Railroad. The records of the Metropolitan Traction Company of New Jersey (unlike many of Whitney's other companies formed in 1892 and 1893) still exist. Since Taylor apparently was not associated with Whitney in 1886, his name does not appear as a stockholder as it does on the records of the Manufacturing Investment Company and the International Sulphite Fibre and Paper Company.

In June 1886, the Metropolitan Traction Company of New Jersey purchased the Houston Street, West Street and Pavonia Ferry Railroad. This was a small company, but controlled the franchises of a large number of other New York Street railway companies.[16] On August 4, 1892, Whitney, Thomas Ryan, and Peter A. B. Widner formed a Philadelphia corporation, the Metropolitan Traction Company. This was a holding company designed to secure control of many street railways. The following year, on November 29, 1893, they formed the Metropolitan Street Railway Company of New York. This company controlled the Houston Street, West Street and Pavonia Ferry Railroad, the Broadway and Seventh Avenue Railway, the Broadway Railroad, and the South Ferry Railroad Company. Whitney appointed Harold Vreeland (the superintendent of the New York and Northern Railroad) president of this company.

Whitney, Ryan, and Widener utilized this company to virtually steal 100 million dollars for their own use in the next nine years from unsuspecting investors. The method employed was to lease various New York street railway companies and then use these leases as assets against which they would issue Metropolitan Street Railway stock. In each case, the cars of the street railways they leased were repainted with the word "Metropolitan" on their sides, so wherever anyone went in New York City one saw Metropolitan Street Railway cars. In addition they made the Metropolitan stock more appealing by using the money from new stock issues to pay high dividends to the holders of older issues. The trio also owned large blocks of stock themselves from which they took large dividends. Large sums of money were also raised by constructing and repairing the lines of the company. The contracts for such work were given to friends of Whitney, Ryan, and Widener, who in turn gave payoffs to the trio.[17]

Considering the large profits made by Whitney from the Metropolitan (almost $35 million), and the fact that Vreeland also became a millionaire, we can see that if Whitney had appointed Taylor president of the company (instead of Vreeland), Taylor also would have been a millionaire within a few years.

Whitney, Widener, Ryan, William L. Elkins, and John D. Crimmins also formed the Consolidated Traction Company of New Jersey on April 10, 1893. Taylor may have been a major stockholder in this company, but the records have disappeared from the files of the Secretary of State of New Jersey.

We are unable to confirm the fact that Taylor may have held large blocks of stock in any of Whitney's companies. Taylor, however, through the Clark family, invested quite heavily in electric railways in the 1890s, including the East St. Louis and Suburban Railway, where Whitney was a large shareholder. Further investments in this company were made both by Taylor and Sanford Thompson in 1902.[18]

After his resignation from MIC, Taylor decided to concentrate on working for Simonds, and to understand this decision we must return to Taylor's relationship with Simonds in the period 1890–93.

TAYLOR'S RELATIONSHIP WITH SIMONDS ROLLING MACHINE COMPANY: THE EARLY YEARS

In the 1880s George F. Simonds of Fitchburg, Massachusetts, observed that circular objects could be formed into any shape by rotating them on their axes between opposite moving surfaces, and in 1884, he secured patents on his rolling machine. Simonds, at the time was the president of the Simonds Manufacturing Company of Fitchburg, which produced saws and cutting tools of every description. He resigned this post in 1886 and incorporated the Simonds Rolling Machine Company. In his biography of Taylor, Daniel Nelson said Simonds acquired the rights to the Taylor forging patent in 1888, and "Taylor took stock in the company rather than cash for his invention."[19] Nelson cites Copley as his source of information, but while Copley states that Simonds acquired Taylor's rights to "rolling machinery on which Taylor held patents" and that his information was that "Taylor received stock in the company" for these rights, Copley did not provide any evidence to support his assertions.[20]

There is no evidence that Taylor acquired Simonds' stock for his inventions, for it appears that Taylor acquired his Simonds' stock through an agreement with Chauncey Smith, Secretary of Simonds, to have the right to sell shares of the firm's capital stock. The directors authorized this agreement on October 21, 1889, stating that Simonds would pay Taylor "as a commission on such sales $13 per share."[21] By April 25, 1890, Taylor had sold 486 shares at $102 per share and 459 shares at $115, earning $3,213.[22] Taylor and his wife only had 100 shares of stock in the company but despite these small holdings he was destined to play an important role in Simonds' affairs.

By August 1890, Taylor assumed even more importance to Simonds in the eyes of George G. Simonds. Simonds liked Taylor because he had invested in the company (not because Simonds had purchased Taylor's forging patent). Simonds wrote Taylor on August 6, 1890:

> I have learned through Mr. Grant that you are not only interested in "The Metal Rolling Machine" financially yourself, but have also placed considerable stock with others and am therefore doubly interested in the quick and full success of the enterprise.[23]

Four days later, Simonds wrote Taylor again about conditions at the company:

> Things are not going well either in the shop or out of it . . . changes should be made to put the business in shape for making money and for this reason I wish to meet with you in private at as early a day as possible.[24]

Taylor did not reply to this letter until September 2, 1890, saying he had just begun his job as General Manager for the Manufacturing Investment Company and was too busy to meet with Simonds. From September to December 1890, several attempts were made to hold a meeting between Taylor and Simonds as well as with the board of directors, but as we have indicated, problems at the MIC mill in Madison, Maine, prevented Taylor from attending a meeting.

By May 7, 1891, Taylor decided Simonds Rolling Machine should enter the manufacturing of track bolts, which were of increasing importance in street railway construction. He wrote Edward Sawyer, manager of Simonds, sending him a sample track bolt and suggesting the company should investigate this line of products.[25] By November 1891, the firm had decided to manufacture track bolts, and simultaneously, Chauncey Smith, Simonds' manager, wrote Taylor that Simonds needed a new superintendent to replace Grant, who had left to form the Cleveland Machine Screw Company. Taylor suggested W. H. Thorne (from Midvale) for superintendent and Smith answered, stating that Thorne should "address himself first to the manufacture of track bolts. . . ."[26] Smith urged Taylor to come to Fitchburg and participate in an interview of Thorne, but Taylor replied that a recent fire at the Madison mill prevented him from coming. Taylor's failure to participate in the selection of a new superintendent was a crucial event on Taylor's part. With Taylor absent, Edward Sawyer, Chauncey Smith, and George Weymouth decided not to hire Thorne, and instead, Weymouth assumed the duties of superintendent as well as manager. With Weymouth as superintendent, the foundation was prepared for future conflicts between Taylor and the Simonds Company, conflicts created by Weymouth. Despite what the officers of Simonds thought of Taylor's abilities, he was still an outsider to the people of Fitchburg. Weymouth, on the other hand, had been a prominent Fitchburg resident since 1882, when he opened a carriage business. He was active in politics, a director of the Fitchburg National Bank, and well liked. The *Fitchburg Sentinel* ran a story of Simonds in 1892, and Weymouth's photograph occupied a prominent place on the page along with photographs of the company plant, but there was no photograph of Taylor or mention of his work. Weymouth, unlike Thorne, did not understand the manufacture of track bolts and consequently they were never produced in large amounts.

The fire at Madison, which prevented Taylor from coming to Fitchburg, was one of many problems Taylor experienced at Madison. On December 18, 1892, Taylor issued a report on the Madison mill: "Report on the Relative Cost of the Madison Mill to That of Other Similar Mills."[27] In this report Taylor said:

> It is the opinion of some people, and I think this opinion is shared by several of the Directors of our Company, that the Madison Mill has been built in a very extravagant manner. The writer has therefore taken pains to look into this matter as closely as possible with a view to determining as nearly as may be the exact facts in the case.[28]

This negative view by the MIC directors of Taylor's efforts at Madison and Appleton, coupled with the difficulty of manufacturing the required amount of pulp per day due to the design of the mills, may have made Taylor wonder if he should remain with MIC. Consequently, while Taylor had found it difficult to travel to Fitchburg the previous month, he now found it easy to meet with Chauncey Smith in Boston. The topics discussed during this meeting are unknown, but one must have been about Taylor's plans for better control of costs in Simonds. When Taylor returned to Madison, he immediately wrote Smith on the subject of costs. Taylor informed Smith that the system could be based on the method used at Midvale and that Simonds, because of its small size, could easily adopt this system. Part of the letter suggested how this method could be used by Weymouth, a suggestion which Weymouth, no doubt, did not appreciate:

> It would seem to me of the greatest importance for Mr. Weymouth to have a sample case in which every article manufactured by us is filed away and all the details entering into the cost of same written out on a card . . . attached to the piece itself. In addition to this cost, which is the proper cost of the article,

there should be attached to the sample, another card showing the limit cost, that is, the money which actually had to be paid out for the manufacture of the article. This cost . . . would include such items as steam, repairs on machine, cost of dies, actual money paid for wages of the workmen, oil, bundling and shipping expenses. This limit cost would show Mr. Weymouth the figure below which, under no condition or circumstances, he could ever go. Better shut down the whole establishment than take work below this cost. . . .[29]

Taylor terminated this letter with the suggestion that Smith could contact him: "if I can be of assistance to you and hoping that this may be of interest to you."

In 1893, when the situation at MIC began to look black, the tone of Taylor's letters to Smith and Sawyer changed considerably. He made every effort to aid Simonds, and in February, when Sawyer told Taylor that George Simonds had been trying to sell the machinery rights "to a new company to be formed by him and Philadelphia parties,"[30] Taylor offered to obtain information on Simonds' backers. We do not know what Taylor discovered, but in March 1893, he told Sawyer that Simonds should enter the field of boot caulks. In May he advised Smith that *Iron Age* for April 20, 1893, had advertised a rolled forging machine made by Tebbetts saying, "I merely wanted to call your attention to it. . . ."[31] In June, Taylor urged the use of piecework and although Smith said Simonds was "On the high road to adopting that plan very soon . . . and . . . it ought to be adopted . . . ,"[32] piecework was not adopted at this time. The continual failure to adopt piecework was a problem that was to plague Taylor both at Simonds and elsewhere.

TAYLOR'S ACCOUNTING SYSTEM

While at MIC, Taylor adopted and refined a system of bookkeeping developed by William D. Basley, the accountant for the New York and Northern Railroad. When Whitney decided to sell this line to the New York Central Railroad in February 1892, he transferred Basley to the New York MIC office at 32

Nassau Street. There Taylor met Basley and became interested in his system of bookkeeping, which used a large number of individual forms to close and balance the books.[33] In May 1893, when Taylor decided to concentrate on working for Simonds and to strengthen his abilities, he made the decision to learn something about bookkeeping. He was impressed by Basley's system of forms which he believed could be used at Fitchburg, and also adapted to fit the problems of other companies.

Late in June 1893, Taylor went to New York. He spent considerable time studying Basley's forms, as revealed by the various notes in his handwriting on Basley Form 207. He also wrote letters to several persons (Sawyer and Smith of Simonds, and Hammond of Forest Paper Company). These letters were almost identical, stressing the flexibility of Basley's system:

> the method of bookkeeping which enables our auditor and the bookkeeper to make out a complete set of exhibits an (sic) close and balance the books with transactions amounting to about $200,000 in two hours (which I saw the last time I was in New York) is quite remarkable. . . . I have regarded it as so valuable that I have been devoting about six weeks to mastering it so as to be able to apply it this fall.[34]

On July 12, 1893, Basley wrote Taylor, outlining the general principles applicable to bookkeeping, stating: "Any other information that you may require, I will gladly furnish you, and if there is anything about the above that you do not understand, I will gladly explain it to you."[35] In examining this letter in detail, we discover that the famous manuscript of Taylor's bookkeeping system titled, "Bookkeeping under the Taylor System" (supposedly created by Taylor), is actually an expanded version of Basley's letter and was no doubt written by Basley himself.[36]

In the Taylor papers at Stevens Institute of Technology, there are two versions of the bookkeeping manuscript: a typewritten copy in Scrapbook #3, without a date, 40 pages long, which we may call "Bookkeeping A," and another version, annotated by Horace K. Hathaway (a Taylor associate) with the statement that the system was developed for a paper mill "about 1893," ("Bookkeeping B"). The latter paper was accepted by Chen and Pan in 1980, as an accurate dating of Taylor's accounting system.[37] In reality, Bookkeeping A is an expanded version of Basley's letter of July 12, 1893; Bookkeeping B was prepared several years later.

By carefully numbering the paragraphs (and portions of each paragraph in some cases) in Basley's letter and comparing it with Bookkeeping A, it becomes clear that portions of the letter were used to write the Taylor manuscript. Since Basley may have explained the letter more fully to Taylor when Taylor visited him in New York in 1893, and because Basley could have written a more detailed explanation of the various paragraphs (that no longer exist), it is possible that the material in Bookkeeping A that parallels Basley's letter is actually Basley's more detailed explanation. We only consider two of the similarities between the Basley letter and Taylor's Bookkeeping A, but there are many others.

Basley Letter	**Bookkeeping A**
All book entries in any kind of business should be made in such a manner that the accounts will of themselves detect errors, ...	The system should be such that no error can be made which will not be indicated from the books themselves within a few days after it occurs.
(Para. 1, lines 1 and 2)	(*a*, p.1)
For instance, taxes (generally paid in advance) is an open account decreased each month by an apportioned charge to operating or manufacture; . . . . Insurance, treated in like manner.	For instance, taxes, which are generally paid in advance and insurance are open accounts which should be decreased each month by an appropriate charge to operating expenses or to manufacture.
(Para. 2*a*, p.1)	(Para. 2, p.5, lines 5–8)

Evidence of a close relationship between Basley's letter and material in Bookkeeping A is found by comparing enlargements of type in both documents with similar type in a carbon copy of Taylor's letter to Chauncey Smith of Simonds on August 4, 1893. These figures reveal the following data:

When we compare specific letters of the words "instance," "taxes," and "generally" in Basley's letter with the same letters of these words found on page 5 of Bookkeeping A, we find that the "i" in "instance" is struck slightly higher than the "n" which follows. The "t" in "taxes" is higher than the "a" which follows, and the "rally" of "generally" is higher than the preceding "gene." On this basis it appears that Basley's letter and Bookkeeping A were typed on the same typewriter, perhaps the one in Basley's office at the MIC in New York. If we compare the letters on lines 1 and 2 with similar combinations of letters in Taylor's letter of August 4, 1893, typed in Madison, Maine, we discover they are not like the ones in lines 1 and 2. In line 3, the "i" in "finished" is at the same level as the "n" which follows, a situation not found in lines 1 and 2. Similarly, the "t" in "state" is almost at the same level as the "a" which follows, again different than the letters in lines 1 and 2. Finally, the "ar" in "particularly" is at the same level as the "ly," a situation not found in lines 1 and 2.

This example of comparison of specific letters from the three documents enables us to conclude that Bookkeeping A was typed on Basley's typewriter in New York City and not on Taylor's typewriter in Madison, Maine.

Further evidence that Basley prepared Bookkeeping A is the fact that it states (on page 3) that the system in Bookkeeping A is Basley's system. When comparing similar pages of Bookkeeping A and Bookkeeping B, we find that the words "Under Mr. Basley's system of bookkeeping" have been eliminated and that the paragraph starts with the word "All." As a result, readers of the later version (namely Bookkeeping B) no longer are able to learn that the Taylor System of Bookkeeping was originally developed by Basley.

On only page 15 of Bookkeeping A, is what appears to be a footnote to the text describing the "General Ledger" in detail. In paragraph 3, we find the remark that "I have made the exhibit *208, page 81,* showing as clearly as may be all the 'general ledger accounts'. . . . "Turning to page 19 of Book-

keeping B, however, this entire paragraph 3 is almost eliminated and the remaining portion (starting with "a certain
part," etc.) is incorporated into the total text. As a result, in
later editions of Bookkeeping what could be seen as a memorandum from Basley to Taylor ("I have," etc.) has been eliminated
and in one more way Basley's connection with the Taylor Bookkeeping System has been removed.

We may conclude that the original Bookkeeping A was
prepared by Basley, typed on his typewriter in New York, and
that subsequent revisions which produced Bookkeeping B
made every effort to eliminate Basley's association with the
system. Taylor was able to convince Smith and Sawyer of Simonds to adopt this system in August 1893, and it was so installed in September 1893.

INDUSTRIAL ESPIONAGE
TO PROTECT SIMONDS

Taylor's activities for the period October 1893 to September 1894
are still a mystery. He may have acted as a consultant to the
International Sulphite Fibre and Paper Company, which still
controlled the Mitscherlich sulphite pulp patents. Taylor held
stock in this company until 1899, even though he stated, on August 25, 1893, that the Mitscherlich process was an "enormous
fraud."[38] There is a possibility that he also may have worked for
the Crescent Steel Company of Pittsburgh in the period September 1893 to September 1894, since he made several trips to Pittsburgh during this period. No details are known of his work there
although Crescent was involved in the later patent suits over the
Taylor–White high-speed steel process in 1906.

From September 1894 to May 1895, Taylor worked for the
William Cramp and Sons Shipyard in Philadelphia, where he
engaged in further metal-cutting experiments. However, while
Taylor was at Cramps, George F. Simonds fell off a train in
Scranton, Kansas, on November 5, 1894, and was killed.[39] This
unfortunate accident made Taylor an important figure to Simonds for four reasons: (1) he was the only engineer with the

firm who, because of his experience in heavy machinery, could possibly improve Simonds' rolling machines, (2) he was considered a person who probably would not sell out to Simonds' rivals, (3) he was the best man to conduct experiments and investigations to ward off the threat of infringement by rival firms, and (4) most important, Taylor had plans for a steel ball combination which he expressed to George Weymouth, the Simonds' superintendent, in April 1895.[40] The American Ball Association was already being formed by Alfred Bowditch of Simonds, who apparently asked Taylor to help by investigating the companies involved; this became Taylor's first task when he returned to Boston.

Nelson informs us that Taylor moved to Boston in March 1895, but "why they went to Boston is unclear. Taylor may have gone back to Simonds. . . ."[41] Taylor's 1895 correspondence, however, reveals that the reasons are not "unclear" and that Nelson's guess was correct. He began working to aid Simonds, and enlisted the aid of Newcomb Carlton, an 1890 graduate of Stevens Institute. Carlton wanted to join the American Society of Mechanical Engineers and asked Taylor for help. Taylor in turn suggested that Carlton could aid him in discovering inside information for Simonds on the companies hoping to be part of the American Ball Association. Carlton's task was to contact these companies and tell them that he represented a company being formed by a group of capitalists, who wished to purchase machines to manufacture bicycle balls in order to profit from the current bicycle craze. As part of Taylor's plan, Carlton was to visit each of the companies on the pretext of examining their production facilities, but at the same time check to see if they were infringing on Simonds' patents and to gauge their output.

In June 1895, Taylor also engaged the services of H. S. Shadbolt of Chicago, Illinois, a detective in mechanical and patent matters, instructing him to obtain a job at a plant he believed was infringing on Simonds' patents. The plant was the Edward Jones and David Roughead Machine Works in Tonawanda, New York. After some difficulties, including getting a finger broken and his foot smashed, Shadbolt discovered they were not infringing.[42] From Tonawanda, Taylor sent Shadbolt to Cleveland, Ohio, to investigate the Cleveland Machine Screw Company. Here, Taylor told Shadbolt not to work in the plant, but to place an advertisement for rolling-machine mechanics in the local paper, telling them to write to a box number. The plan was a success and Shadbolt wrote Taylor: "Your scheme of advertising worked fine, as all your schemes do. . . . Now, Mr. Taylor, I am now thoroughly convinced (after interviewing mechanics) that they are not using your process for making balls."[43]

Simultaneous with the Simonds' patent infringement investigations, Taylor had been asked by the Northern Electric Manufacturing Company in August 1895, to improve their bookkeeping system. Since he was deeply involved in his investigations and also preparing for a series of steel ball experiments in the Fall, Taylor had to improvise. He altered the Simonds' bookkeeping methods for use by Northern Electric by adding the words "delivery and erection" at appropriate points in his instructions.[44]

In October 1895, Taylor conducted a series of experiments at Fitchburg with the Bundy dies that were being used by the Hathorn Fancy Forging Company (later renamed the Hathorn Manufacturing Company) to infringe on Simonds' patents and which Hathorn claimed anticipated Simonds' invention. As Taylor reported in December 1896 (one year after his experiments):

> In many respects, the Bundy dies closely resemble those of Simonds. Fortunately for us, however, the Bundy dies are entirely inoperative if made as illustrated by him. . . . I have had dies made exactly like those shown in Bundy's drawings . . . and found it entirely impossible to roll a ball with them either from steel or lead.[45]

Taylor conducted these experiments on October 15 and November 21, 1895, at the shop in Fitchburg.[46]

In November 1895, Taylor discovered that the Pope Manufacturing Company of Hartford, Connecticut, (bicycle manufacturers) might also have been infringing on Simonds' patents. Taylor tackled this new problem and (either through Shadbolt or by himself) located an employee, Ernest V. Kendall, who was willing to prepare an affidavit stating Pope had infringed on the Simonds' patents since 1890.[47] The original affidavit was prepared by Taylor, a method he repeated a second time in the *Simonds* v. *Hathorn* deposition, which will be discussed shortly.

SANFORD THOMPSON AND TAYLOR'S HANDBOOK ON SPEED OF WORK

In the Taylor biography, Copley said that "the story of the development of details of Scientific Management is sometimes more the story of one of Taylor's associates than of Taylor himself."[48] This is especially true in the case of Sanford Thompson, the person who developed the tools required for the successful development and application of time study in industry.

In 1895, Taylor conceived of the idea of publishing a series of handbooks on the time to accomplish tasks in the building trades. The origins of this idea were outlined in his 1895 paper on "A Piece Rate System":

> What is needed is a handbook on the speed with which work can be done. . . . Such a book should describe the best method of making, recording, tabulating, and indexing time-observations, since much time and effort are wasted by the adoption of inferior methods.

Taylor, On December 30, 1895, hired Sanford Thompson under written contract to secretly collect data and prepare manuscripts for such a handbook. In this contract, Thompson pledged to give his entire time and services for the purpose of "gathering information for writing a book, books, articles, or several articles . . . (on) . . . the time required for doing various kinds of work."[49] In addition, the information and any material Thompson wrote would become the "sole property of Taylor," to be published or not published at Taylor's discretion.[50] Finally, he agreed to "use his best endeavors to prevent other parties from knowing the nature and objects of the work upon which he was engaged."

Taylor, in 1903, in discussing time study, said the art of studying unit times "has its own peculiar implements and methods" and that Thompson had "developed what are in many respects the best implements in use, . . ."[51] He also explained briefly Thompson's six-year investigations into the construction industry.

> Mr. Sanford E. Thompson, C.E., started in 1896 with but small help from the writer, except as far as the implements and methods are concerned, to study the time required to do all kinds of work in the building trades. In six years he has made a complete study of eight of the most important trades—excavation, masonry (including sewer-work and paving), carpentry, concrete and cement work, lathing and plastering, slating and roofing, and rock quarrying. He took every stopwatch observation himself and then, with the aid of two comparatively cheap assistants, worked up and tabulated all of his data ready for the printer. The magnitude of this undertaking will be appreciated when it is understood that the tables and descriptive matter for one of these trades alone take up about 250 pages.[52]

In his writings, Taylor discussed the "implements" associated with time study in the following order: Thompson's time-study forms, watch book, and stopwatch. Here, although we will discuss these items, our discussion shall follow their actual historical development. This is a vital necessity, because each of these items was created by Thompson to meet problems associated with his study of the building trades.

Stopwatch
At the start of the six-year study of the building trades, Taylor told Thompson he should make his observations with a stopwatch, which he described to Thompson as: "arranged so that by pressing one spring the hand will fly back to 0, or, by pressing another spring they go ahead from the point at which they were last stopped."[53] While Thompson correctly understood the type of watch Taylor desired, Taylor had only vague knowledge of the watch; he wrote Thompson:

> Your understanding in response to the function of the watch is correct . . . except . . . my impression is that the whole watch

Stopwatch with decimal face from Taylor's *Shop Management* (1911: Harper & Brothers), p. 155.

was started and stopped. It, however, had a minute hand as well as a second hand, so it would record at least 60 minutes in addition to the regular number of seconds. I am afraid you will find difficulty in getting just the right kind of watch.[54]

Although he hunted for the correct watch, Thompson found it difficult to find the one he needed because the only watch available would not be a "fly back." Thompson then decided to obtain a common stopwatch that recorded 30 minutes and have it rebuilt to one like Taylor wanted, but while it was being rebuilt, Thompson asked Taylor the specific location he wished to have the spring to make the watch "fly back." In his letter, Thompson included a drawing of this watch saying the spring could be placed "anywhere along dotted line. I had mine placed at *A* because I shall use it chiefly with the left hand. For right hand or pocket use, the *B* location might be better."[55]

On March 2, 1896, Taylor wrote to Thompson:

I have yours of the 25th (February 25, 1896). Am very glad indeed to hear that you have the stopwatch, and it works very satisfactory. I think it would be a good idea to put the additional hand and spring on as you suggest, although in many cases this might not be useful, since it is frequently desirable for one to know not only the average time for performing an operation, but also the quickest time in which it can be done, as well as the slowest rate at which the man is working.[56]

While this watch was being made, however, Thompson accidentally discovered the very watch Taylor wanted.[57] Now that he had found the watch, Thompson began searching for dials divided into hundredths of a minute and informed Taylor of this fact.[58] Taylor asked Thompson for two of these watches.[59] By 1903, Thompson had developed the decimal watch and attempted to secure a patent on such a watch, but he failed. This watch is illustrated in "Shop Management," with the drawing reproduced there being the same one Thompson used in his rejected patent application.[60]

The Watch Book

One of the problems faced by Thompson in making observations of workers in the building trades was the difficulty in secretly timing their work. As a result, Taylor and Thompson decided it was necessary to devise a way of concealing both the watch and the forms for recording observations. Thompson's solution to the problem was the creation of the "watch book" which held a watch and small forms for recording actual times. He developed this book in 1896 after describing it to Taylor in 1895. On January 8, Taylor suggested that Thompson order "a good book with a place for a stopwatch in it such as we spoke of."[61] Thompson went to work and by February 21 he had the watch book which he described as follows:

> I have . . . had made . . . a combination case and notebook to carry in my pocket. This is substantially as we talked when you were in Boston. It is made to imitate a notebook with a cover on it to protect the "leaves." As it opens, the right-hand part consists of a hollow box, containing the watch, the edges of which are of wood cut away where the springs of the watch come. The left-hand part is a plain cover but so arranged at the back (or hinge) that it will hold a thin block or pad. Over both parts is

Watch book for time study from Taylor's *Shop Management* (1911: Harper & Brothers), p. 153.

a light leather cover. . . . A fly leaf will cover the watch when desired.[62]

Thompson's drawing of this first watch book, taken from his letter, appears in the 1903 "Shop Management" paper and in the 1911 book.

Time-Study Forms

Because of the size of the watch book, it was necessary to have small forms to record the observation, but they also had to be large enough to handle the various data Thompson was recording. Thompson solved this by designing a form 4 by 7 inches, which he described to Taylor as follows:

> I intend to have some of Form A1 printed to start with. I have divided a large number of operations into elementary divisions and it seems to me that Form A1 will cover almost any simple work. Form A2 which with others I shall probably have printed later, modified by my experiments with A1, will cover almost every kind of shoveling, including unloading cars, loading carts, and digging holes. My sheets will have to

be small so that the case containing them and the watch will not attract attention.[63]

After examining Form A1, Taylor told Thompson that he did not allow enough room on his blanks:

for the various descriptions of the work and the operations, and I feel you will have to have other blanks, say, folding over or enlarged, in order to give you sufficient room to be sufficiently specific in your description.[64]

Thompson already had found Form A1 too small and designed a new one, Form B2, which was twice the size.

After he had developed these three elements, Thompson, throughout 1896, concentrated on studying other aspects of the building trades: plastering, lathing, brickwork, concrete, etc. When Taylor assumed control of the Simonds shop in December 1896, he subsequently employed Thompson for other studies.

TAYLOR AT THE JOHNSON COMPANY: 1896

In 1895, the Johnson Company of Johnstown, Pennsylvania, manufacturers of street railway motors and owner of the Steel Motor Company, which also manufactured street railway motors, shifted their manufacturing facilities from Cleveland to buildings they owned in Johnstown. At Johnstown they hired men, rebuilt the plant, and made plans to reorganize all plant operations. To accomplish this reorganization, Arthur Moxham, co-owner and manager of the Johnson Company, began a search for a suitable person.

While Moxham was engaged in this search, William C. Whitney was in the process of reorganizing the Metropolitan Street Railway of New York into a citywide railway system. He was ordering railway motors, but we do not know if he may have suggested Taylor to Moxham. In addition, Taylor was purchasing street railway and railroad stock at the time and may have become a stockholder in the Johnson Company, as in previous cases. In any case, Taylor was hired to reorganize the company.

Taylor's main work at Johnson was to install the bookkeeping methods developed by Basley. In installing this system, Taylor became aware of the complete lack of any organized system of the materials needed for production. He wrote Casper Goodrich on June 3, 1896:

> Some hundred and fifty thousand dollars worth of valuable stores and supplies dumped down in a shed helter skelter, without even protection from the weather, and each workman dived into this pile for whatever he wanted without rendering any account to anyone of what he wanted.[65]

Taylor told Moxham the company needed "an accurate running balance of raw materials, merchandise, and stores throughout all of your establishments."[66]

By September 1896, Taylor had succeeded in introducing a large number of forms to keep track of both raw materials and semi-finished products. By October, Taylor had succeeded in completing the installation of his first systematic stores-keeping system and also applied his differential piece rate in the electric motor plant. His problem, however, was that Johnson had used a contract system where a contractor hired the men, supervised them, and paid them a day wage. The contractor made a personal profit on his "contract" by reducing costs in the firm. The continual effects of the 1893 depression had weakened the "contract" system and because of this Taylor was able to abolish the "contractors," making them salaried foremen, and to introduce the differential piece rate. Taylor reported the success of this work stating that:

> in the classes of work to which it has been applied the cost has been fully cut in two. We have saved enough in armature winding alone to pay for all the costs of introducing the system and running it.[67]

Despite these reforms, the Johnson Company was suffering financial reverses. In July 1896, Taylor was asked to curtail his activities and by October 1896, the plant was virtually closed. Taylor ceased his work at Johnstown and returned to Fitchburg to handle the new problems at the Simonds Rolling Machine Company.

SIMONDS ROLLING MACHINE COMPANY: 1896–1898

Earlier, in February 1896, Simonds obtained evidence that the Hathorn Company (which had desired to sell to Newcomb Carlton's mythical rolling machine company) was infringing on Simonds' patents. On February 26, 1896, Alfred Bowditch of Simonds informed Taylor that a former Hathorn Company employee, A. B. Purington, claimed that Hathorn was not only infringing on the Simonds patents, but that he, Purington, had developed the first Hathorn ball-grinding machine that was based entirely on Simonds' patents.

In his letter, Bowditch said he was sending Taylor drawings of the Hathorn machines. On a subsequent trip to Johnstown, Purington helped Taylor make detailed drawings of the machines for Bowditch, and Taylor suggested he should hire Purington to make more rolling machines:

> Purington, I think, will prove a valuable man for us. He offers to make us a complete rolling machine for I think $300.00 to $400.00 exactly like the Hathorn machine. . . . He says the pattern for this machine belongs to one of the machine shops in Bangor. I have also made accurate sketches of the Hathorn ball-gauging machine which seems to me far superior to ours.[68]

At the same time Taylor was working in Johnstown he was also deeply involved in the production problems of Simonds. He continually urged the adoption of piecework because "it not only cheapens our output, but at the same time increases the quantity of same."[69] He suggested that the employees, not the foreman, keep track of their own time. However, Bowditch did not agree, and Taylor wrote him explaining the task of the foreman.

In preparing this data for Bowditch, Taylor described the role of the foreman both in relation to timekeeping and as a leader of men in a way very similar to that found in Metcalfe's report to Lyford on November 11, 1880, cited earlier.[70]

Metcalfe wrote:

> Foremen should not be expected, nor in fact allowed to do any but the most abundantly necessary clerical duties . . . their

business, even of the best of men, is not to record events but to drive, and lead men to actual results.[71]

Taylor wrote:

> My reason is that the foreman is the last man in the place who should be burdened with clerical work. Upon the energy and ability to hustle of the foreman depends, in my mind, the success in manufacturing more than on any other one element and if the foreman is busy any appreciable portion of his time in time-keeping, he is neglecting to that extent far more important duties.[72]

It is interesting to note that Taylor made no effort to use his functional foremanship concept because it probably was not developed at this time sufficiently to be used successfully.

Taylor's efforts to have piecework installed, and the continual delays and excuses by George Weymouth, led the Simonds' Board of Directors, on October 14, 1896, to pass a resolution supporting piecework and a few months later, on December 11, 1896, turning over to Taylor "the entire charge of our shop at Fitchburg."[73] The Board especially urged Taylor to "get out all the balls which possibly could be produced."[74]

Although Taylor was in charge of the shop at Fitchburg, Weymouth was still responsible for all purchasing and selling and in this area he was helpful in getting Congress to pass a tariff on the importation of antifriction balls. This tariff was necessary due to the decline of the ball market in America.[75] Meanwhile Taylor was faced with a new group of problems at Simonds.

Almost immediately after he assumed control of the shop, Taylor discovered that the Hathorn Company was turning out one million balls a week on nine forging machines. Fortunately, Taylor knew that George Hathorn was willing to sell the rights to his "lightening grinder."[76] Taylor made efforts to purchase this machine for Simonds, but was not successful.

As a delaying tactic, until he could get Hathorn's "lightening grinder," Taylor relied on the use of the differential piece rate to increase output in the grinding department.

But Taylor did not use time study, hence he was not using scientific management as he was to espouse it later. Taylor estimated high rates (which he guaranteed for three years) and low rates which he continually lowered "until each workman finds it for his interest to work fast and do the best quality of work only."[77] By March 1897, through the aid of Sanford Thompson (who commuted from Newton Highlands to Fitchburg, Massachusetts), all of the grinding departments were on the differential piece rate. The result was that the number of balls produced in March was three times the average monthly output of 1896.

The problem, however, was quality and Taylor had to ensure that Simonds' balls were better than Hathorn's. To ensure this quality, Taylor introduced an elaborate system of inspection, described by Thompson as "systematic supervision." An effective method of increasing the output was instituted:

> An accurate daily record, both as to quantity and quality, was kept for each inspector. . . . This enabled the foreman to stir the ambition of all the inspectors by increasing the wages of those who turned out a large quantity and good quality, at the same time lowering the pay of those who fell short, and discharging others who proved to be incorrigibly slow or careless. An accurate time study was made through the use of a stop watch and record blanks, to determine how fast each kind of inspection should be done.[78]

While Thompson was working to improve the inspection process, Henry L. Gantt was hired by Taylor as a consultant to develop a ball-grinding machine and a ball-hardening machine. The latter produced 250,000 one-quarter-inch balls per hour, the amount a skilled hardener could produce in a day. After Weymouth resigned in June, Taylor appointed Gantt superintendent.[79]

The Simonds–Hathorn suit made it necessary for Taylor to conduct further tests on the Bundy dies in 1897; these tests proved the dies were inoperative. Despite these problems, events elsewhere were moving to make it possible for Taylor to have an opportunity to introduce his management methods.

TAYLOR'S WORK AT BETHLEHEM

In 1897, the Bethlehem Iron Company had the problem of reducing production costs to meet the federal government's demand for lower prices for armor plate. The president of Bethlehem, Robert Linderman, asked his subordinates how to solve the problem. Russell Davenport, Taylor's old friend from Midvale and second vice president of Bethlehem, urged the employment of Taylor as a consultant, and in November 1897, Linderman authorized Davenport to contact Taylor in regard to "the proposed establishment of [a] piecework system in our machine shop."[80]

During December 1897, Taylor negotiated with Davenport on the possibilities of installing piecework at Bethlehem. By December 18, 1897, after Gantt had perfected his grinder, Taylor informed Hathorn he was leaving Simonds, and the "Lightening Grinder" was no longer needed by Simonds because the firm was making money. Taylor said he had been able to:

> ... get them systematized and running smoothly, so as to be able to manufacture cheaper than other companies, and having accomplished this, I shall leave before long. I have already made arrangements for my next job which will be in the West.[81]

On January 4, 1898, Taylor wrote Linderman that before piecework could be installed several steps were required. The first was taking all control of the machines from the machinists. The second was:

> ... a careful study of each type of machine should be made so as to ascertain its driving and feeding power ... and a table should be made for each machine which indicates the best cutting speed, feed, etc., for doing work, as well as the time required to do it.[82]

On January 8, 1898, he sent Linderman details on how the machine shop had to be reorganized:

> The whole method of putting orders into the shop and the inspection and payment for the work, and of making up your labor returns must be overhauled and improved before piecework can be introduced ... (This program would take) nine months to two years. ...[83]

Taylor left Fitchburg in May of 1898, and moved to Bethlehem, Pennsylvania. To secure suitable backing for his changes, Taylor managed to have Davenport appointed Superintendent of Manufacturing.

We should recognize the enormous problem facing Taylor. Not only did the majority of Bethlehem executives oppose his program, but the entire plant was very large. The Armor and Gun Plant was modern. The 1,155 foot Open-Hearth and Forging building had been built in 1897, along with the 846-foot Hammer Shop, and the 1,250-foot long Machine Shop (Machine Shop No. 2). There was also a large railyard, one mile from Machine Shop No. 2 called the "farm," for loading and unloading iron and steel. Although Taylor had been hired to install piece rates in Machine Shop No. 2, through Davenport his authority extended to the Open-Hearth, Treating, and Forging Departments. In fact, in Taylor's mind he was planning to reorganize the entire works.[84]

When Taylor studied Machine Shop No. 2 in 1898, he concluded that the present organization of the shop was bad and that it required reorganization. The first step was in the direction of specialization: "Which is the essence of functional foremanship and the planning department was to group all of the machines in accordance with kind and size and place a gang boss in charge of 'each group'."[85] This plan of functional organization can be illustrated by a chart of Taylor's "Functional Plan of Organization for the Bethlehem Steel Company," shown on the next page.

Frank Gilbreth used a simplified version of the functional foremanship as illustrated below. Under this plan, Taylor had four executive functional bosses in the shop: "(1) gang bosses, (2) speed bosses, (3) inspectors, and (4) repair bosses."[86] The gang boss was in charge of the preparation of all work before it was placed in the machine. At Bethlehem the "preparation" activities of the gang bosses included the preparation of work for the machines, the disposition of the work, and the securing of tools and appliances. The speed boss, said Taylor, "must see that the proper cutting tools are used for each piece of work, that the work is properly driven, . . . and that the best speeds

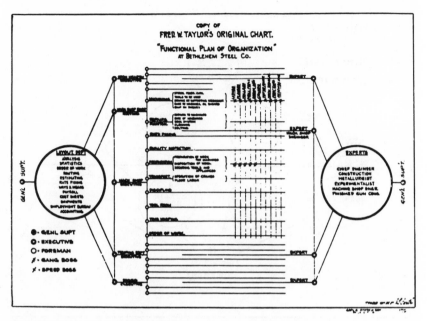

Taylor's functional plan of organization.

and feeds and depth of cut are used."[87] At Bethlehem, there were speed bosses for the lathes, planers, milling machines, drill presses, and boring machines.

Taylor's plan was to use the functional foremanship concept as the basis of a planning department to run the entire machine shop, the open hearth, treating, and forging departments. The development of a special slide rule and the modification of his high-speed tools for everyday use were also part of his plan.

With Davenport's backing, Taylor proceeded to ensure the proper feed and speed for the lathes in the machine shop. Taylor began this work in February 1899 by hiring two assistants, Joseph Welden and James Kellogg. Their task was to re-speed the machine tools in Machine Shop No. 2.

The next step was to develop a reliable method of determining the correct feed and speed. At first, Taylor hired Griswold Knox of Lehigh University to develop a slide rule for this task.

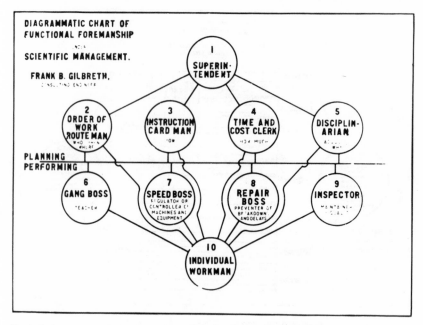

Taylor's functional foremanship as published frequently by Frank B. Gilbreth.

Unfortunately, this slide rule was not as successful as Taylor had hoped and he eventually hired Carl Barth to help develop a suitable slide rule.

Part of the plans for increasing the output in Machine Shop No. 2 included improving the maintenance of tension on the belt-driven lathes. The method utilized in industry was accomplished by a "belt fixer" who:

> . . . carried a heavy tension scales clamp to each machine whose belts needed tightening, attached the clamp to the belt in its working position, and turned a crank until the required tension showed on the scales.[88]

An assistant to Barth, Gulow Gulowsen, however, had designed a belt bench to perform this job. Gulowsen's proposal was to bring the belt to a bench where the clamps were permanently attached. At this bench, Gulowsen had:

two pulleys, one fixed and the other movable; the belt was stretched around the pulleys, its ends pinched in the clamps, and a crank was turned until the scales registered the required tension; then the belt was cut to length and the job was completed.[89]

This device enabled constant monitoring of the tension of belts throughout Machine Shop No. 2. The Gulowsen belt bench is pictured in the illustration section of this book.

THE PIG-IRON HANDLING EXPERIMENTS

Although Taylor had been hired to reorganize and improve production in Machine Shop No. 2, he soon became interested in studying the work performed by the yard laborers at the "farm." Taylor's attention was drawn to these workers for several reasons: (1) he was experiencing difficulty with the Bethlehem officials, (2) he had problems with installing his differential piecework in the machine shop, and (3) they offered an opportunity to continue Sanford Thompson's studies of shoveling, etc.

Taylor first planned to study the shoveling work performed at Bethlehem in 1898 simply because Thompson, in April 1898, had returned to the study of shoveling. Thompson had made considerable observations of shoveling in 1896, but in 1898 he was studying shoveling by employing a laborer to "dig holes, etc., and fill them up again," in order to "obtain such fundamental data as average capacity of a shovel, differences in volume, between earth in excavation and in carts, etc."[90] By June, Thompson completed a report on these experiments, reporting the hardest part was "obtaining the fundamental data as to the capacity of a shovelful. . . ."[91] Although this report was forwarded to Taylor, its fate is unknown. The fact that Taylor began his discussion of piece rates at Bethlehem Steel (in "Shop Management") with the work of men "unloading from railway cars and shoveling on to piles," demonstrates his first concern was with shoveling because Thompson had a multitude of data on the topic.[92] However, the shoveling studies were ultimately postponed until 1899.

The opportunity to conduct studies of a different form of work, and have these laborers work on piecework, occurred because of an increase in the price of pig iron in February 1899. These studies were destined to become Taylor's most famous work. Taylor, himself, was puzzled by the fame which his work with the pig-iron handlers had achieved:

> For some reason, I don't know exactly why, this illustration has been talked about a great deal, so much, in fact that some people seem to think that the whole of scientific management consists in handling pig iron.[93]

Before considering Taylor's studies of the pig-iron handlers we must explain what the term *pig iron* means. Pig iron is formed when melted iron is allowed to flow into a gridiron of damp sand. In this gridiron of sand, the "smaller bars . . . (were called) . . . 'pigs'; the larger one that is to nourish the rest is the 'sow'."[94] The pieces of pig iron formed by this procedure weighed about 92 pounds for a "full pig" and 46 pounds for a "half pig." The pig iron was moved manually by gangs of laborers.

Because Taylor said there was a "science of handling pig iron," his story of the study of the pig-iron handlers has been described as the "Pig Iron Experiments." The most colorful (and most often cited) version of these "experiments" appears in Taylor's *Principles of Scientific Management* (1911). The following is an excerpt from this book:

> The Bethlehem Steel Company had five blast furnaces, the product of which had been handled by a pig-iron gang for many years. This gang, at this time, consisted of about 75 men. They were good, average pig-iron handlers, were under an excellent foreman who himself had been a pig-iron handler, and the work was done, on the whole, about as fast and as cheaply as it was anywhere else at that time.
>
> A railroad switch was run out into the field, right along the edge of the piles of pig iron. An inclined plank was placed against the side of a car, and each man picked up from his pile a pig of iron weighing about 92 pounds, walked up the inclined plank and dropped it on the end of the car.
>
> We found that this gang were loading on the average about

12½ long tons per man per day. We were surprised to find, after studying the matter, that a first-class pig-iron handler ought to handle between 47 and 48 long tons per day, instead of 12½ tons. This task seemed to us so very large that we were obliged to go over our work several times before we were absolutely sure that we were right. Once we were sure, however, that 47 tons was a proper day's work for a first-class pig-iron handler, the task which faced us as managers under the modern scientific plan was clearly before us. It was our duty to see that the 80,000 tons of pig iron was loaded on to the cars at the rate of 47 tons per man per day, in place of 12½ tons, at which rate the work was then being done. And it was further our duty to see that this work was done without bringing on a strike among the men, without any quarrel with the men, and to see that the men were happier and better contented when loading at the new rate of 47 tons than they were when loading at the old rate of 12½ tons.

Our first step was the scientific selection of the workman. In dealing with workmen under this type of management, it is an inflexible rule to talk to and deal with only one man at a time, since each workman has his own special abilities and limitations, and since we are not dealing with men in masses, but are trying to develop each individual man to his highest state of efficiency and prosperity. Our first step was to find the proper workman to begin with. We therefore carefully watched and studied these 75 men for three or four days, at the end of which time we had picked out four men who appeared to be physically able to handle pig iron at the rate of 47 tons per day. A careful study was then made of each of these men. We looked up their history as far back as practicable and thorough inquiries were made as to the character, habits, and the ambition of each of them. Finally we selected one from among the four as the most likely man to start with. He was a little Pennsylvania Dutchman who has been observed to trot back home for a mile or so after his work in the evening about as fresh as he was when he came trotting down to work in the morning. We found that upon wages of $1.15 a day he had succeeded in buying a small plot of ground, and that he was engaged in putting up the walls of a little house for himself in the morning before starting to work and at night after leaving. He also had the reputation of being exceedingly "close," that is, of placing a very high value on a dollar. As one man whom we talked to about him said, "A penny looks about the size of a cartwheel to him." This man we will call Schmidt.

The task before us, then, narrowed itself down to getting Schmidt to handle 47 tons of pig iron per day and making him glad to do it. This was done as follows. Schmidt was called out from among the gang of pig-iron handlers and talked to somewhat in this way:

"Schmidt, are you a high-priced man?"

"Vell, I don't know vat you mean."

"Oh, yes, you do. What I want to know is whether you are a high-priced man or not."

"Vell, I don't know vat you mean."

"Oh, come now, you answer my questions. What I want to find out is whether you are a high-priced man or one of these cheap fellows here. What I want to find out is whether you want to earn $1.85 a day or whether you are satisfied with $1.15, just the same as all those cheap fellows are getting."

"Did I vant $1.85 a day? Vas dot a high-priced man? Vell, yes, I vas a high-priced man."

"Oh, you're aggravating me. Of course you want $1.85 a day—everyone wants it! You know perfectly well that that has very little to do with your being a high-priced man. For goodness sake answer my questions, and don't waste any more of my time. Now come over here. You see that pile of pig iron?"

"Yes."

"You see that car?"

"Yes."

"Well, if you are a high-priced man, you will load that pig iron on that car tomorrow for $1.85. Now do wake up and answer my question. Tell me whether you are a high-priced man or not."

"Vell—did I got $1.85 for loading dot pig iron on dot car tomorrow?"

"Yes, of course you do, and you get $1.85 for loading a pile like that every day right through the year. That is what a high-priced man does, and you know it just as well as I do."

"Vell, dot's all right. I could load dot pig iron on the car tomorrow for $1.85, and I could get it every day, don't I?"

"Certainly you do—certainly you do."

"Vell, den, I vas a high-priced man."

"Now, hold on, hold on. You know just as well as I do that a high-priced man has to do exactly as he's told from morning till night. You have seen this man here before, haven't you?"

"No, I never saw him."

"Well, if you are a high-priced man, you will do exactly as this man tells you tomorrow, from morning till night. When he tells you to pick up a pig and walk, you pick it up and you walk, and when he tells you to sit down and rest, you sit down. You do that right straight through the day. And what's more, no back talk. Now a high-priced man does just what he's told to do, and no back talk. Do you understand that? When this man tells you to walk, you walk; when he tells you to sit down, you sit down, and you don't talk back at him. Now you come on to work here tomorrow morning and I'll know before night whether you are really a high-priced man or not."

This seems to be rather rough talk. And indeed it would be if applied to an educated mechanic, or even an intelligent laborer. With a man of the mentally sluggish type of Schmidt it is appropriate and not unkind, since it is effective in fixing his attention on the high wages which he wants and away from what, if it were called to his attention, he probably would consider impossibly hard work.

What would Schmidt's answer be if he were talked to in a manner which is usually under the management of "initiative and incentive"—say as follows:

"Now, Schmidt, you are a first-class pig-iron handler and know your business well. You have been handling at the rate of 12½ tons per day. I have given considerable study to handling pig iron, and feel sure that you could do a much larger day's work than you have been doing. Now don't you think that if you really tried you could handle 47 tons of pig iron per day, instead of 12½ tons?"

What do you think Schmidt's answer would be to this?

Schmidt started to work, and all day long, and at regular intervals, was told by the man who stood over him with a watch, "Now pick up a pig and walk. Now sit down and rest. Now walk—now rest," etc. He worked when he was told to work, and rested when he was told to rest, and at half past five in the afternoon had his 47½ tons loaded on the car. And he practically never failed to work at this pace and do the task that was set him during the three years that the writer was at Bethlehem. And throughout this time he averaged a little more than $1.85 per day, whereas before he had never received over $1.15 per day, which was the ruling rate of wages at that time in Bethlehem. That is, he received 60 percent higher wages than were paid to other men who were not working on task work. One man after another was picked out and trained to handle pig iron at the rate of 47½ tons per day until all of the pig iron was handled at this rate, and the men were receiving 60 percent more wages than other workmen around them.[95]

The above account, prepared by Taylor's assistant Morris L. Cooke, is very colorful, but the actual experiments were different. The experiment began in March of 1899 and lasted into June of that year. The actual pig-iron loading experiments were conducted by two men, Hartley C. Wolle and James Gillespie, who reported directly to Taylor.

James Gillespie came to Bethlehem in 1899 when Henry Gantt brought him from Simonds. Wolle had joined Bethlehem in 1878, and because of his familiarity with yard laborers, he was asked to work for Taylor. Our understanding of the true experiments comes from a report that Gillespie and Wolle submitted to Taylor on June 17, 1899. According to the report, the method of loading pig iron was to have pig iron gangs of 8 to 12 men; each gang loaded a separate railroad car. An inclined plank was placed against the car, using some pig-iron blocks to support the plank. For loading, two men were in the car and from six to eight men carried the pig iron up the planks to the side of the car "where it was taken from them by the two men before mentioned and piled in the car."[96]

The report mentions that since there were so many men involved, the workers got in each other's way. The initial part of the study from March 1 to March 18, 1899, was an attempt to find out what was the average amount of pig iron being handled per man per 10-hour day. They found that 12.8 tons were hauled per 10-hour day, costing nine cents per ton. On March 13, 1899, Gillespie and Wolle selected 10 of the *very best men* that they could find from Foreman John Haack's "Pig-Iron Gang," which consisted of "large powerful Hungarians" who had loaded pig iron for a number of years, and put them to work loading pig iron in the usual manner, that is, two men in the car with eight carrying the pig iron. These men were *told to work* at their *maximum speed*. It turned out that in 14 minutes they loaded 16 tons of pig iron, or an average of 71 tons in a 10-hour working day per man. But Gillespie and Wolle noticed the men seemed to be totally exhausted.[97] From their observations, Gillespie and Wolle decided that if these men could work a 10-hour day moving at approximately the rate they were moving they would have been able to load about 75 tons per man. From the 75 tons "we deducted 40 percent for rest and necessary delays and set the amount to be loaded by a first-class man as 45 tons per day."[98] So Gillespie and Wolle claimed a "first-class man" could load 45 tons. Taylor, for some reason, used 47 tons a day as first-class work.

Gillespie and Wolle presented their findings to Davenport and Taylor, who set a rate of $.0375 per long ton for loading pig iron from a larger pile of 6,000 or 7,000 tons, with the understanding that as conditions changed and the iron became more difficult to load (due to the increased height from the pile to the car and the greater distance to be traversed), new rates would be established.[99]

Taylor supposedly said he wanted to select scientifically a workman who was not only physically able to load 47 tons a day but who was also motivated to perform the task. In his story, Taylor said he finally chose "a little Pennsylvania Dutchman who has been observed to trot back home for a mile or so after work in the evening who was about as fresh as when he would come trotting down to work in the morning" and who "was engaged in putting up the walls of a little house. . . ." This man Taylor called "Schmidt." Research has revealed that Schmidt actually existed, but his name was Henry Knolle (also spelled Noll). Schmidt, or Knolle, was 28 years old at the time of the experiments, having been born in Shimersville, Pennsylvania, on May 9, 1871. But it appears that Knolle was not scientifically selected in the way that Taylor implies. What happened was simply that some of Haack's men, 8 or 10 men, were selected to load pig iron and told they would be loading on a piece rate basis. The next morning when they arrived to do the work they refused to load by the piece rate, and to avoid a strike, Gillespie and Wolle allowed them to continue on day work.

That evening, however, Robert Sayre, Jr., the assistant general superintendent of the company, told Gillespie and Wolle to discharge any man who refused to load iron on piecework. This is exactly what happened the next day, March 17, 1899, and further observations were necessarily postponed for the next nine days. In the meantime, the iron was loaded on day work by men from other gangs.[100]

During this period Gillespie and Wolle were aided by one John Enright, foreman of a gang loading iron by the day in the stockyard of Mill No. 2. Enright told Gillespie and Wolle that he could convince some men on his gang to start on the piece rate system. Gillespie and Wolle gave him the go-ahead, and on March 29, 1899, seven of Enright's men volunteered to start working on piecework the next day. Since the composition of this gang, and future Gillespie and Wolle gangs became important to further observations, the names and nationalities of the men must be reviewed. The seven volunteers were: Henry Noll, John Strohl, Evan Miller, and Preston Frick (all Pennsylvania Dutch), and Robert Skelly, Mike Morgan, and Tom McGovern (all of Irish descent).

On March 30, 1899, the next morning, only Noll, Strohl, Miller, Frick, and Skelly appeared for work.[101] That the volunteers were of Pennsylvania Dutch and Irish descent may seem unimportant today; however, the fact points to the difficulties that Gillespie and Wolle had in obtaining and retaining men in their piecework gang. Haack's Hungarians who had been discharged on March 16 were threatening other laborers and preventing them from volunteering to load iron by the ton. As a result, Gillespie and Wolle had to rely on Pennsylvania Dutch and Irish workers who were not under social obligation to the Hungarians.

The five volunteers began loading iron in the usual manner (two men in the car, three carrying iron), with the understanding that they would not be forced to continue if they found the work too difficult. At the end of 10 hours they had loaded 32 tons per man, earning $1.19 each. Gillespie and Wolle noted that the men must have found the task difficult since they all appeared fatigued,[102] and their fears were substantiated because on the next day, March 31, only three men (Noll, Frick, and Skelly) reported for work, making it impossible to load iron in the usual manner.

Gillespie and Wolle solved the problem by assigning each man a separate car to load. This method also enabled Gillespie and Wolle to observe readily the ability of each man. Because none of these volunteers were as well fitted physically for this work as the Hungarians from Haack's gang who had been discharged (Noll in particular, being of slight build, his weight not exceeding 135 pounds), Gillespie and Wolle were surprised at the tonnage loaded. Noll loaded 45¾ tons (earning $1.71), Frick 35½ tons (earning $1.33), and Skelly 38 tons (earning $1.44).[103] Skelly felt unable to continue and was allowed to leave. Gillespie and Wolle also believed that Frick, because of his youth and slight build, might have to quit. So on the afternoon of March 31, it looked as if their "gang" would consist of only one man: Henry Noll. That evening, John Dodash, a Hungarian, volunteered. John Dodash and his brother Joseph were hired on April 1; although they were physically strong enough for the task, they continued to load iron without earning a fair day's wage until Gillespie and Wolle relieved them on April 8.[104]

For April 1 and 3, the piecework gang consisted of Noll, Frick, John Dodash, and his brother Joseph. Noll loaded the greatest amount on both days, 36 tons (April 1) and 49 tons (April 3). On April 4, George Robe, another Hungarian from Haack's group, joined the gang. He loaded 36 tons, Noll loaded 55 tons! On that day Gillespie and Wolle decided that Frick was unfit for the work, and they gave him a job in Machine Shop No. 2 "in recognition for his volunteering for the work and effort to continue same, although unable to make a fair day's wages."[105]

On April 5, a new man, Ambrose (no first name given), was added to the gang. After a few hours both Ambrose and Robe asked Gillespie and Wolle if they could return to their former jobs because "their lives were in danger from the men who had been discharged from Haack's gang . . . (who) had threatened them with bodily harm if they worked by the piece."[106] By April 10, five of the Hungarians discharged in March were rehired by Haack, and the opposition partially subsided.

With the many changes in the membership of their piece-work gang, Gillespie and Wolle came to depend on Henry Noll and toward the end of their report expressed their gratitude for both his loyalty and hard work:

> We also think that the work of Henry Knolle should be appreciated, as this man was the only one who continued with us from the start and at times constituted our whole piecework gang. He worked to his maximum from the beginning and by this means demonstrated that a good day's wages could be made at the existing rates by a good man.[107]

The Gillespie and Wolle report, on which Taylor marked in his own handwriting "not adopted," sheds new light on the law of heavy laboring used by Taylor to explain the percentage of rests in handling pig iron and other work. Several of their conclusions illustrate their contribution to Taylor's "discovery" of such a law:

1. That the tiring effect of work upon a man is not necessarily in proportion to the number of foot pounds of energy which he has exerted.

2. That a man can load as much iron with a walk of 15 feet on level as with a shorter walk, but if the walk be greater than 15 feet the amount of iron loaded falls off with the greater length of walk.

3. That where the elevation does not exceed one in five, as much iron can be loaded at this elevation as on a level— in other words, an elevation of 1 foot is equivalent to a walk of 5 feet.

4. The main tiring factor in loading pig iron is the "picking up" of the pig.[108]

Let us review Taylor's story of his search for a law of heavy laboring. It began at Midvale Steel in the 1880s with a study of the tiring effect of heavy labor upon a first-class worker. Two first-class men were selected, paid double wages, required to perform a variety of tasks, and records were kept of the number of foot-pounds of work each man did each day. Neither of these studies nor a second series of experiments, however, revealed any uniform relationship between foot-pounds of energy exerted and the tiring effect of the work upon the individual. Despite these negative results, Taylor said that some years later "a third series of experiments was made . . . and two college men devoted about three months to the experiments."[109] The Gillespie and Wolle report reveals that this experiment was actually part of *their* pig-iron observations, since they note that along with the

> . . . establishment of piecework rates for loading iron, Mr. Taylor desired to have compiled, from the many records, a table showing the amount of energy expended under the different conditions of height and distance reduced to foot-pounds.[110]

For more than two months Gillespie and Wolle kept records of those pig-iron loaders, Noll, Simon Conrad, and Emerick Auer. After analyzing these records Gillespie and Wolle discovered that "as the walk and lift increased, the foot-pounds of energy increased very materially."[111] As a result, they concluded that Taylor's theory regarding heavy laboring and foot-pounds of energy was not applicable to pig-iron loading, because the amount of iron loaded depended (1) on the ability and endurance of the man to lift a certain number of pigs (Gillespie and Wolle considered this to be the main tiring factor) and (2) the length of the walk was next in importance as a tiring factor.[112]

A table constructed by Gillespie and Wolle to examine these results revealed:

1. With a walk of 6 to 15 feet, other conditions remaining the same, the same amount of iron was loaded after walking 15 feet as when only walking 6 feet.
2. With a walk of 15 to 21 feet, the amount of iron carried was reduced.
3. With a walk of 21 to 30 feet, the amount of iron carried was reduced significantly.

4. Where the iron was carried up a gangway of 1 to 5 feet in elevation, the amount of iron carried was the same.

5. Where the iron was carried up a gangway of 6 feet or greater elevation, the amount of iron carried was reduced.[113]

Although Taylor always said the pig-iron experiments were conducted to establish piecework rates, he also desired to use the study of pig-iron loading as a way of obtaining more information for a series of handbooks and tables on the time required to perform physical work. He and Sanford Thompson had initiated a series of studies into this subject in 1895. During his preliminary investigations into the topic, Thompson made a study of material filed under the title of "man-power" in the Boston Public Library. He informed Taylor of his findings on February 10, 1896:

> I find that Thurston in the book which I purchased and also Kent, quote their tables from Rankine's "Steam Engine" while the latter apparently quotes them from Poncelet. I found the last edition of his "Mecanique Industrille" (in French) in 1880, and find that he quotes from French experiments made still longer ago, several of which I looked up.[114]

On April 3, 1899, Taylor returned to this problem and informed Thompson that he was about to commence some studies on a general formula of what constituted a day's work:

> My attention has recently been called to the desirability of determining, if possible, some general formula for what constitutes a big day's work in different styles of labor—for instance, to find what a day's work consists of in the way of walking empty and then walking with various loads, . . . and to find what constitutes a day's work in foot-pounds of energy, both in the way of lifting, say pig iron or shoveling dirt. . . . I read, with a great deal of interest, the notes which you forwarded me in the latter part of March, but have not quite finished them. You refer there to a good many books giving data regarding laboring work at various times. Will you not give me the publishers' addresses of these various books. . . . I want to purchase all of them for my own small library.[115]

We know little about Thompson's work in this area; however, if Taylor ever purchased the books on laboring they were never preserved after his death, since no books of this nature were donated by the family to the Taylor Collection at the Stevens Institute of Technology (although many of Taylor's books were taken from the family library by his disciples before the remainder of the collection was given to Stevens).

To determine such a formula, Taylor ordered Gillespie and Wolle to compile from the records on pig-iron loading "a table showing the amount of energy expended under the conditions of height and distance reduced to foot-pounds."[116]

To determine the number of foot-pounds of energy expended in the loading of pig iron, Gillespie and Wolle concluded it was necessary to consider not only the height the laborer had to lift the pig, but in addition, the height the man had "to lift his body and the energy expended in bending his body and throwing the pig."[117]

As a first step in making the necessary calculations, Gillespie and Wolle had to ascertain both the average weight of the pig and the average weight of the man loading the pig iron. They discovered these to be: average weight of pig, 92 pounds; average weight of the man, 165 pounds. The next step was calculating the energy expended in lifting the pig. To learn this they developed the following formula:

$$92 + \frac{165}{2} \times 2 \text{ feet} = 349 \text{ foot-pounds}$$

Here the weight of the pig (92) plus half the weight of the man (165 × .5), raised the height of two feet (× 2) gave the energy required to lift the pig: 349 foot-pounds.

To obtain the additional data for their study, Gillespie and Wolle conducted a number of experiments, but only two of them are discussed in their report, "Walking and Throwing Experiments."

The data gathered by Gillespie and Wolle while studying the task of walking with a pig or throwing a pig, was subjected to a quantitative analysis.[118] The results of this analysis are of interest.

Walking Experiments

Gillespie and Wolle state it "was found by experiment that a man walking and taking a step of 27 inches, raised his body at each step 1½ inches.[119]

$$\frac{165}{12} \times 1^{1}\!/_{12} \text{ inches} = 20.6 \text{ foot-pounds}$$

To learn the energy expended by a man walking on a grade, they did an experiment on a man walking up a plank and concluded that on a grade, the energy expended was "equal to that expended when walking on a level plus his weight and load multiplied by the height he rises."[120]

Throwing Pig Experiments

Gillespie and Wolle said the energy expended in throwing a pig into a car could be estimated based on the following considerations:

> Each pig falls from a man's hand an average distance of 2 feet, 6 inches, and he throws it from him an average distance of 3 feet, hence he must impart to that pig in throwing a velocity sufficient to carry it 3 feet horizontally while it is falling 2½ feet vertically.[121]

From the data Gillespie and Wolle gathered, they determined the energy for throwing a pig into a railway car as 209 foot-pounds. They summarized their results as follows:

Energy of walking, 1 foot empty   = 9.16 foot-pounds
Energy of carrying 1 pig 1 foot   = 5.11 foot-pounds
Energy of lifting 1 pig   = 349 foot-pounds
Energy of throwing 1 pig into car = 165.5 foot-pounds[122]

Gillespie and Wolle then prepared a table to illustrate the basis for their final conclusions.

They also prepared a table to indicate the quantity of pig iron which could be loaded per day by a first-class man under different conditions. Gillespie and Wolle included a diagram representing the number of tons of pig iron loaded at different distances (up to 30 feet), by a laborer in a day. In this diagram, the ordinates represented tons and the abscissas represented the distance the iron was carried. The line representing tons is horizontal up to 15 feet, indicating that the same amount of pig iron was loaded at 15 feet, as at a shorter distance. After 15 feet, however, the amount of pig iron loaded decreased almost in proportion to the increased distance.

From the data in the chart, Gillespie and Wolle drew the final conclusions concerning the loading of pig iron.

When Taylor gave a talk on the pig-iron experiments in Philadelphia on June 4, 1907, he said that he had to convince a "Pennsylvania Dutchman," Henry Knolle, to handle 47 tons of pig iron per day:

> I picked out a Pennsylvania Dutchman. It is up to me now to get that fellow convinced and get him to handle that pig iron sure. I went to him and said, "Noll, are you a high-price man?" He said, "I don't know what you mean." I said, "Of course, you know what I mean. Are you a high-priced man?" "I don't know what you mean," he said. I said, "Don't trifle with me. Of course, you know what I mean. I want to know whether you are really a high priced man, or one of these cheap workers, satisfied with $1.15 a day," the wages paid up there at that time. He said, "I would like more money." "Of course, I know every man wants more money, but I want to know whether you are really a high-priced man. I am looking for fellows I can pay $1.85 a day to." He said, "I will take $1.85 a day any time." "You are making a joke out of this thing. You are not treating this matter seriously. I want to know whether you are a high-priced man. You know what I mean." "I don't know what you mean. I will take $1.85 a day." "You seem to be very stupid. There is something wrong with you. I want to find out whether you are a high-priced man. If you are, see that pile of pig iron? See that car? If you are a high-priced man you can load that iron on that for $1.85 a day." "Will I get $1.85?" "Yes. I don't care whether you do it particularly. I am not going to have men around me who can't earn $1.85 a day. Unless a man can earn $1.85 he will have to get out sooner or later. That is all there is to it."

When Taylor's *Principles of Scientific Management* was published in 1911, Taylor gave Noll the name of "Schmidt" and described him as a "man so stupid that he was unfitted to do most kinds of laboring work. . . .[123] Because this portion of Taylor's book was written by his associate Morris L. Cooke (who had originally had a stenographic report made of Taylor's 1907 talk), it appears that he utilized Taylor's words "You seem to be very stupid" from that talk to prepare the statement in the 1911 book. In reality, Henry Knolle did attend grammar school until age 11, or perhaps longer, and could read and write.[124]

Because the men in the experiment were earning good wages, it appears that from the middle of May 1899 the prejudice against piecework seemed to grow less and Gillespie and Wolle had less difficulty in obtaining men for the experiment. From June 1 to June 15, we have the records of the employees' tonnage. On June 2, Henry Knolle loaded 68.3 tons of pig iron, earning $2.57 for the day, but on June 1, Simon Conrad turned 70.7 tons, and on June 3 turned 70.9, earning on that day $2.68.[125] (See chart below.) Gillespie and Wolle attributed the lessening of prejudice to the fact that when any men were injured or tired from excessive work, they were not forced to lose time but were given easier work until they could return to loading pig iron.[126] We must note that in his version of the pig-iron experiments Taylor mentioned the use of rest periods for his manual laborers. As you will remember, he is quoted as saying to the worker Schmidt, "Now pick up a pig and walk. Now sit down and rest. Now walk—now rest." In a footnote in *Principles of Scientific Management*, Taylor stated,

> . . . the men were made to take a rest, generally by sitting down, after loading 10 to 20 pigs. This rest was in addition to the time which it took them to walk back from the car to the pile.[127]

Taylor, instead of using Gillespie and Wolle's straightforward explanation for the lessening opposition to piecework, created an elaborate tale concerning the hiring of a special force of men to load pig iron. In his Boxly talks, Taylor said that these men were obtained by spreading the word outside the Bethlehem plant that he was looking for "high-priced men" to load pig iron. The local newspapers, said Taylor, opposed him, but "the newspapers, even in ridiculing us, did us the greatest service . . . and gave us the

TABLE III-1
Wages and Tonnage of Pieceworkers June 1–June 15, 1899

		Employee: Simon Conrad Piece		Employee: Henry Knolle Piece		Employee: Emerick Auer Piece	
Rate	Date	Tons	Wages	Tons	Wages	Tons	Wages
$.0375	6/1	70.7	$2.65	48.0	$1.80	—	—
$.0375	6/2	55.7	$2.09	68.3	$2.57	50.7	$1.90
$.0375	6/3	70.9	$2.68	39.7	$1.49	30.1	$1.13
$.0375	6/5	48.0	$1.80	36.3	$1.36	49.1	$1.84
$.0375	6/6	51.7	$1.94	59.5	$2.23	54.7	$2.05
$.0375	6/7	65.1	$2.44	50.1	$1.88	63.2	$2.37
$.0375	6/8	48.0	$1.80	35.5	$1.33	50.7	$1.90
$.0375	6/9	50.7	$1.90	30.7	$1.15	46.6	$1.74
$.0375	6/10	46.4	$1.74	46.6	$1.74	48.0	$1.80
$.0375	6/12	48.0	$1.80	47.7	$1.79	—	—
$.0375	6/13	52.3	$1.96	42.9	$1.61	52.3	$1.96
$.0375	6/14	55.7	$2.09	—	—	—	—
$.0375	6/15	53.6	$2.01	—	—	53.6	$2.01
Average		55.1		45.9		49.9	

Note: Data from Gillespie and Wolle (12, p. 7).

best advertisement all over."[128] Indeed, according to him, they got him all the men he needed, men who wanted to find out if they were "high-priced men."

The issues of the *South Bethlehem Globe* and the *Bethlehem Star* for the period February 1898 to January 1901 fail to mention Taylor's work at Bethlehem, much less the handling of pig iron! It is sad, but true, that Taylor's newspaper story is also a fabrication. The *Globe* and *Star* are filed in the Archives of the Moravian Church, Bethlehem, Pennsylvania. The only entry related to Taylor's work is an announcement by Robert Linderman that the new piece rate system would increase employee wages at Bethlehem.[129]

The later stories of Schmidt are of interest. According to Copley, in 1910, a report was circulated by opponents of Taylor and Scientific Management claiming that Schmidt had died of overwork. In 1913, when the Taylor method was being introduced in the Ordnance Department of the Army, another report was circulated also claiming that "Schmidt had been killed by his task of handling 47 tons of pig iron in a day."[130] Taylor hired a detective to find Schmidt and commissioned a physician to report on Schmidt. The report stated, "I find him to be 44 years old and . . . in good physical condition."[131]

Henry Knolle was to live another decade and died February 25, 1925, at the age of 54. Also Knolle's little house which was immortalized in the Taylor story as being built in 1899, was not on the 1901 maps of Bethlehem, but first appears on the 1903 city maps; therefore, it was impossible for Knolle to be building his home during the experiments, as Taylor claimed.[132] The house was built after the experiments were finished, probably in 1902, but the story of the house building added color to Taylor's account.[133]

The information gathered by Gillespie and Wolle proved important to Taylor's search for a law of heavy laboring. While he never gave them credit, their comments on the effect of lifting and distance probably gave Taylor the idea of initiating a new series of studies. Carl Barth, who had come to Bethlehem late in April 1899, was assigned the task of reviewing the past experiments conducted at Midvale, the Gillespie and Wolle data, and designing a series of new experiments.

The new experiments were conducted by Atherton B. Wadleigh in December 1899, and by Mr. Wyckoff in March 1900. The subjects were two "Extraordinary Laborers," John Hahn (or Hohn) and Gansberger (first name not given).[134] Barth, according to Taylor, took the data gathered and reduced it to a series of curves. From these curves Barth discovered the law Taylor was seeking. It was directly related to Gillespie and Wolle's comments on the ability of a man to lift and carry a pig, but Taylor described it as the law of heavy laboring, saying:

> The law is confined to that class of work in which the limit of a man's capacity is reached, because he is tired out. It is the law of heavy laboring, corresponding to the work of the cart horse, rather than that of the trotter. Practically all such work consists of a heavy pull or a push on the man's arms, that is, the man's strength is exerted by either lifting or pushing something which

TABLE III-2
Results of Pig-Loading by Two "Extraordinary Laborers,"
1899-1900

		Distance Moved (in feet)					
		0	5	10	20	30	40
Tons carried	Full pigs	90.0	79.0	70.2	56.0	44.5	35.0
Tons carried	Half pigs	110.0	82.5	65.8	46.2	34.7	27.1
Percentage of rest	Full pigs	57.5	56.5	55.0	54.8	55.2	58.2
Percentage of rest	Half pigs	31.0	35.0	37.0	41.0	48.0	51.5

Data from C. Barth Papers, Chart 157A, Harvard University.

he grasps in his hands. And the law is, that for each given pull or push on the man's arms it is possible for the workman to be under load for only a definite percentage of the day.[135]

The data gathered by Barth on the number of tons carried (given in both full and half pigs, 92 and 46 pounds, respectively); the distance carried (in feet); and the percentage of rests are shown above.

The data provides revolutionary insight into Taylor's figures on the time required for rest under the law of heavy laboring. The time for rests was derived by Taylor by following the idea of Gillespie and Wolle of selecting the time for rests at "the lesser" and "greater" distance. He then used the average of these two figures to obtain the percentage of rests for full pigs (56 percent) and half pigs (42 percent).[136] Taylor's method of calculating was to select from Barth's curves the figures for percentage of rests at 0 and 40 feet and then calculating as follows:

Percent of Rests

	0 Feet		40 Feet
Full pigs	57.5 + 58.2	= 115.7 ÷ 2 = 57.3 or 57%	
Half pigs	31.0 + 52.5	= 83.5 ÷ 2 = 41.8 or 42%	

Taylor (described by Lyndall Urwick[137] as a man of integrity) readily gave these figures as those applicable to pig-iron loading, but never said they were based on the work performed by two extraordinary workers (Hahn and Gansberger) or that they included the distance pig iron was carried. Most important, he never acknowledged his debt to Gillespie and Wolle for providing the needed insight into this problem.

In the 1911, "Principles of Scientific Management" manuscript version of the tale, one finds an addendum in the handwriting of Alfred Barter of Plimpton Press, printers of the Harper edition—"and at regular intervals was told by the man who stood over him with a watch, 'Now, pick up a pig and walk. Now sit down and rest. Now, walk. . . now, rest, etc.' " Below this note appears another note on a separate sheet of paper in Morris L. Cooke's handwriting:

> This seems to be rather rough talk. And indeed it would be if applied to an educated mechanic or even an intelligent laborer. With a man of the mentally sluggish type of Schmidt it is appropriate and not unkind since it is effective in fixing his attention on the high wages which he wants and away from what if it were called to his attention he probably would consider impossibly hard work.

This statement by Cooke is used by Taylor in the body of the book.[138]

An analysis of Barth's work shows that his "percentage of rest" was derived from curves marked "return walk considered rest." This reveals that there was no rest pause of the type usually attributed to Taylor. Instead, the return walk, empty-handed, was considered a rest. This explains Taylor's remark that if a worker is carrying a full pig (92 pounds) he must be entirely free from load during 57 percent of the day,[139] i.e., walking back empty-handed after loading a pig on a car. In brief, the rest periods that authors have been describing with such assurance for the past 60 years never existed!

As Taylor's biographer, Copley noted that:

> in his papers and over and over again in his informal talks at Boxly and on the platform throughout the country, Taylor used

what he accomplished with these pig-iron handlers as an illustration of the value of scientific methods.[140]

The accomplishments have been analyzed, and we find that Taylor has fallen into the category of authors about whom the historiographers warn us. He has told his story with such an:

> abundance and precision of detail, (that) though they produce a vivid impression on inexperienced readers, (they) do not guarantee the accuracy of the facts, they give us no information about anything but the imagination of the author when he is sincere, or his impudence when he is the reverse.[141]

Whether imaginative or impudent, the fact is that Taylor seems to have believed that the end justified the means.

THE SHOVELING EXPERIMENTS

We don't know when and how Taylor first came to the conclusion that shoveling offered fertile ground for improvement of productivity. On December 30, 1895 he signed a contract with Sanford E. Thompson of Newton Highlands, Massachusetts, to gather information and to assist in writing articles or books. The salary was $100 per month plus expenses. This initial contract was the beginning of a 15-year close relationship between the two. The original contract, in part, reads,

> Thompson agrees to give his entire time and services, as far as it is practicable for him to do so, during the period of one year, beginning February first, 1896, to the work of gathering information for writing a book, books, articles, or series of articles for publication, and to recording and tabulating such information, and in assisting Taylor in writing said articles or book. The subject matter of said articles or book being the time required following various kinds of work.[142]

The book Taylor was contemplating concerned the cost to do work and it did not take Taylor and Thompson long to concern themselves with shoveling work. From Johnstown, Pennsylvania, Taylor wrote Thompson on February 15, 1896 (with typos corrected here).

> Regarding the question of shoveling coal, I do not feel that we yet have all the information desired. . . . For example, I want to know how much of the time is consumed in pushing the shovel into the pile. I think we should also know just how many minutes during the 10 hours the man is actually actively at work, and how much of this time he is resting, and I shall ask Mr. Coonahan to make a number of practical observations on this point.
>
> I return you herewith the data which you ask for regarding the unloading of coal. . . . I note your figures on the foot-pounds of energy in unloading coal. I think, however, you are perhaps a little wrong on one point. The coal, as it is unloaded over the side of the car leaves the shovel while the latter is turned almost upside down. It is not thrown, for instance as most laborers would throw dirt into a cart, that is, keeping the dirt always over the shovel and shooting the shovel out in the air at an angle of about 45 degrees in a comparatively straight line.
>
> Of course, you will remember that in pushing the shovel underneath the coal there is a good deal of force expended; all of this pressure, however, is given on the end of the shovel by the leg of the operator; it is never done by hand. The center of the coal pile is six feet from the outside edge of the car, and of course the average position of the man in the car is in the center of same. From this you can get the average throw. The pile starts at nothing and comes up to about the top of the side of the car over which the coal is thrown, so that its average height would be half way between these two. The average weight of the coal in a shovel is 18 lbs. This does not include the weight of the shovel. I think I should get at the weight of the shovel by merely weighing the one which you have in your cellar; this will come close enough to the facts, I think.[143]

On March 2, 1896, Taylor again wrote to Thompson:

> In figuring out the coal-shoveling data, I think it desirable of course, to figure the horsepower, which a man exerts when he is shoveling at his usual gate (sic) and is actively engaged in work. You will remember that Mr. Coonahan wrote me that a man shoveling 40 tons of coal per day worked at the rate of 12 shovelsful per minute, while he was actively at work. If I

remember rightly the same man averaged throughout the day, about $7\frac{1}{2}$ shovelsful per minute, this shows that the actual horsepower developed by the man when actively shoveling was $\frac{2}{3}$ greater than his average horsepower. This should, of course, be carefully noted.

I would suggest that as soon as you have taken sufficient observations, and have the data at hand that it would be well to work up the data which you have, into as nearly as possible the form in which you think it should be published. That is put it into tabulated form giving the various elements and data which you think we should insert when booked. I think that the operation of reducing your data to practical working form will show up any defects that there may be in the information which we have at hand, and will very materially assist you in making further observations.

I think each table should contain say a column showing the work which can be done by a *first-class* man when working at his best through an average of 10 hours, possible also the rate at which this man works when he is actively engaged in the work; it should also show the amount of work which an *average* man will do, probably also the cost per unit of work if done by the *first-class* man who earns $1.00 a day, and if done by the *average* man who earns $1.00 a day, and possibly some remarks as to the pay of different man (sic) in different parts of the country for this class of work. The table for shoveling dirt or coal or ashes, as the case may be, should, I think give the above data for varying heights to which the material has to be thrown, and it strikes me that it would be well to give a table showing the time for picking a given amount of the material to be shoveled under varying conditions of hardness. You understand, of course, that the above suggestions are merely rough ideas, as they occur to me. When you come to think them over more carefully, I have no doubt that you will develop others and modify these suggestions.

I take pleasure in enclosing you herewith a check for $100.00 for the month of February. Will you kindly send me a statement of your expense, etc., and I will immediately forward a check for same.[144]

In 1899, Taylor finally turned to his previously planned study of shoveling. At Bethlehem there was a lot of shoveling.

Men shoveled snow, iron ore, ashes, gravel, and sand. Taylor hired Atherton B. Wadleigh, a family friend, of Lehigh University to do this work. Wadleigh's shoveling data was subsequently analyzed by Thompson in 1902, in preparation for the proposed Taylor-Thompson booklet on times to perform work.

In final preparation for his June 1903 "Shop Management" paper, Taylor requested data on shoveling, etc. From Sanford Thompson's letter press book, we find a copy of Thompson's letter to Taylor of April 3, 1903, which illustrates the depth of research which Taylor and Thompson were pursuing.[145] One should note that Thompson is sending Taylor new pages to replace older ones sent on April 7, 1903, and that he is informing Taylor how some of the elements were arrived at. Note that "contract" is day work. Thompson wrote:

THE ENCLOSED PAGES DIFFER SLIGHTLY FROM THOSE SENT YESTERDAY AND SHOULD BE SUBSTITUTED FOR THEM.

I have omitted the formula for clay (shoveling) on page 6b in the forms copy, and have corrected it. I have inserted in the table values for carrying earth on a shovel instead of throwing. I have omitted the values for clay because I find that there is a slight disagreement in values, due probably to the fact that clay is slightly sticky, and therefore the time throwing may be is different from other materials.

My values for walking with shovel are made up entirely from combination of elements. I have no times for walking with a shovel of earth, but I have estimated the time per foot from other classes of work. Since for the distances which I have selected the time for back walk is greater than 30 percent of the total time, I have assumed the percent of rest to be 5 percent, which I consider to be an extreme minimum for necessary delay.

A comparison of average contract times which may be expected on this kind of work in piecework may be of interest. This comparison is based on selections from the data on Bethlehem Steel Works. I have assumed that gravel corresponds to die.

Filling shovel. Average contract net times are about 68 percent greater than piecework net times.

Throwing shovelful. Contract and piecework times are the same.

Walking with shovel. Contract times are about 33 percent greater than piecework time.

Percentage of rest. In contract earthwork is about 30 percent and in piecework about 25 percent.

(one line of illegible penmarks is followed with:)

I do not consider shoveling earth to represent the advantages of unit times so much as some other subjects on account of the difficulty in classifying earths, but I have been rather surprised at the way I have been able to separate my times per shovelful (which include throwing) into the separate elements of "filling" and "throwing."

I trust that the matter which I am sending will prove to be that which you wished, and if there is too much of it that you can throw part away without much trouble. I thought you might like it in just the form I have given.[146]

Taylor did use Thompson's data for his paper on "Shop Management" and the material also appears in the 1911 book of the same title. The manuscript to "Shop Management" finds Taylor utilizing Thompson's page 6b in its entirety, merely adding a few notes in the written description.[147]

The studies at Bethlehem, coupled with Thompson's data, enabled Taylor to determine that the most work could be done in a 10-hour day with a shovel that could handle 21½ pounds of material with each thrust. In his 1907 talk at Boxly, Taylor described the science of shoveling and how the proper-sized shovel was determined at Bethlehem:

> Shoveling is a much larger art than pig-iron handling. Though most people would think there was not very much art in handling it, there is quite an art in it. It never occurred to any contractor I ever talked to to investigate what the proper load of a shovel was, what load a first-class man, properly built for shoveling, would do a maximum day's work with. Yet it must be perfectly evident that there is a maximum shovel load, a shovel load of so many pounds resting on the shovel, at which a man will do the greatest amount of work. One of our first tasks when we came to make an art of shoveling was to find out just what that load was for a first-class man. It required a large number of accurate experiments, continued for days and days, and we found that was about 21½ pounds. That is to say, a

first-class man, well built for shoveling, a skillful shoveler, would do more work with 21½ pounds shovel loads than with 18 pounds or 24 pounds. You see there are reasons why that must be so. There is some maximum. It is very evident a man handling a one-pound shovel would not do as much as a man handling ten. I thought it was about 14 pounds, and was very much surprised to find it was 21½ pounds. It is an art, and that requires a lot of experiment and a lot of data.[148]

By 1912, Taylor developed a more complex and colorful account of the shovel experiments, which he described on January 30, 1912, to the Special Committee of the House of Representatives when they investigated "The Taylor and Other Systems of Shop Management":

Mr. Taylor: I have not the slightest doubt that different size shovels and implements for handling dirt have been in existence for hundreds of years. I do not know it, but I have not the slightest doubt of it. What I was trying to indicate in my testimony was that it became the duty of the management to supply the man with exactly the right implement to do each kind of work, and that the proper implement was only supplied to the men, and could be only supplied to the men, after the science of shoveling had been carefully studied, and that this was one of the results of the study of the science of shoveling.

The Chairman (William B. Wilson): I simply say, Mr. Taylor, that more than 40 years ago I worked for a large coal company that required men to do shoveling, sometimes shoveling slates and shales, which are heavy, and sometimes shoveling coals, which are light. They maintained different sizes of shovels for use in shoveling the different kinds of material, an old-style No. 2 shovel being the style for handling the heavy materials and an old-style No. 5 or No. 6 for handling the lighter material or coal, the 5 and 6 being simply used for the different capacities of men, and that was before any furore had arisen with regard to shop management.

Mr. Taylor: It seems to me, Mr. Chairman, that you came very close to working under scientific management about 40 years ago yourself.

Mr. (John G.) Tilson: I desire to ask a question. In regard to the 21½ pound load for shoveling, does that apply regardless of the bulk to 21½ pounds? Is that the most economical load, regardless of the bulk?

Mr. Taylor: Yes, sir; regardless of bulk.

Mr. Tilson: Do you take into account any difference in effect on the man, as the load varies?

Mr. Taylor: I think the load remains the same; whether the bulk is large or small the load remains the same.

Mr. Tilson: My question is just this: You found, as I understand it, that at 38 pounds to the shovel that was not an economical load?

Mr. Taylor: Not an economical one if it was too heavy a shovel load and prevented the man from doing a proper day's work.

Mr. Tilson: That is, your dirt pile grew as the size of your shovel went down?

Mr. Taylor: The pile of dirt shoveled in a day grew larger and larger as the shovel load starting with 38 pounds per shovel went down until we reached a 21½ pound shovel load, at which load the men did their largest day's work, and then again the dirt pile grew smaller and smaller as the shovel load became lighter and lighter than 21½ pounds.

Mr. Tilson: What I was trying to get is this: You have told us the effect on the pile. What about the effects on the man? Was the man as well off when he was shoveling the 21½ pound load?

Mr. Taylor: Yes; he took his natural gait all day long in each of those kinds of shoveling. The workman regulated his own pace. No one regulated it for him. The fact was that when he was shoveling with a heavy load of 38 pounds it tired him to such an extent that he went much slower, naturally. He took fewer shovel loads, and he had to rest more between shovel loads.

Mr. Tilson: Then take it on the other side, if it was very light, not more than 10 or 15 pounds?

Mr. Taylor: In order to shovel the same amount with a light load of 10 or 15 pounds that he shoveled with a 21½ pound load, he would have to work so quick—to make his motions so quick— that they then became tiresome.

Mr. Tilson: So you figure out that regardless of bulk the easiest load for a man to handle is 21½ pounds with a shovel?

Mr. Taylor: Yes, sir.

The Chairman: Would that be true irrespective of the distance that the dirt had to be thrown?

Mr. Taylor: No, sir. I am very glad that you asked that question. That again opens another large element of the science of shoveling, and I did not wish to burden you unnecessarily with the science of shoveling. Now, that holds true up to about 4 feet in length and 5 in height; that 21 pounds is the best load. When you rise about 5 feet in height, say, the combination of 5 feet in height and 4 feet in length, and go higher than that, then you must have a lighter load. The load again falls off. You understand, Mr. Chairman, that in my direct testimony, in speaking of the science of shoveling, I only spoke (broadly speaking) of the effect of that one element of the science. I want to assure you, gentlemen, again that the true science of shoveling is quite a large affair, but I will be glad to go into it if you care to go further and tell you more about it. It is quite a large affair.[149]

The studies of the yard laborers and the introduction of piecework continued throughout 1899, by Wadleigh (after Wolle and Gillespie had resigned) and although they were not as scientific as Taylor may have later claimed, they did achieve successful results. For the period April 1900 to April 1901, the use of piecework (instead of day work) had reduced the cost of labor to move shoveled material in the yard from 7.2 cents per ton on any day work to 3.3 cents per ton on piecework.[150] Despite this success in reducing costs, Taylor, by 1901, was unsuccessful in achieving increased output in Machine Shop No. 2. A partial solution to this problem was the utilization of a new method of pay developed by Gantt who had come to Bethlehem from Fitchburg in December 1898.[151] Gantt suggested to Taylor that a daily bonus be used:

A daily bonus of fifty cents to be offered to every man who accomplished the task set for him on his instruction card. At the same time, he would have an incentive for reaching the standard called for on his instruction card.[152]

This method proved successful, but the general opposition to Taylor's work by Bethlehem executives led Linderman to terminate Taylor's contract on May 2, 1901.

Although Taylor's work at Bethlehem was less successful than he wished, the experience gained by Barth and Gantt proved useful in later industrial applications of Taylor's management concepts.

Copley explained that Taylor retired from active work in 1901 to "serve the cause of science in management" and "due to considerations for his health."[153] The actual health problems were never discussed, but his testimony in some recently discovered court documents throws new light on the reasons for Taylor's retirement. Testifying in 1906, Taylor said:

> I had a bad nervous breakdown several years ago and have been unable to do active business since, and am under strict orders from my doctor not to work more than three hours a day.[154]

In this testimony, Taylor does not mention retiring to concentrate on spreading his ideas on management. Instead, he definitely states that because of his nervous breakdown he was "unable to do active business."

TAYLOR AND HIGH-SPEED CUTTING TOOLS

Frederick Taylor was the holder or co-holder of 45 U.S. patents, including a power hammer; golf clubs, both driver and two-handed putter; scoop handle tennis racket; molding machines; and his most famous high-speed steel used for high-speed cutting tools.[155] He claimed this discovery occurred at Bethlehem in the fall of 1898, but as we shall see, the exact date and actual discoverer of this heat-treating method is still a mystery.

Considering Taylor's background with the manufacture of armor-piercing projectiles at Midvale in 1889, he would have recognized the value of an improved heat-treating method for steel. In the manufacture of such projectiles it was necessary to forge shells capable of piercing naval armor and these forging methods were described in the published literature of the 1889–90 period:

> Forged steel armor-piercing shells are cut from steel bars of proper size. They are hammered to the general form of the shell, and afterward turned and tempered. . . . The shells are first

brought to a cherry-red throughout, plunged in oil and kept immersed until cold; they are then again brought to a cherry-red, hung with the head, as far as the front band, in cold water for ten minutes, and afterward immersed in oil.[156]

The cherry-red color of the shell was later identified as 1,500 degrees Fahrenheit.

Taylor's story of the development of the heat-treatment methods must be examined in order to understand the extent of the mystery concerning this discovery.

In his "Art of Cutting Metals" Taylor claimed that,

> During the winter of 1894–95, (he) . . . conducted an investigation in the shop of Wm. Sellers & Co., at the joint expense of Messrs. William Cramp & Sons, shipbuilders, and Messrs. Wm. Sellers & Co., to determine which make of self-hardening tool steel was, on the whole, the best to adopt as standard for all of the roughing tools of these two shops.
>
> As a result of this work, the choice was narrowed down at that time to two makes of tool steel: (1) the celebrated Mushet self-hardening steel . . . and (2) a self-hardening steel made by the Midvale Steel Company.[157]

Shortly after Taylor arrived at Bethlehem in 1898, he decided to establish standards for the tool steel he wished to use to increase the speed of metal cutting in the machine shop. Taylor favored the Midvale self-hardening tool steel, but wanted to investigate other makes of tool steel to discover the most efficient to use.

A large powerful, electrically driven lathe was installed and experiments made during the summer of 1898. At the conclusion of this work, Taylor still believed the Midvale steel was the best and arranged a demonstration to show this superiority to Bethlehem officials. The demonstration, however, proved a failure since the Midvale Steel tools had to be operated at slower machine speeds.

Taylor said he first believed the tools had been overheated by the Midvale blacksmiths, but they told Taylor they had been extremely careful not to overheat the tools. Convinced that Midvale steel was still the superior tool steel, Taylor decided to launch a new series of experiments, and to secure the aid of Bethlehem's metallurgist Maunsel White in performing the tests. White became associated with Taylor in this work on October 23, 1898. Maunsel White was Taylor's age, born March 15, 1856, on his grandfather's Louisiana plantation. He attended neither grade school nor high school, but was personally tutored on the plantation. He graduated as class valedictorian from Georgetown University, and received a degree in metallurgy from Stevens Institute in 1879. It was claimed he had a photographic memory and was able to recite *Hamlet* from memory. After Stevens, he went to work for the Bethlehem Iron Company.[158]

The results of these new experiments performed with White were described by Taylor's associate Morris L. Cooke in 1909:

> For this purpose there was started a carefully laid out series of experiments, in which tools were to be heated at temperatures increasing by about 50 degrees all the way from a black heat to the melting point. These tools were then to be ground and run in the experimental lathe upon a uniform forging, so as to find:
>
> *a.* That heat at which the highest cutting speed could be attained (which our previous experiments had shown to be a cherry red).
>
> *b.* The exact danger point at which if ever heated, these tools would be seriously injured.
>
> *c.* Some heat treatment by which injured tools could be restored to their former high cutting speeds.
>
> These experiments corroborated the former ones in showing that the tools were seriously broken down or injured by overheating to, say, somewhere between 1550 degrees F. and 1700 degrees F. But to the great surprise of everyone, tools heated up to or above the high heat of 1725 degrees F. proved better than any of those heated to the best previous temperature, namely, a bright cherry red; and from 1725 degrees F. up to the incipient point of fusion of the tools, the higher they were heated, the higher the cutting speeds at which they would run. Thus the discovery that phenomenal results could be obtained by heating tools close to the melting point, which was so completely revolutionary and directly opposed to all previous heat treatment of

tools, was the indirect result of an accurate, scientific effort to investigate as to which brand of tool steel was, on the whole, the best to adopt as a shop standard. No one connected with the experiments had the slightest idea that overheating beyond the bright cherry red would do anything except injure the tool more and more, the higher it was heated.[159]

Taylor claimed that following the discoveries in the fall of 1898, he and White devoted eight to nine months with more experiments to determine how to make practical use of the new tools. On October 20, 1899, the two men filed a patent application for the "Process of Treating High-Speed Tool Steel," receiving patent number 668,269 on February 19, 1901. A second patent for the process was filed on August 10, 1900, and patent number 668,270 was issued on February 19, 1901. These patents were sold to Bethlehem Steel for $50,000 by Taylor and White after some controversy between them and the company.

The high-speed tool steel patents would eventually pit Bethlehem against Taylor's old company, Midvale. But that story brings us back to 1886. For in late 1886, the Navy Department called for bids to manufacture armor plate for three ships, the *Puritan, Texas,* and *Maine.* Midvale was not prepared to compete with the Carnegie Steel Company or the Bethlehem Iron Company for this contract, but prepared plans to build an armor plant capable of competing with them for future contracts.

Under Charles Harrah, plans for a new armor plant were purchased abroad and an extensive armor-manufacturing facility was constructed. Because anyone familiar with the construction of such a plant was associated with Midvale's competitors, Midvale had to build the plant with its own resources. In 1904, the *North American* newspaper in Philadelphia, said:

> This new armor plant was a "monument to the untiring energy, the unflagging faith and the superb ability of Messrs (Charles) Harrah, (James F.) Sullivan and the inventor (of Midvale's armor plate), George H. Chase.[160]

In 1903, Midvale submitted its first bids (in competition with Carnegie and Bethlehem) for 8,000 tons of armor plate for the battleship *New Hampshire* and the cruisers *Montana* and *North Carolina*. At this time, Bethlehem Steel recognized that to compete with Midvale and Carnegie for this contract it would be to their advantage to have secure control over the high-speed steel patents and to prevent infringements on them.

In 1903, the Niles-Bement-Pond Company, a machine tool manufacturer that operated plants in Ohio, Pennsylvania, and New Jersey, began to use the Taylor–White process without a license from Bethlehem Steel, and Bethlehem filed a suit against them. The case lasted for five years with a final decision against the two patentees on January 29, 1909. The difficulties Taylor and White experienced with the heat-treating patents arose, primarily, because of the startling claims they made in their original patent application. These claims concerned the "breaking-down point" in the process of heat-treating chrome-tungsten steel. Taylor claimed during the trial:

> Our invention is based on our discovery that, while it is true that tools made of air-hardening steels all rapidly deteriorate at temperatures in excess of a bright cherry red (although it must be understood not all at the same temperature) it is also true that when air-hardening steels are made with certain constituents in ascertained proportions, this deterioration only prevails during a limited range of temperatures above the bright cherry red—that is to say, from about 1,550 to about 1,700 Fahrenheit—and our further discovery that above this range of temperatures, which we call the "breaking-down point," and from 1,725 Fahrenheit up to a temperature at which the steel softens or crumbles when touched with a rod (approximately 1,900 to 2,000 Fahrenheit), the efficiency of tools of such special steels—that is, their cutting speed . . . is greatly increased.[161]

The judge in the case said Taylor and White claimed they had discovered the existence of a "breaking-down point" between 1,550 degrees and 1,725 degrees Fahrenheit. In addition, they said:

> the fact that steels could not be heated above a bright cherry red or a temperature of about 1,500 Fahrenheit was thoroughly recognized in the art, and that their discovery consisted in ascertaining that by passing beyond that hitherto seemingly impass-

able boundary and heating the steel up to 1,725 Fahrenheit and far higher, its hardness, toughness, and cutting quality were greatly increased.[162]

The judge observed that no publication was offered by patentees to prove the existence of such a "breaking-down point." Further was the testimony of a large number of expert witnesses, who said that the existence of such a "breaking-down point" was a myth, not sustained by the facts.[163]

In reviewing the various claims regarding the existence of a "breaking-down point" at 1,700 degrees Fahrenheit, Judge Joseph Cross included the results of tests made to prove the claims of Taylor and White. These were made at the Bethlehem Steel Company in the presence of the lawyers and experts of both sides. Cross described these tests as follows:

> Turning to the results of these tests, it will be found that they did not at all accord with the theory and statements of the patent. What they did show was that at a heat of 1,500, regarded by the patent as the highest point of efficiency in the prior art, was indeed the lowest point of efficiency; that from 1,550 to 1,600 the same degree of efficiency, or rather inefficiency, was substantially maintained; and that from and after a temperature of about 1,600, and not 1,725 as called for by the patent, marked improvement was shown. In short every material assertion of the patent bearing upon the point in question was disproved. In the presence of open tests, the private tests of either party must, to some extent, give way, because they are relatively unsatisfactory; that is to say, experts' tests will almost invariably be found to support the theory of the party making them.[164]

Before the high-speed steel suit began, however, Bethlehem received the stunning news that on December 20, 1904, Midvale armor plate performed well in an unofficial trial at the Indian Head Proving Grounds. On December 22, 1904, Rear Admiral N. Mason, Chief of the Bureau of Ordnance said this test:

> means ... the Midvale people have made good and are equipped to enter into the manufacture of armor plate for the government.[165]

In fact, the *North American* published a cartoon depicting Midvale's victory.

In the early stages of the *Bethlehem Steel* v. *Niles-Bement-Pond* suit, Taylor testified about the Taylor-White patent in Philadelphia on January 23, 1906. Taylor proved to be a frustrating witness since he seemed incapable of recalling anything about the original discovery, the date it occurred, or the discoverers, as excerpts here illustrate.

Question 4:   You are the Frederick W. Taylor who on October 20, 1899, filed an application for Letters Patent of the United States for metal-cutting tool and method of making the same, are you not?

Answer: I am unable to state without seeing a copy of the application whether I am the Frederick W. Taylor whom you refer to or not. I have entirely forgotten the date on which I filed an application for any patent relating to tool steel.

Question 5:   Did you on or before October 20, 1899, make or think that you had made an improvement in the art of treating steel?

Answer: I was engaged as employee of the Midvale Steel Works for about 10 years, and during that time made many improvements in the art of treating steel. I also made improvements in the art of treating steel while employed by the Bethlehem Steel Co. but without referring to memoranda or copies of patents I am unable to state whether such improvements were made before October 20, 1899.

Question 6:   Do you remember whether at any time during 1899 you made, or thought that you had made, an improvement in the art of treating steel which consisted as to an essential or important feature in raising the temperature of steel to a point at which the surface thereof was pasty or crumbling?

Answer: I remember that Mr. Maunsel White in conjunction with myself made an improvement such as

you state. I cannot, however, without reference
to memoranda made at the time, or to patent
applications made by us, state whether the invention was made during the year 1899.

Question 7:   Your memory is "rather hazy" on all points
connected with this matter to which you have
just referred isn't it?

Answer: For several years I have had no practical connection with the improvement made by Mr. White
and myself. I, therefore, am not willing to swear
positively as to exact dates or facts, without referring to accurate memoranda or documents
made during the making of said improvement.[166]

The reasons for Taylor's strange behavior were unknown at
the time, but subsequent events were to provide evidence that
would prove a virtual bombshell in the courtroom.

Taylor's vague answers in January were followed by similar answers from Maunsel White in February 1906. White was
questioned in the New York offices of F. P. Warfield and H. S.
Duell, the lawyers for Niles-Bement-Pond on February 1, 3, 6,
7, 8, 1906.

White was asked to relate the events that resulted in the
discovery of the heat-treating method described in the Taylor–
White patent. White said the heat treatments:

consisted in the use of various temperatures of final heating, and
the test of tools was by taking their cutting speeds. This is a
general description of the method, the details were a matter of
record made at the time, which I cannot trust my memory to
give.[167]

White was asked if he could:

give the name of anyone present during these experiments, or
any part of them, who would be able to make an intelligent,
definite statement as to what was done, why it was done, and
the results?[168]

He said no one; that Mr. Taylor and himself were the only
ones involved in the early stages of the development of the

heat-treating method at Bethlehem. White also revealed that he had very little association with the actual experiments or the tests of the heat-treated tools in the special lathe:

> As a matter of fact, the men who were directly connected with the experiments that were made in the development of this patent, I very seldom came into direct contact with, as I would consult with Mr. Taylor with regard to the steps to be taken in the blacksmith's shop, and devoted most of my time to this end of it, and it would be impossible for me to say, at the present time, who were in charge of the lathes where the experiments of cutting speeds were made. The two blacksmiths at whose fires we did most of our work were Schultz and Nowack. I might state that Mr. Sandmeyer, who is now in our employ, and has charge of the crucible furnaces, came to our works subsequent to the issue of this patent, and therefore had no connection with it.

> Question 3:   It wasn't necessary, then, that you personally superintend the lathe tests?

> Answer: It was not, as I got a daily report of the records made on the lathes, and in the case of special tools I would go to the lathe, and verify for myself the cutting speed; generally in company with Mr. Taylor.[169]

White was asked how he and Taylor determined the order in which they would conduct the experiments and also to produce the records of their early results. White replied:

> We made, for instance, our first experiment, then Mr. Taylor and myself took the results and consulted over what would be the next best step to pursue; having determined upon this, another experiment was made, and so on, until the final development of the patent.[170]

In regard to the records, White said he had turned the records over to his secretary, H. S. Snyder, years ago and did not know where they were at present.

Upon learning that White did not know where the records were, the lawyers for Niles-Bement-Pond—Warfield and Duell—asked the lawyers for Bethlehem Steel to produce these records. The Bethlehem lawyers replied that the statements in patent

668,269, would provide the best information on the development of the process. This suggestion led Warfield and Duell to claim:

> Defendant's counsel has noted that complainant's counsel does not care to have any facts relating to this invention, or the way in which it was made, brought before the Court in this case, except such as have been carefully prepared and approved as fit to stand the light of day, and set forth in the patent itself. He, however, insists that all the facts should be before the Court, and gives notice that he will, as the only way remaining by which the rights of the defendant can be protected, urge upon the Court at the hearing, in the default of the production of such records, that complainant by its refusal to produce such records, admits that the subject matter of such records would furnish facts contrary to defendant's contention in this case, on *first*, the question as to whether or not the alleged invention, or inventions of the patent or patents in suit, was an invention; and, *second*, on the question as to who were the inventors, or who was the inventor, of the alleged invention in question. Defendant makes this statement in order that there may be no question of doubt as to its position, or any question of surprise.[171]

Warfield and Duell followed this line of thought and on February 19, 1906, interviewed John S. Hay in Philadelphia. Hay was born in Johnstown, Pennsylvania, on April 14, 1872, and lived there until moving to Pittsburgh in 1888. In 1906, Hay said he was formerly a metallurgist at the Crescent Steel Works of the Crucible Steel Company of Pittsburgh, and that he had developed a similar heat-treating method in 1897. Hay, however, failed to supply any real information because although he had applied for a patent, there was an interference declared with the Taylor–White patent. When Duell asked Hay, "did you sell out to the Bethlehem Steel before the date at which you would have had to disclose facts relative to when you conceived your invention, etc., in order to contest the interference?," Hay replied he had.

Duell also asked Hay what he received for his invention and he said a free license for the Carnegie Steel Company plus a "cash payment."[172] Hay did not disclose the cash amount he received, but it apparently was enough to enable him to retire from Crescent in 1904, and purchase a 25-acre farm and a large house at Woodlyn Station, Pennsylvania.[173] From 1904 to 1916, Hay operated a crucible furnace in Homestead, Pennsylvania, and manufactured alloys used in armor plate. Unfortunately, this plant was destroyed by fire in 1916, and Hay retired to Woodlyn, where he died on May 3, 1943.[174]

It is apparent that Bethlehem's action in purchasing the rights to Hay's invention was designed to bury whatever evidence might exist on the development of a method of heat-treating tools prior to Taylor and White's discovery.

A strange twist to Hay's testimony was evidence presented by Duell that when Hay had originally met with him in January 1906, he said that "neither yourself or Messrs. Taylor and White, or either of them, made the invention which you believed that you had made at the time you made it . . . but that a certain individual, now deceased, made it." Duell asked Hay that person's name and residence.[175] Hay said he did not know the name but added:

> I know part of his name. He was called "Lewis" and I never believed him and simply mentioned this matter in a reminiscent way, and also to throw Mr. Duell off me, as he would bother somebody else and not me.[176]

At the present time we know nothing else about this mysterious "Lewis" or whether Hay was telling Duell the truth about this individual.

Taylor's vague answers in 1906 weakened Bethlehem's position regarding Hay's 1897 discoveries, and Taylor's position was dealt another blow when the men who had worked with Hay all testified that Hay indeed had developed a method of heat-treating tools. Bethlehem first tried to discredit Hay's work by "Scouring the Alleys and Saloons" (of Pittsburgh) to find former Crescent employees who would testify that Hay had never developed a heat-treating method like Taylor and White's.[177]

Their next step was to utilize Taylor's apparently poor memory as a way to create a story about a mysterious "Taylor" who had originally performed tool treatment experiments at Crescent in 1897 and 1898. This story implied that the "Taylor" who came to Crescent was Frederick W. Taylor. In 1907,

two witnesses testified about the work of this "Taylor"—
George Keim (40 years old) and Oliver M. Kenyon (38 years old).
Keim said "Taylor" worked in a special place in the blacksmith
shop where he did his work in secret. Keim described Taylor's
activities when Attorney George H. Parmelee asked him:
"Please describe what you saw Taylor do in treating tools made
from this self-hardening steel." Keim replied:

> Well, for a time after he was there he had this place in secret,
> and then he treated his tools openly, and didn't seem to care
> whether anyone seen them, and he would heat this tool up to a
> yellow scaling heat and give it a bath in hot water.[178]

Similar testimony was also given by Oliver M. Kenyon, who
explained that the normal tool-treating process was changed to
primarily the method of treating the nose of the tools after
Taylor appeared. Kenyon said:

> I saw a man by the name of Taylor experimenting in an enclo-
> sure—a stall around the fire, or something like that. He would
> take the tool and heat it to a high fluxing heat and then dip it
> into a mix. The tool was then taken to the machine shop and
> ground, and experimented with in taking large cuts on the lathe.
> That was continued for some time.[179]

Kenyon also said that prior to Taylor's experiments, Crescent
had never heat-treated tools at such a high heat.[180]

Aside from the testimony of Keim and Kenyon there is no
other evidence that a person by the name of "Taylor" conducted
such experiments in 1897 and 1898, at Crescent. It may be a
coincidence that this individual had the same last name as Taylor, but that he would also develop a method of heat-treating tools
almost at the same time as Frederick W. Taylor, seems almost
impossible. Only further research will unravel this mystery.

In compressing the large amount of evidence gathered during Bethlehem's suit against Niles-Bement-Pond, Judge Cross
said that "high-speed steel" as a process:

> was carried on at the Crescent works of the Crucible Steel
> Company of America, and is testified to by seven witnesses. The
> period of the alleged use is defined with accuracy; that is, with

such accuracy that there can be no reasonable doubt that the use prevailed for two years prior to the time when the application for the patents in suit were filed.

The steel there treated was chrome-tungsten steel of a composition within the terms of the patent. It was treated for tool purposes, and so tested as to leave no room for doubt that it was uniformly subjected to temperatures which exceeded not only the breaking-down point of the patent, but in many cases the highest heat suggested in the patents.[181]

Although Bethlehem Steel said the use of this heat-treating method was not public use, Judge Cross rejected this suggestion, stating it was:

The uniform and systematic method of steel treatment followed in the Crescent works for a number of years. The employees all knew of the method pursued, and there was never, at any time, any injunction of secrecy placed upon them; the only possible suggestion of secrecy lay in the fact that the general public was not admitted to the works without a permit from the office, but this was done to avoid the risk of accident, and is a rule commonly enforced in factories.[182]

Judge Cross also criticized both Taylor and Charles H. Halcomb (of the Sanderson Brothers Steel Company) for initially failing to fully reveal what they knew about the heat-treating process:

It is with regret that, before closing, I feel constrained to give expression to the following criticism. The complainant's case, aside from the testimony of its expert witnesses, rests in no small degree upon that of a witness who, in the first instance when called by the defendant, showed a lack of memory, and an unwillingness to testify, as to matters concerning which it would seem as if he must have had more knowledge than he chose to reveal. However, when this same witness was called by the complainant, a marked improvement in his attitude and memory is noticeable, and he became a mainstay of its case. The record discloses, and it is undisputed, that not only this witness, but another important one, refused to testify for the complainant, until after it had entered into an agreement with them by which, in consideration of their testimony, if the patents in suit were sustained, they were to have

licenses there-under. The testimony of witnesses whose compensation is contingent upon the success of the party in whose behalf
they testify, whose contingent compensation is furthermore an
interest in the very subject-matter of the litigation, who refuse to
testify until after such contingent consideration is promised, who
thereupon testify pursuant to the arrangement, and subsequently
demand and accept such contingent compensation, cannot but be
impaired.[183]

Cross continued, being very critical about Taylor, who in
1906 originally demanded a fee for his testimony:

> Nor is this all, for the first of the witnesses referred to, in the
> first instance, demanded a pecuniary consideration for testifying,
> which he admits he regarded as prohibitive, while the second
> threatened to withdraw his testimony because of some delay in the
> delivery of the license which he was to receive as compensation. It
> is not merely that such witnesses are interested, for that does not
> fully express their status; it is rather the character of their interest
> and the method of its acquirement; they dickered with the com-
> plainant for an interest in the rest as the condition of their testi-
> fying. Their compensation, so far as they knew, was dependent
> upon the strength of their testimony, and they had every induce-
> ment to make it effective. Furthermore, when testimony is first
> bartered for by a complainant in a court of equity, under circum-
> stances like the above, and the testimony given pursuant to the
> bargain is accepted and used, not only its equitable standing, but
> the strength of its case, is likewise impaired, for the suggestion
> will not down that, if some witnesses have testified under such an
> arrangement and for such a consideration, other witnesses in the
> case may have done the same thing.[184]

The judge's constrained language concerning the testimony of Taylor failed to give the details of the strange events
surrounding this case. These events were reported in the *New
York Times* of February 8, 1909, which revealed that Taylor's
testimony in support of the Bethlehem Steel claims was made
only after the company had granted him special concessions
regarding his future use of the patents.

The *New York Times* article revealed that some months
earlier the counsel for Niles-Bement-Pond had obtained copies
of confidential letters between Bethlehem and Taylor:

Counsel for the Niles-Bement-Pond Company had in some way procured certain blotters . . . (books of records) . . . containing copies of correspondence which tended to show that the Bethlehem Steel Company had promised certain valuable concessions in case the testimony should tend to support the allegations made by the steel company.

The paper also said:

> . . . When Mr. Taylor was examined he admitted that such concessions had been made, although he preferred to call them agreements and explained them by saying that he gave his testimony as an expert, and not as a manufacturer. But he admitted the authenticity of an agreement made some time in the Spring of last year by which he was to receive a favorable license from the Bethlehem Company authorizing him and his successors to manufacture or treat metal-cutting tools by the methods described in the patent.[185]

According to the *Times*, Taylor and Charles H. Halcomb refused to testify until Bethlehem Steel "entered into an agreement with them by which, in consideration of their testimony, they were to have favorable licenses in case the patents in suit were sustained."[186]

Judge Cross also said that the successful use of the Taylor–White prepared tools at Bethlehem was due, in great part, to the other changes Taylor introduced at Bethlehem. Utilizing evidence presented during the case, he illustrated how the ability of the tools to remain efficient despite high working temperatures was made possible, in part, by Taylor's shop management methods: "Whatever advance has been made in this direction has been by means of apparatus or shop facilities, and methods not involved in the patents."[187] Furthermore, said Cross, the testimony revealed that shop rights or licenses were granted to U.S. firms, and similar rights sold abroad for large sums of money:

> An analysis of the testimony upon this point will show, however, that with the shop rights and licenses, and included in the consideration, paid therefore, were licenses under various other patents for furnaces and other apparatus used in the practice of the patented process.[188]

In his summary of the entire case, Cross said:

> The case, then, may be summarized as follows: The prior art was radically different from what the patent would lead us to believe. There was no such thing known to the art as a "breaking-down point"; on the contrary, it is established that given a new steel, particularly if the composition were unknown, it was customary to experiment with and test and try it, and thereby ascertain the best method of treating it; that, in pursuing this course, the method of the patent was substantially followed, and temperatures as high as any mentioned therein, or higher, were, not in isolated cases, but in ordinary practice, resorted to. Moreover, as a matter of fact the patentees themselves, in making their alleged discovery, simply adopted the experimental rule which other workers in the art both before and since adopted and used, and if, in the race, the patentees have surpassed others, it has not been through novelty of procedure, but by means of special facilities, apparatus, and methods not embraced in the patents.[189]

Under the above conditions, he declared the Taylor–White patents invalid and Bethlehem Steel lost the case.

Considering the severe rebuke from Judge Cross about the concessions that Halcomb and Taylor obtained from Bethlehem in exchange for their favorable testimony in the case, one may wonder why Taylor entered into such an agreement. Copley said that when Taylor left Bethlehem in 1901, "he had got all the money those need who care nothing about display."[190] But by 1907, six years had passed, Boxly had been built in Chestnut Hill (the full cost is unknown, but rebuilding of the gardens alone cost $17,000), and Taylor was utilizing much of his spare money to promote his management ideas. In light of this situation, we can see that he could use an additional source of money.

Taylor's need for additional funds can be seen in a letter he wrote to his friend Herbert L. Clark in 1909:

> Now, during all these years I have spent every cent which could be spared from my income in furthering this cause and during a considerable part of the time I have been obliged every

year to encroach upon my principal in order to carry on the work I am doing.[191]

It is possible that Taylor saw the money he would derive from the concessions he received from Bethlehem as a fund for the promotion of management concepts. The money he would earn in this manner would have been considerable as revealed by the "copies of correspondence" mentioned in the *New York Times* article of February 8, 1909.

The copies of the letters between Taylor and Bethlehem Steel have apparently not survived, but copies of the letters between Halcomb and Bethlehem still exist. Halcomb had negotiated an agreement with Bethlehem for the use of the high-speed steel patents, prior to Taylor's testimony, if they were upheld by the court. The possibility of a separate agreement with Taylor bothered Halcomb. The correspondence between Halcomb, his lawyer, and Bethlehem Steel concern Taylor's agreements and Halcomb's reaction to them.

Halcomb was disturbed simply because under the license agreement between Halcomb and Bethlehem, Halcomb only had to pay five cents a ton for all the high-speed steel he produced where others would have to pay ten cents. In a conference with Bethlehem Steel's lawyer, Mr. Thomas Bakewell, and their vice president H. S. Snyder, on February 9, 1907, Halcomb's lawyer friend Alfred Wilkinson discovered Bethlehem was unhappy with this agreement. Wilkinson subsequently wrote Halcomb on February 11, about Bethlehem's attitude, and Halcomb replied on February 12, saying he did not like the spirit displayed by Bethlehem concerning his testimony and agreement. Halcomb also commented about his testimony:

> I was asked if I would be willing to testify in a suit under certain conditions. I went over these conditions and an agreement was drawn up. . . . I have nothing further to say on the subject. I stated the terms under which I was willing to give my evidence and those terms still stand and I have performed my share of the agreement.[192]

Halcomb signed the final agreement with Bethlehem on April 6, 1907. The copy of the actual license, dated April 4,

1907, included with Halcomb's testimony reveals that the first of the six conditions specified in this agreement said "The license was not exclusive." This statement left Bethlehem free to negotiate with other individuals on the use of the high-speed steel treatment process under special conditions.

In a few months Halcomb's lawyer discovered Bethlehem had signed a similar agreement with Taylor. In informing Halcomb of this fact, on November 18, Wilkinson also remarked that Taylor had some absurd idea of using high-speed steel to make separable teeth for milling cutters. Halcomb replied on November 21, saying Taylor's idea was a useful one. Further, Taylor may have much more in mind and if this were so then his agreement with Bethlehem would be threatened:

> I do not understand your reference to Bethlehem giving Taylor a license. Isn't he still with the company and, as part owner with White in the patents, doesn't he have a right to use the patent without a license?
>
> I see nothing at all absurd about making separable teeth for Milling Cutters. Quantities of Milling Cutters are built up that way already, and there was a firm called H. A. Williams & Co., of Taunton, Mass., who made Twist Drills from Carbon Steel by twisting them into shape from a flat bar. I won't say that he was over-successful and he stopped making them long ago but Taylor will be simply trying to apply the process with Carbon Steel to High Speed Steel. I am inclined to think that more might be involved than appears on the surface. If a High Speed Drill made from a flat bar twisted should be a success, I do not know why by some means a patent might not be taken out for that and then Taylor might have a big company making quantities of Drills, which nobody else could make but himself, and he would have got a license which might be quite detrimental in the end.[193]

Wilkinson replied immediately, telling Halcomb that in his conversation with Bakewell, he discovered Bethlehem had signed with Taylor not only to obtain his good will, but for other purposes:

> As I understood his proposition, they wanted Taylor's good will for some reason or other. Perhaps he has some testimony in his

possession and therefore they wanted to trade with him or else make a present and keep him in line. I did not understand, that coming at this late date, it was a matter of particular importance, but Mr. Bakewell is of course tremendously interested in this case and put it up to me, that he knew you would be interested too, and of course he would not do anything without informing you and also asking your advice where he could get it.

As I understand, Taylor & White sold out to Bethlehem their entire interest, but there was some question whether or not they did have the right to use these inventions for their own particular purposes. Perhaps Mr. Bakewell had it in mind to settle that question definitely and without making trouble to Bethlehem or its licensees.[194]

In his reply, Halcomb asked for more data concerning Bakewell's proposition regarding Taylor. Halcomb had to wait several months for any information since Bakewell waited until January 18, 1908, to phone Wilkinson. After talking with Bakewell, Wilkinson wrote Halcomb on the subject:

Mr. Bakewell telephoned me yesterday and asked if you had agreed to the proposed arrangement with Taylor, as he wished to take Taylor's testimony and get ready for argument quickly as possible; he spoke as though we were holding him back, where as we ought to help. (This is the first I have heard of the matter since I wrote you a month or more ago.) I told him how much you were interested in his success in the suit, that you certainly wouldn't interpose any obstacle and that we had tried to get him twice in the last two months, when you were in New York.[195]

Replying to Wilkinson on January 20, 1908, Halcomb said he was anxious to do anything to help Bethlehem win their suit and had:

no objection to their giving Taylor a license in order to get his testimony, if they give it to him on the same terms as they gave me mine. He certainly should have to pay a royalty but it will be satisfactory to me if that royalty is made the same as mine, that is, half what other licensees may have to pay.[196]

In his reply of January 25, 1908, Wilkinson sent Halcomb a copy of Bethlehem's proposed agreement with Taylor. He said

Bakewell wanted to know if Halcomb had any objections as soon as possible, since Taylor would give his testimony shortly. Wilkinson said that under the agreement with Taylor, both Taylor and Halcomb could make steel for "detachable milling cutters and for these particular twist drills" and that Halcomb would have to admit that his license fee would not be affected by the license given to Taylor.[197]

Wilkinson also explained the special arrangement Bethlehem had made with Taylor:

> The situation seems to be just as though, to put it in other words, they gave him a license at 5 per pound and then turned back to him all the cash received therefrom, which in a certain sense they could do without reference to your license, and as a recompense for his testimony. If they wished to pay him a lump sum all they would have to do to avoid your license would be to discount the royalty to be received and estimate the equivalent lump sum.
>
> In view of the present terms of this license it does not seem pertinent to raise the questions you raised over the telephone the other day, that it ought to be limited to Taylor making it for himself.[198]

Halcomb apparently was not satisfied with the fact that he could manufacture steel for milling cutters and twist drills on the same basis as Taylor and explained this fact to Wilkinson:

> To be brief, I haven't any objection to Mr. Taylor's being licensed even if he has to be licensed on the same terms as the Bethlehem Steel Co., in other words, at an advantage of 2½ a lb. below me but, in view of my having already a broad license, I can't consent to its being circumscribed or restricted by giving Mr. Taylor any exclusive rights by which he can limit the sale of my steel by his refusing to license other people to make Detachable or Built-up High Speed Milling Cutters or Flat Twisted Drills. In other words, the field must be kept open. Let Mr. Taylor come in as a competitor and I have no objection, but do not let him come in as a monopolist.[199]

In replying to Halcomb's letter on January 29, Wilkinson explained that Taylor had originally wanted $3,000 to $4,000 in cash for his testimony, but Bethlehem offered him a free license:

> As I understand it, they want to give Mr. Taylor a free license by way of consideration and no modification of that is possible by way of Mr. Taylor paying any license fee, because as Mr. Bakewell told you over the telephone, he first asked $3000 or $4000 cash, which they refused but in place thereof offered him this free license.[200]

Taylor's agreement to accept a license in lieu of money probably occurred because of Taylor's previous experiences with both Bethlehem and Wm. Sellers & Company in collecting money for the Taylor–White tool steel rights. In 1902, Taylor wrote Maunsel White about this problem, saying Sellers was paying them $3,000, 41 percent of which ($1,230) was due White. He said he had difficulties collecting from Sellers. In addition, he said that there also was a check due to them from Bethlehem for the high-speed steel royalties but it also was delayed.[201]

At this point, Halcomb was frustrated by Wilkinson's and Bakewell's apparent failure to recognize that Taylor's agreement with Bethlehem would give him a monopoly. On January 30, he immediately wrote Wilkinson, explaining that because he had a broad license to sell high speed steel to anyone in the country he had the same rights as Taylor. Therefore "my right shall not be limited by not being allowed to sell High Speed Steel for Built-up Cutters or Flat Twisted Drills."[202]

By February 4, Bethlehem had arranged to have Taylor testify on February 12, 1908, and they were eager to settle affairs with Halcomb. Consequently Wilkinson wrote Halcomb on February 4, stating that Bethlehem thought many of Halcomb's criticisms of Taylor were justified. In addition, he said Bakewell believed the arrangements with Taylor were complete and he wished to confer with Halcomb on the telephone on the matter.

From Bakewell, Halcomb learned that Taylor would not testify unless he were given the sole monopoly to sell high-speed steel for a specific purpose. For his part, Halcomb demanded a private agreement with Bethlehem. Under this agreement, whatever steel orders Taylor would send to Bethlehem would be secretly divided equally between Bethlehem and Halcomb.

Halcomb explained the entire agreement in a letter to Wilkinson on February 8, 1908, saying he was allowing Taylor to limit his own license. Further he was "making this concession at a decided loss to myself in order that the Bethlehem Steel Co. may have the benefit of Mr. Taylor's testimony."[203]

This agreement was divided into two parts. First, Taylor was given the exclusive right to sell high-speed steel for inserted teeth in built-up milling cutters, but had to purchase this steel either from Bethlehem or Halcomb. Second, Halcomb entered into a secret agreement with Bethlehem which he explained in detail to Wilkinson:

> SECOND. That in consideration of my consenting to Mr. Taylor's being the sole licensee of the Bethlehem Steel Co. for selling High-Speed Steel for Inserted Teeth for Built-up Milling Cutters, wherein it is stipulated that said Taylor shall give his orders for such steel to the Bethlehem Steel Co. or myself, that the Bethlehem Steel Co. shall enter into an agreement with me whereby such orders shall be eventually divided, as to weight, between the Bethlehem Steel Co. and me.
>
> You see the point of this. Without such an agreement as to equal division of orders, the Bethlehem Steel Co. might prevail on Mr. Taylor to place all his orders with them and I would be cut out of valuable trade.
>
> Then the private agreement between Bethlehem and me provides that, even though Mr. Taylor should send all the orders in to Bethlehem, they shall equally divide those orders with me.[204]

All this correspondence reveals that Taylor was planning to manufacture inserted teeth for built-up milling cutters, using high-speed steel. To achieve this goal he made an agreement with Bethlehem. In this agreement he would have an exclusive license for such manufacture if he would testify in Bethlehem's behalf in the high-speed steel suit. Taylor, however, was unaware that Halcomb gave up his right for such manufacture only when he entered into a secret agreement with Bethlehem.

Under this agreement, although Taylor believed he was ordering his steel from Bethlehem, he did not know that Bethlehem was secretly dividing his orders with Halcomb.

Despite the defeat of the patents, it is apparent that the heat-treating method, coupled with all the changes in the shop in regard to belt-tightening, standardization of operations, and other improvements, improved conditions in the machine shop. Taylor's own testimony during the patent suit demonstrated this fact:

> When we were finally ready to introduce these tools on a large scale into the machine shop, the main lines of shafting in the shop were speeded up from 96 revolutions per minute (their speed before the introduction of our new tools) to 225–300 revolutions per minute. It was our wish to speed up these lines of shafting even to a higher speed than those just given, but in this case we were limited in the possible speed of our main lines of shafting by the vibration caused in the shop through these extraordinary high speeds. In addition to this increased speed in the main lines of shafting, in a great many cases we increased the speed ratio also of the countershafting of the machine to that of the main line, thus running the machines at even a higher cutting speed than that indicated by this increase in the speed of the main lines of shafting.
>
> The output in poundage of the principal machine shop of the Bethlehem Steel Company was more than doubled, and this means that the machines during the time when they were actually cutting metals worked much more than twice as fast as they did before, since, as everybody knows, a great part of the time consumed in a machine shop is taken up with putting the work into the machines, taking it out, adjusting the speeds, measuring it for size, and also for taking the final finishing cuts for which class of work, namely taking finishing cuts, our high-speed tools were not suited.[205]

The machine shop problems were limiting production. Throughout Bethlehem the improvements introduced by Taylor, especially the high-speed steel tools, increased production since rough forgings could now be handled, thereby reducing the work previously performed in the hammer shop and forging department.

NOTES

1. Whitney papers, 1885, Box 1, Vol. 3.
2. Gallo and Kramer, 1981, p. 11–14.
3. Copley, I, p. 364.
4. Fannon to Marshall, April 21, 1916, p. 5.
5. Goodrich, 1915, p. 2.
6. *New York Times*, October 1, 1886, p. 1.
7. Fannon to Marshall, April 21, 1916, p. 5.
8. Fannon to Marshall, April 21, 1916, p. 6.
9. Fannon to Marshall, April 21, 1916, p. 8.
10. "Reports Digester," November 7, 1892.
11. Taylor to Hammond, May 18, 1893.
12. Taylor to Hammond, May 18, 1893.
13. McCleod, 1974, p. 17.
14. Copley, I, pp. 386–87.
15. Records of the Secretary of State of New Jersey, West Trenton, New Jersey.
16. Henry J. Carman, The Street Railway Franchises of New York City, 1919, pp. 206–07.
17. Burton J. Hendrick, "Great American Fortunes and Their Making: Street Railway Financiers—III," *McClure's Magazine*, XXX, no. 1 (November 1907), pp. 323–38.
18. Thompson to Taylor, December 22, 1902.
19. Nelson, 1980, p. 55.
20. Copley, I, p. 392.
21. Simonds to Taylor, August 16, 1889.
22. Sawyer to Taylor, April 25, 1890.
23. Simonds to Taylor, August 16, 1890.
24. Simonds to Taylor, August 20, 1890.
25. Taylor to Sawyer, June 30, 1891.
26. Smith to Taylor, November 9, 1892.
27. Rhode, 1981.
28. Taylor, December 19, 1892.
29. Taylor to Smith, December 28, 1892.

30. Sawyer to Taylor, February 27, 1893.
31. Taylor to Smith, May 1, 1893.
32. Smith to Taylor, June 6, 1893.
33. Wrege, 1983.
34. Taylor to Hammond, August 4, 1893. Similar letters can be seen in Taylor to Smith, August 4, 1893, and Taylor to Sawyer, August 4, 1893.
35. Basley to Taylor, July 12, 1893, p. 5.
36. Wrege, 1983.
37. Chen and Pan, 1980.
38. Taylor to Hammond, August 25, 1893.
39. *Osage City News*, 1894; *Boston Transcript*, 1894.
40. Taylor to Weymouth, April 20, 1895.
41. Nelson, 1980, p. 58.
42. Shadbolt to Taylor, September 22, 1895.
43. Shadbolt to Taylor, November 13, 1895.
44. Taylor Notebooks.
45. *Simonds* v. *Hathorn*, 1898.
46. *Simonds* v. *Hathorn*, p. 402.
47. Affidavit, E. A. Kendall, December 4, 1895.
48. Copley, I, p. xxvi.
49. Taylor-Thompson Contract, 1895, p. 1, para. 1.
50. Taylor-Thompson Contract, 1895, p. 2, para. 7–8.
51. Taylor, 1903, p. 1424.
52. Taylor, 1903, p. 1424.
53. Taylor to Thompson, January 9, 1896.
54. Taylor to Thompson, January 13, 1896.
55. Thompson to Taylor, February 21, 1896.
56. Taylor to Thompson, March 2, 1896.
57. Thompson to Taylor, March 6, 1896.
58. Thompson to Taylor, March 19, 1896.
59. Taylor to Thompson, March 24, 1896.
60. Taylor, 1903, p. 1427.
61. Taylor to Thompson, January 8, 1896.
62. Thompson to Taylor, February 21, 1896.
63. Thompson to Taylor, February 14, 1896.
64. Taylor to Thompson, March 6, 1896.
65. Taylor to Casper Goodrich, June 3, 1896.
66. Taylor to Arthur Moxham, February 21, 1896.
67. Taylor to Fox, October 22, 1896.
68. Taylor to Bowditch, March 24, 1896.

69. Taylor to Bowditch, March 24, 1896.
70. Metcalfe, 1880.
71. Metcalfe, 1880, pp. 12, 15.
72. Taylor to Pratt, March 12, 1896.
73. Bowditch to Taylor, December 11, 1896.
74. Report on Progress, 1907.
75. Weymouth to Taylor, March 18, 1897.
76. Hathorn to Taylor, April 19, 1897.
77. Taylor, December 29, 1896.
78. Taylor, *Shop Management*, 1911, p. 88.
79. Alford, 1934, p. 66.
80. Davenport to Taylor, November 22, 1897.
81. Taylor to George Hathorn, December 18, 1897.
82. Taylor to Robert Linderman, January 3, 1898.
83. Taylor to Robert Linderman, January 8, 1898.
84. Taylor to Robert Linderman, May 1898.
85. Copley, II, p. 123.
86. Taylor, *Shop Management*, 1911, p. 100.
87. Taylor, *Shop Management*, 1911, p. 101.
88. Bjork, 1947, p. 307.
89. Bjork, 1947, p. 307.
90. Thompson to Taylor, June 8, 1898.
91. Thompson to Taylor, June 24–27, 1898.
92. Taylor, 1903, p. 1357.
93. "Testimony," BTS, p. 110.
94. Rose, 1884, p. 46.
95. Taylor, *Principles*, 1911, pp. 42–47.
96. Gillespie and Wolle, 1899, p. 13.
97. Gillespie and Wolle, 1899, p. 14.
98. Gillespie and Wolle, 1899, p. 14.
99. Gillespie and Wolle, 1899, p. 2.
100. Gillespie and Wolle, 1899, pp. 3–4.
101. Gillespie and Wolle, 1899, p. 4.
102. Gillespie and Wolle, 1899, p. 4.
103. Gillespie and Wolle, 1899, p. 4.
104. Gillespie and Wolle, 1899, p. 5.
105. Gillespie and Wolle, 1899, p. 5.
106. Gillespie and Wolle, 1899, pp. 5–6.
107. Gillespie and Wolle, 1899, pp. 6–7.
108. Gillespie and Wolle, 1899, p. 11.
109. Taylor, *Principles*, 1911, p. 55.

110. Gillespie and Wolle, 1899, p. 7.
111. Gillespie and Wolle, 1899, p. 7.
112. Gillespie and Wolle, 1899, pp. 7–8.
113. Gillespie and Wolle, 1899, p. 8.
114. Thompson to Taylor, February 10, 1896.
115. Taylor to Thompson, April 3, 1899.
116. Gillespie and Wolle, 1899, p. 7.
117. Gillespie and Wolle, 1899, p. 7.
118. Hsu and Wrege, 1984.
119. Gillespie and Wolle, 1899, p. 1a.
120. Gillespie and Wolle, 1899, Table 1.
121. Gillespie and Wolle, 1899, pp. 1–2a.
122. Gillespie and Wolle, 1899, p. 2a.
123. Taylor, *Principles of Scientific Management*, 1911, p. 62.
124. Whiting, 1983.
125. Gillespie and Wolle, 1899.
126. Gillespie and Wolle, 1899, p. 7.
127. Taylor, *Principles of Scientific Management*, 1911, p. 61, footnote 1.
128. *Engineering News*, October 19, 1899, pp. 50–51.
129. *South Bethlehem Globe*, May 17, 1898, p. 1.
130. Copley, II, p. 55.
131. Copley, II, p. 55.
132. Wrege, 1976.
133. Wrege and Perroni, 1974.
134. Barth, "Fixing Rates," 1900; Barth, "Observations," 1900.
135. Taylor, *Principles*, 1911, p. 57.
136. Taylor, *Principles*, 1911.
137. Urwick, 1959, p. 5.
138. Taylor, *Principles of Scientific Management*, 1911, p. 46.
139. Taylor, *Principles of Scientific Management*, 1911, p. 57.
140. Copley, II, p. 38.
141. Langlosis and Seignobos, 1966, p. 162.
142. Taylor-Thompson Contract, 1895.
143. Taylor to Thompson, February 15, 1896.
144. FWT to Thompson, March 2, 1896.
145. Thompson, No. 10, 1903, pp. 273–74.
146. Thompson to FWT, April 9, 1903.
147. Taylor, "Shop Management," 1903, pp. 1432, 1434, and *Shop Management*, 1911, pp. 163, 165.

148. Report of conversation by and questions put to Mr. F. W. Taylor, June 4, 1907.
149. House Resolution, 1912, pp. 1477–79.
150. Taylor, *Principles*, 1911, p. 71.
151. *The Week*, December 3, 1898.
152. Copley, II, p. 128.
153. Copley, II, p. 167.
154. *Bethlehem* v. *Niles–Bement–Pond Company*, 1909; Frederick W. Taylor, "Testimony," January 24, 1906, p. 54.
155. Hayward, 1951.
156. Califf, 1889, p. 453.
157. Taylor, 1907, p. 50.
158. Neck and Bedeian, 1988.
159. Cooke, 1907–1910, pp. 47–48.
160. *North American*, Philadelphia, December 27, 1904.
161. *Bethlehem Steel* v. *Niles-Bement-Pond Company*, 1909, p. 884.
162. *Bethlehem Steel* v. *Niles-Bement-Pond Company*, 1909, p. 885.
163. *Bethlehem Steel* v. *Niles-Bement-Pond Company*, 1909, p. 887.
164. *Bethlehem Steel* v. *Niles-Bement-Pond Company*, 1909, p. 888.
165. *North American*, February 12, 1905.
166. Frederick W. Taylor, "Testimony," January 23, 1906.
167. Maunsel White, "Testimony," February 3, 1906, p. 153.
168. Maunsel White, "Testimony," February 3, 1906, p. 161.
169. Maunsel White, "Testimony," February 3, 1906, p. 162.
170. Maunsel White, "Testimony," February 3, 1906, p. 164.
171. Maunsel White, "Testimony," February 3, 1906, p. 166.
172. Hay Testimony, February 19, 1906, pp. 5–6.
173. *Atlas of Delaware County*, 1910, Plate 19; *Chester Times*, July 1, 1955, p. 1.
174. Hay, Suppes Families, 1923, p. 86; *Chester Times*, May 3, 1943, p. 2.
175. Hay Testimony, February 19, 1906, pp. 10–11.
176. Hay Testimony, February 19, 1906, p. 11.
177. F. P. Warfield, "McDonald Testimony," p. 2.
178. George Keim, "Testimony," 1907, pp. 5–6.
179. Oliver Kenyon, "Testimony," 1907, p. 5.
180. Oliver Kenyon, "Testimony," 1907, p. 5.
181. *Bethlehem Steel* v. *Niles-Bement-Pond Company*, 1909, pp. 892–93.
182. *Bethlehem Steel* v. *Niles-Bement-Pond Company*, 1909, p. 893.
183. *Bethlehem Steel* v. *Niles-Bement-Pond Company*, 1909, p. 897.

184. *Bethlehem Steel* v. *Niles-Bement-Pond Company,* 1909, p. 897.
185. *New York Times,* February 8, 1909, p. 3:5.
186. *New York Times,* February 8, 1909.
187. *Bethlehem Steel* v. *Niles-Bement-Pond Company,* 1909, p. 895.
188. *Bethlehem Steel* v. *Niles-Bement-Pond Company,* 1909, p. 895.
189. *Bethlehem Steel* v. *Niles-Bement-Pond Company,* 1909, p. 896.
190. Copley, II, p. 167.
191. Copley, II, p. 235.
192. Halcomb Testimony, 1908, pp. 17–18.
193. Halcomb Testimony, November 2, 1908, p. 47.
194. Halcomb Testimony, November 2, 1908, pp. 47–47A.
195. Halcomb Testimony, November 2, 1908, p. 51.
196. Halcomb Testimony, November 2, 1908, pp. 51–52.
197. Halcomb Testimony, November 2, 1908, p. 53.
198. Halcomb Testimony, November 2, 1908, p. 53.
199. Halcomb Testimony, November 2, 1908, p. 53.
200. Halcomb Testimony, November 2, 1908, p. 56.
201. Taylor to White, January 14, 1902.
202. Halcomb Testimony, November 2, 1908, p. 58.
203. Halcomb Testimony, November 2, 1908, p. 58.
204. Halcomb Testimony, November 2, 1908, pp. 60–61.
205. Copley, II, p. 112.

PART IV

THE SYSTEM SPREADS

IMPLEMENTATION

The Taylor system of management was only used in its entirety in two plants: Link Belt Engineering Works and Tabor Manufacturing Company. In each case, Taylor's system was installed because of a personal relationship between Taylor and the presidents of these two companies.

In the case of Link Belt, James Mapes Dodge adopted Taylor's methods because of a long-standing friendship between Taylor's family and Dodge through their mutual membership in the Unitarian Society of Germantown. At Tabor, Taylor's aid was solicited because he and Tabor's president Wilfred Lewis, had been friends for 25 years. In addition, Taylor had his assistants help solve Tabor's production problems and help Lewis financially by purchasing Tabor stock.

Taylor at Link Belt

In 1884, James Mapes Dodge (1852–1915) moved from Indianapolis to Philadelphia. He formed a partnership with Edward H. Burr as the Link Belt Engineering Works. This company became the Philadelphia representative of the Ewart Manufacturing Company of Indianapolis, manufacturers of William P. Ewart's link belt chain. A factory was built adjacent to Midvale Steel between the Richmond Branch of the Philadelphia and Reading Railroad and Nicetown Lane (now Hunting Park Avenue). At first Dodge employed one of Taylor's early assistants, Lewis Wright of Manayunk, Pennsylvania (south of Germantown), as superintendent. Although Wright, according to Dodge, installed a "number of exceedingly clever things" at Link Belt, he died suddenly in 1895.[1]

Between 1895 and 1899, Dodge made little effort to improve operations at Link Belt, but in 1900, he witnessed Taylor's demonstrations of heat-treated, high-speed steel at Bethlehem. Dodge decided to utilize high-speed steel tools at Link Belt, although he used cast steel in his products and did not really need high-speed steel tools. The introduction of increased cutting speeds created problems due, primarily, to the uneven power to the lathes that was caused by of the use of steam as a source of energy.

Dodge, under the influence of Oberlin Smith of the Ferracute Company, determined to correct this condition, not by any changes in overhead belting, but by converting to individual direct motor drive. This task was given in September 1899 to Conrad Lauer, with assistance provided by two young engineers: Dodge's son Kern Dodge and his friend Charles Day. They were so successful in their conversion that Charles Day and Kern Dodge decided to form a company, Dodge & Day, to modernize other factories. Dodge & Day were successful in this business especially through Day's diagrams illustrating the alternatives in the modernizing process. The diagrams created by Day were influential in determining the diagrammatic methods used by Carl Barth in installing the Taylor system in companies.

In his 1903 "Shop Management" paper, Taylor briefly mentioned the novel contributions of Dodge and Day:

> It is, however, a good sign for the future that a firm such as Dodge & Day of Philadelphia, who are making a specialty of standardizing machine shop details, find their time fully occupied.[2]

Day was a devoted follower of Taylor and the firm of Dodge & Day advertised themselves as "Modernizing Engineers" specializing in "Shop Management, Shop Equipment and Motor Drives."[3] An important feature of their services was the issuing of reports outlining how they would achieve this modernization. These reports were titled "Betterment Reports."

The first modernizing work done by Dodge & Day, outside of Link Belt, was in 1902 for the Jeaneusuille Iron Works Company, which was building a new plant at Hazelton, Pennsylvania. This was followed by the modernization of the New Haven Manufacturing Company, a machine-tool manufacturing company. The first "Betterment Report" was issued for this company.

Dodge & Day described the "Betterment Reports" as being:

> written with two things in view, a policy to follow for future growth, and the immediate betterment of present conditions with the least possible outlay.[4]

Day recognized there was value in depicting the problems associated with decisions concerning shop organization in graphic form. The graphic models he created were expressed in the form of a "network," which indicated the various alternatives involved in decision making. In 1903, Day described his graphic method as follows:

> We have found the graphical presentation of complex problems facilitates greatly a study of their various elements . . . the mind can grasp the problem as a whole.[5]

Day's "network" model was included as part of a paper on "The Machine Shop Problem," which he presented before the American Society of Mechanical Engineers in June 1903. In the introduction to this paper, Day acknowledged his debt to Taylor, stating that Dodge and Day were introducing the Taylor system into machine shops. Day then proceeded to outline the value of his special "network" diagrams to illustrate machine shop problems.[6]

Constructing networks of this nature helped Day think through the various steps required to complete the modernization of factors. Unfortunately, as far as published material is concerned, there is no evidence that Day applied a time factor to each activity necessary for success. This may have occurred in Day's everyday practice, but may not have been put into print to give Dodge & Day a competitive edge.

In summarizing the advantages of his "network" diagrams, Day said they could be used to show "the number of courses which may be open for fulfilling the conditions in view."[7] This statement by Day in 1903 can be compared to Herbert Simon's 1960 definition of a decision:

> Decision making comprises three principal phases: finding occasions for making a decision; finding possible courses of action; and choosing among courses of action.[8]

Day's diagrams were designed to fulfill the last two items in Simon's definition.

From 1904, until Taylor's death in 1915, Dodge and Day had a working relationship with Taylor and they frequently employed Taylor's associates (Carl Barth, Morris L. Cooke, Horace K. Hathaway, and Sanford Thompson) as consultants to aid in various phases of their shop modernization work. Because of this association, Day's concepts of graphic models was adopted by Carl Barth and, in turn, Day probably adopted some of Barth's concepts of paperwork flow diagrams into his own models.

In 1906, the Crocker-Wheeler Company of Ampere, New Jersey, hired Dodge & Day at an annual fee of $6,000 to completely modernize their plant. Day moved to Jenkintown, Pennsylvania, in 1906, because it was an express stop on the Reading Railroad to Newark, which enabled him to reach the Crocker-Wheeler plant in Ampere. This move was important to Day because at the Jenkintown station one day he met an old college classmate, John Zimmermann. The meetings at the station became more frequent, and in 1907, John Zimmermann joined the firm, which at this time had 40 employees. Zimmermann's entrance into the firm brought new resources, new capital, and new contacts. This resulted in reorganizing the firm by placing a member of the firm or one of the principal engineers in actual charge of each job that came into the office. The work on a job was either done by this man or supervised by him.

By 1911, the firm had become so large that the workload of each member increased greatly, and as a result Kern Dodge decided to withdraw from the firm. His interest was acquired by the two remaining partners and the name changed to Day & Zimmermann. Lauer and Nicholas G. Roosevelt were added to the partnership and the business was divided into four departments: Industrial, Engineering and Construction, Investigation, Reports and Public Service Management. By 1915, Day & Zimmermann had been contacted by the United States Navy to conduct an investigation of the Philadelphia Naval Yard and develop management systems related to fire control on naval vessels. We do not know, however, if any of Day's diagrams were employed in this work.

LINK BELT

In 1903, in an effort to improve conditions at Link Belt, Dodge consulted with Taylor, who suggested Carl Barth for the job. Barth's work at Link Belt represented the further development of Taylor's basic ideas concerning management. This installation was an illustration of Horace Drury's 1916 observation, that "Taylor himself had comparatively little experience with the introduction of his own system."[9] Barth's reorganization of Link Belt required five years. The first two years were devoted to installing Taylor's methods of tool maintenance and various "handling facilities."

By 1905, Barth turned to the installation of three functional foremen in charge of two lathes in the machine shop. In fact, the special efforts Barth made to prepare the lathe operators for the new methods were remarkably like present methods of preparing employees for changes in organizations:

> The two men who were used in the introduction of the system were taken into the superintendent's office and talked to by me personally in the presence of the three functional foremen appointed to run them. . . . I set forth the whole principle on which we proposed to treat them into the future.[10]

During the period 1905–1908, Barth introduced a great many innovations. He made slide rules, initiated time studies, constructed a planning department, reorganized the tool room and storeroom, and converted the Link Belt accounting system to the Taylor–Basley system of bookkeeping. Barth also installed the differential piece rate. By 1910, under the Taylor system, output per employee had doubled and costs had been reduced 20 percent.

THE TABOR MANUFACTURING COMPANY

The Tabor Company, since 1889, was a successful marketer of molding machines that were actually manufactured by other companies such as the William Sellers Company. In 1900, the Tabor family persuaded Wilfred Lewis (then employed at Sellers) to resign his position and become president and part owner of Tabor. Under Lewis's direction, the company would manufacture its own products and become a New Jersey company.

As a manufacturing site, Lewis rented space in a corner of Sellers' building as an assembly area. To manufacture the actual molding machines, Lewis purchased second-hand machine tools from Sellers. Because he basically was an engineer and not familiar with production methods, the production of molding machines was inadequate, with only six machines being assembled each month for the first two years (or 72 machines a year).

In 1901, the Tabor workers had formed a union and declared a strike, seeking shorter hours and higher wages. To settle the strike, Lewis reduced the length of the working day if the workers would continue to produce 72 machines a year.

By 1902, however, it became evident to Lewis that the company was headed for bankruptcy. At this point Lewis appealed to Taylor for aid. Taylor suggested that Tabor should add Taylor–Newbold high-speed saws to its product line and adopt Taylor methods in order to salvage the company and make it profitable.

While Taylor saw the utilization of his methods at Tabor

primarily as a method of advertising and perfecting his system of management, he also saw it as a training center for new disciples. In succession, Dwight Merrick, Horace King Hathaway, and Robert Thurston Kent were trained at Tabor. Later on, Sanford Thompson sent all new engineers for the Thompson-Lichtner Company to Tabor to be trained in Taylor's methods.

Taylor sent Barth to Tabor in January 1903. He spent three months preparing slide rules and then returned to Link Belt. Taylor was forced to work at Link Belt alone until December 1904. Luckily, Link Belt had hired Horace King Hathaway in the fall of 1904, and he was assigned to help Barth. When Barth returned to Tabor in December 1904, Hathaway was loaned to Tabor and the development of the Taylor system became the responsibility of Hathaway.

In 1911, the Tabor Manufacturing Company was reorganized as a Pennsylvania corporation with 100 shares of stock, with Taylor owning a major share.[11]

At Tabor, Hathaway and Barth finally were able to install many of the management methods Taylor had described in 1903. The first steps were made by Taylor who improved the machines and installed his belting maintenance methods and a tool room. Hathaway and Barth first concentrated on cutting tools and then Taylor's other mechanisms. They established a planning room operated by an order-of-work clerk, a route clerk, a cost clerk, a balance-of-stores clerk, an instruction card clerk, and a move clerk. On the production floor they had four functional foremen: gang bosses, speed bosses, inspectors, and repair bosses. The last step was the use of time study and incentive wages, either the differential rate or the task and bonus system.

CLOTHCRAFT—AN EXAMPLE OF SCIENTIFIC MANAGEMENT

Midvale, Tabor, and Link Belt have always been held up as outstanding examples of the Taylor system. Each of the firms were intimate with Taylor; friends and relatives held control at Midvale, and in the latter two, Taylor himself held a strong financial share, enabling personal control. But perhaps it was the Clothcraft Shops of Cleveland, Ohio, in which Taylor had no financial hold, only a philosophical one, which offers the best example of what Taylor perceived as Scientific Management.

Although the company began implementing time study and office organization as early as 1910, more human-oriented changes took place after Taylor died, and illustrates concerns for the worker which Taylor claimed was central to his philosophy. We are not claiming that Taylor would have designed a structure similar to Clothcraft—but Clothcraft illustrates the type of structure of which Taylor often spoke.

The focus on the human side was initiated by Richard A. Feiss, who managed Clothcraft and who, after 1913, was aided in his work by a remarkable woman, Mary B. Gilson. Although he was a working businessman faced with important problems and decisions every day, Feiss in 1910 deliberately set out to understand, aid and encourage the personal growth and development of his employees. During the years 1910–25, Feiss constructed an organization that successfully combined the elements of scientific management and Feiss's own concepts of "Personal Relationship." This marvelous structure was destroyed in 1925 by financial problems in the clothing industry and a clash of personalities among the executives of Clothcraft. Feiss's work was recognized as unique by his contemporaries, and Horace Drury in 1918 said that at Clothcraft Feiss's "chief contribution toward the development of the science of management has been the scientific study of the human element."[12] An overall view of Feiss's contribution was provided by Gilson in 1940:

> He was a pioneer and many things he said and did in the early part of this century are now being discussed as though they were newly discovered phenomena in the field of human relations and factory management. He belonged to that unfortunate species of human beings—the man who is ahead of his time.[13]

To appreciate Feiss's efforts we must remember he did his work before the development of the behavioral sciences as we know them today.

Richard A. Feiss was born in Cleveland, July 1, 1878. He graduated from Harvard Law School in 1903. He practiced law in New York until 1904, when he returned to Cleveland to join his father in the business of manufacturing men's and boy's clothing. By 1904, they had constructed their own factory and were actively working to eliminate the evils of the "outside" shop system. In 1907, the name Joseph & Feiss was adopted along with the trademark, "Clothcraft." In 1909, Feiss became works manager and formulated plans to improve production and working conditions by "Improved Methods of Production," and "Establishing a System of Personal Relationships" (which contained many elements associated with present-day personnel practices and the concept of human relations). To understand the problems Feiss faced in carrying out his plans, a brief survey of the men's clothing industry in Cleveland in the 1910–15 period is in order.

The processes used in the industry consisted of five categories: cutting, trimming, sewing, pressing, and examining. All of them were influenced by the changes and innovations Feiss introduced at Clothcraft. Cutting determined not only the fit and appearance of the clothing, but also the number of pieces obtainable from a given bolt of material. Trimmers gathered and marked the cut pieces into the proper order for the sewers. Sewing was divided into two divisions: machine sewing (primary method) and hand sewing (making buttonholes, sewing on buttons, etc.). Ironing and pressing were two essential steps in clothing manufacture. Ironing in most plants was by gas irons requiring constant lifting and putting down (Feiss used electric irons on a movable arm to reduce fatigue). Steam presses were used in most factories (Feiss used electromagnetic presses heated by gas but operated electrically). In examining, all suits were checked during manufacture and after the suit was finished. In brief, Feiss not only had the problem of standardizing many different operations, each dependent upon the preceding one, but also required a steady force of workers to realize his goal of 2,000 suits a day.

Feiss installed adaptations of Taylor's methods to improve his production: improvement of machinery, routing and scheduling, and time and motion study. Improvement of equipment was marked by purchase of the most modern equipment for cutting, sewing, and pressing garments, and Feiss explained his improved equipment as follows:

> Fully 30 percent of the different machines at Clothcraft Shops are not, as far as is known, used by any other establishment in the industry, and practically every machine in use has been developed so as to be specially adapted for its particular purpose in the hands of the individual who uses it.[14]

The most important operation improved was the handling of batches of clothing, or routing and scheduling. Under the old system the batches were thrown into boxes regardless of their order; deciding who got the next batch was haphazard and depended on the yells of the operators, which enabled the foreman to know who should get the next batch.[15] The new system of handling batches was via routing and scheduling:

> The batches were arranged in numerical order and workers knew the planning department couldn't have designs on any individual. A worker got the number which the route board indicated was next in order.[16]

In assigning batches of clothing, Feiss patented a special "Price Slip on Piecework," which enabled any operator to easily keep track of work completed and money earned during the day.[17] Time studies were first made at Clothcraft in 1914, after Feiss corresponded with Taylor. In March 1914, Feiss wrote Taylor that he believed the exact amount of time required for an operation was the best basis for time study: "I am confident that this is the only element upon which any additional percentage of time for unavoidable delays can be based. . . ."[18]

Feiss also studied the need for relaxation during the work cycle, and found (instead of rest periods) that if the operator left the work position and picked up his own work, this provided the relaxation.[19]

In 1918, Horace Drury in his in-depth study of scientific management, concluded that

> possibly more clearly than Taylor, Feiss recognizes the fact that people do not usually do their best work for pay alone.

Combined with good pay there should also be the element of personal interest.[20]

The vehicle Feiss utilized to develop his ideas on personal relationships was his Employment and Service Department. Feiss believed no person could succeed with any method of management "affecting people in an organization unless he has the people affected absolutely with him," and that this could only occur through democracy, possible only when everyone had "a great deal to say with respect to the actual conditions under which they work and live."[21] Democracy was installed at Clothcraft through the concept of personal relationships. Feiss discussed this idea many times, describing it as face-to-face contact with people, thorough discussion of problems and solutions, together with a personal interest in the development of people. In 1919, Feiss lectured on his ideas of personal relationships and stressed the role of management:

> (Managers) . . . will agree that there is only one way you can solve a human problem, and that is by sitting down together and solving it, not by issuing bulletins or creeds or making fine speeches . . . but . . . in sitting down, man to man, and working it out.[22]

He said the shop committee at Clothcraft was very democratic:

> . . . in our plant we have a shop committee that is so democratic that a very well-known president of a well-known labor union (Sidney Hillman) said it went too far in its democratic tendencies, but it is a real shop committee. It is a medium for discussion among ourselves and the operators.[23]

The committee did not take the place of management, but could veto any management plans it felt unacceptable:

> It does not take the place of management but it cooperates and helps. They have a right to propose in writing . . . anything of common or collective interest, to the management, and the management has absolute right to veto it. . . . If there is anything of interest to the common welfare, relative to conditions, poli-

cies, etc., we do the same thing. We put it straight to them and they veto or accept it.[24]

These comments by Feiss reflected his belief that management concern itself "with the establishment and development of a personal relationship that will lend itself to a progressively better understanding between management and men."[25]

To build a democratic work environment Feiss created the concept of "organizational fitness." In most organizations only the worker's fitness for work was considered, but Feiss believed there were two kinds of fitness: fitness for position and fitness for the organization. To him, fitness for every member of any organization was to have the character (or have one capable of being developed) to match the character of the organization. Feiss was vitally interested in what is currently labeled "corporate culture." He considered this vital because;

> No matter how skilled or fitted one may be to do a given piece of work, if he is out of harmony with the spirit or character of the organization, he will be an everlasting detriment to himself and all others in the organization who come in contact with him.[26]

Feiss gave Mary Gilson, as Superintendent of the Employment and Service Department, full responsibility to develop methods to ascertain fitness for position and the organization. She determined both of them could be decided by personal interviews at the time of hiring and counseling during home visits after the employee joined Clothcraft.

The name Employment and Service Department was selected to reflect its dual role in developing personal relationships. "Employment" covered the selection, examination, and training of workers, and "service" covered "anything for the comfort and improvement, intellectual or social, of the employees. . . ."[27] The specific methods employed by Gilson in Employment and Service and their relationships to the "personal relationship" went well beyond what most scientific managers developed. Feiss was one of the first to select workers via psychological tests, but until they were developed, Gilson utilized an application form and held individual interviews.

Of the items on this application form, three were very important: (1) "Languages Spoken": This was vital since 31.3 percent of Cleveland's foreign residents did not speak English and this was detrimental both to Clothcraft and the individual. Speaking English was not only important in order to understand instructions, but also required for the democratic environment Feiss sought, since there could be no common understanding without a common language. If the applicants did not speak English they had to agree to learn English at classes given at Clothcraft. (2) "Wage Contribution": This was important since many young workers (primarily women) were required to give all their pay to the head of the family even if not essential to the family. Gilson determined this custom not only caused worker inefficiency, but also reduced the individual's personal freedom. She used a home visiting system with the family to help reach an agreement where a portion of the worker's pay went to the family, "and the remainder of the earnings kept by the employee."[28] (3) "Information on Past Employment": This was used both as a record of experience and earnings, and to encourage employees to actively search for new workers suitable for the special character of Clothcraft.

Because the practical aim of Employment and Service was to keep all positions filled with fit men and women, physical and mental examinations were conducted. The examinations were used to determine the employee's manual dexterity, ability to follow instructions, and intelligence. Gilson wanted tests to help uncover any errors in the original selection process and to help the development of the workers. The latter was possible at Clothcraft since all positions (clerical or executive) were filled from within.[29] A final reason for psychological tests was Gilson's desire to advance women into higher positions; she believed tests would demonstrate their abilities. Clothcraft's climate was favorable to the development of women because the question of sex did not arise when persons were selected for executive positions, e.g., Mary Hennan was production supervisor in 1920.

Gilson developed a special interview program designed to examine, among other things, "the character of the organization and its policies, and the responsibilities of the organization to the employee as well as the responsibility of the employee to the organization."[30] Gilson conducted this interview and it covered the responsibility of the organization to the worker (evaluation of earning opportunities, regularity of employment, cooperation in development of physical and social well-being), and the responsibility of the worker toward the organization (maintenance of physical and moral conditions, regularity of attendance, and development of character). The interview was followed by an orientation program.

After the interview, an instructor was assigned to the new employee. This instructor had a dual role: (1) to instruct the employee in the correct method of performing work, and (2) to help the employee become adjusted to the factory:

> If a new employee has no friends in the organization it is the duty of the instructor to see that he become acquainted. . . . In fact, the instructor's responsibility in helping new workers to take root in an organization to "get a right start" is unlimited.[31]

At the end of the day, before leaving the factory, new employees were interviewed again by the Employment and Service Department to discover their reactions to the day's work and to be reassured if there were any doubts about the job. These friendly, informal interviews were held until the difficulties of adjustment were over. The primary objective was an:

> aim to impress the worker with the fact that there are people in the organization who are definitely and vitally interested in him as a human being, and that our services are at his command if we can do anything to help him to secure steady and good earnings and to further the development of him and his family.[32]

Irregularity of employment was high in Cleveland's clothing industry, but Feiss corrected this condition by standardizing the production of suits so that enormous quantities could be made during the off season, resulting in no shutdowns throughout the year. The steady employment of workers also depended on the regular attendance of employees. To accomplish this, Gilson initiated a system of home visiting and counseling:

Our home visiting is a very important part of the service work. You cannot separate all the elements that go to make up the life of an individual. The attitude in the home is a big factor in the efficiency produced at the factory.[33]

Gilson also explained the importance of home visits:

The health and well-being of . . . (Mr. Feiss's) . . . people are fully as dependent upon the conditions which confront them outside the factory as upon those existing within. He recognizes, too, that these conditions outside of their work constitute fully as important factors in their steadiness and efficiency as any working conditions he may provide.[34]

The origin of home visiting and counseling was Gilson's daily absence report. Each absence was investigated by the Home Visiting Service to discover the cause of the absence and this work led to employee counseling:

Every absentee is visited in his home, and . . . as fruitful as anything are the intimate friendly chats . . . (about) . . . a thousand and one home and business problems.[35]

Reports of the home visits were returned to Employment and Services so the information was available when the individual returned to work the next day, and no absentee was allowed to return to work unless he or she was interviewed. In brief, the system of home visits and counseling was designed to maintain a steady force of workers, and to help the employee solve personal problems that might influence performance at work and hinder development of the individual.

The installation of eating and rest facilities was a common feature in large factories at this time, but at Clothcraft such facilities were also utilized to further the work of Employment and Service to create the "character" of the factory. Men and women had separate locker rooms with bath and shower rooms. There were separate dining rooms for men and women, with each employee having his or her own seat. This latter feature was utilized by Gilson to form the "Heads of Table Conferences." Separate recreation rooms were provided for use during inclement weather with outside recreation grounds for baseball, basketball and quoits. The recreation rooms were also used for parties given by the different departments. The parties were also used as opportunities to build a working spirit at Clothcraft.[36]

At Clothcraft the employees participated in the decision-making activities through three groups: Foremen Meetings, The Employee Advisory Council, and the Heads of Tables Conferences. All of these groups met to discuss questions of policy and general interest to the employees. They all had the proposal and veto power we discussed earlier. The overall importance of Employment and Services was acknowledged by Feiss in 1916:

> One of the most important functions of the employment and service department is to develop organization spirit and free expression of personal and public opinion . . . (and) . . . the development of that intimate personal contact so necessary to management.[37]

A NEW PLANT AND NEW PROBLEMS: CHANGES AT CLOTHCRAFT

As Feiss succeeded in standardizing the manufacture of clothing the need arose for a new plant to meet the production level of 700,000 suits a year. Construction began on November 1, 1919, and a new plant opened on May 13, 1921. The advanced nature of this building and Gilson's Employment and Service was featured in a special eight-page section of the *Cleveland Plain Dealer* on May 15, 1921, with the statement that it was the largest and best-equipped individual plant in the world manufacturing men's clothing. The construction of the plant was a large investment and was, unfortunately, completed at a time when the men's clothing industry was in a deep recession. The recession continued for the next three years, and in November 1924, Feiss had a nervous breakdown and was forced to take a rest. He returned to Clothcraft in 1925, but financial conditions grew worse, and during a reorganization of the firm,

Feiss resigned on July 5, 1925. In 1926, he moved to Boston, opening a consulting firm, Richard A. Feiss, Inc. In 1940, he moved to California and died in Los Angeles, June 8, 1954. From the time he left Clothcraft, he never mentioned his innovative work again since the trauma of abandoning his work was too much and his pioneer work was almost forgotten, yet it was one of the most complete institutions of scientific management ever attempted.

BARTH AND PAPERWORK FLOW CHARTS

After 1904, Taylor grew to rely more upon Barth and Horace King Hathaway to do the actual installation of the Taylor system in various factories. One result of this decision by Taylor was the development of new elements for the Taylor system. The most novel of these developments was Barth's development of paperwork flow charts and decision point symbols.

In 1908, when Barth reorganized the H. H. Smith and M. A. Furbush & Son Machine Company of Camden, New Jersey, independent of Taylor, he created detailed diagrams depicting not only the importance of Taylor's planning department in a scientifically managed organization, but also the flow of paperwork through the organization. Prior to this time, Taylor had frequently described the role of the planning department but had never produced a diagram of the paperwork flow essential to the successful operation of such a department.

TAYLOR 'S WRITINGS

Two books on management appeared under Taylor's name in his lifetime. Although Taylor had presented a number of papers before the American Society of Mechanical Engineers during the period 1886–1902.[38] He found writing these papers a difficult chore. In preparing his next papers, he sought the aid of two of his associates: Sanford Thompson and Morris L. Cooke.

The preparation of these papers (which eventually appeared as books) is linked to the changes in Taylor's life after 1901.

"SHOP MANAGEMENT"

We must remember that Thompson and Taylor had signed an agreement, in 1895, for Thompson to help Taylor prepare manuscripts. After the close of the work at Bethlehem, Taylor turned to Thompson with plans to publish three books, *Handbook of Unit Times, Bricklaying,* and *Earthwork,* the manuscripts of which Thompson had in progress.

The origins of Taylor's "Shop Management" can be traced to various reports which Thompson began to send to Taylor in 1901. On November 25, 1901, Thompson sent Taylor a report on piecework at Bethlehem. Thompson told Taylor that in his opening summary he had included the "Economic Results," followed by a brief outline of the methods employed in introducing piecework at Bethlehem and, finally, "a number of General Conclusions," and "Laws," followed by a detailed discussion of the work at Bethlehem.[39] Taylor did not reply until January 1902, informing Thompson that:

> it might be better to put the report in the form in which you would perhaps publish it in our book rather than in a form of a report applying especially to the Bethlehem Steel Works.[40]

Seventeen days later Taylor wrote a second letter, commenting that the report, instead of being "a history of the difficulties met with at Bethlehem" in introducing piecework, should outline the best method of introducing piecework.[41] Seven months passed before Thompson forwarded the report telling Taylor he was sending:

> a copy of a chapter on "Method of Establishing Piecework." This is in accordance with the suggestions in your letter of January 23rd, and I have followed the outline you gave me in that letter, enlarging it as I went along.[42]

Taylor studied this description carefully, informing Thompson that:

the general criticism I have to make on your report is that it is a description of what happened locally at Bethlehem. I think what we ought to describe is the proper method of introducing piecework under these conditions, describing the necessary procedure and warning anyone against wrong methods.[43]

As the year 1902 came to an end, Taylor decided to prepare a paper on "Shop Management" for the ASME meeting in June 1903. Daniel Nelson, commenting on this paper, said that it "was a remarkably disjointed presentation, especially for a work whose central message was the virtue of system and careful organization."[44]

Our knowledge of Thompson's work for Taylor will help us understand why Nelson found "Shop Management" so disjointed a document. Nelson observed that this paper, "Shop Management," was "a series of four separate but interrelated essays reflecting Taylor's concerns of 1901 and 1902."[45] Further, said Nelson, Taylor treated various "features of scientific management in seemingly random and haphazard fashion. He changed topics abruptly, with little or no transition."[46]

In February 1903, Taylor wrote Thompson for aid in helping him prepare "Shop Management" as a paper for the ASME meeting in 1903. Thompson replied that to help Taylor he was sending a description of his "note sheets," or if this was not satisfactory, he could substitute "handling pig iron" or "boxing bicycle balls," and that he was only too glad to help Taylor prepare his paper.[47] This letter serves as an introduction to the fate of some of Thompson's reports, as the following indicates. On February 16, Taylor asked Thompson for information on a number of subjects for his paper and Thompson forwarded six reports, as follows:

1. Application of piecework to yard labor for year ending April 30, 1901.
2. Material handled by Brown Hoist during year ending April 30, 1901.
3. Report of comparison between quality and balls done by day work and by piecework.
4. Report of the effect of introducing piecework and of

shortening the hours of labor in the inspecting room.

5. Effect of shorter hours of labor (describing reduction of hours at Fitchburg).

6. Method of operating watch book (a copy of directions which I furnished with books for Bethlehem Steel Co. and Simonds R. M. Co.).[48]

Many of these topics are covered in "Shop Management" on the following pages:

Topic	"Shop Management" (1903) Paper
Piecework and yard work	pp. 1357–63
Comparison of quality of balls under day work and piece rate	p. 1385
Effect of shorter hours of labor	pp. 1383–86
Piecework and shortened hours of labor	pp. 1384–85
Method of operating watch book	pp. 1424–26

Thompson also provided Taylor with tracings of the patent drawings of his watch book and decimal dial and hoped Taylor would find these sufficient for his paper.[49] On April 9, 1903, Thompson wrote Taylor another letter stating he was sending Taylor six new pages of information for his paper, which were used directly by Taylor, becoming pages 143 through 149 of the manuscript. Another page, "B.S. 14," which Thompson had sent Taylor in 1901, became page 166.

Taylor also included a discussion of "elementary times" in "Shop Management," on pages 1422–41. This material is similar to the report on "Elementary Times" Thompson forwarded to Taylor on July 22, 1902. Thompson said, "This will enter more fully into our method of elements, and will be followed by a table giving values for all of the elementary times used."[50] A table of this type was utilized by Taylor in "Shop Management," as Figure 297, page 1433. In addition, Taylor also had a time-study form on the operation of "Wheel-Barrow Excavation" as Figure 293, page 1425. This form is dated "March 10, 189_," with the observer's name as "James Monroe." This is actually a time study made by Thompson in March 1896.

"Shop Management" was read before the ASME at the Saratoga, New York, meeting in 1903, and published as paper

"1003" in Volume XXIV of the *Transactions*, covering pages 1337–1456, with pages 1456–80, the published discussion on the paper. The paper was reprinted as a book as companion to *The Principles of Scientific Management* by Harper and Brothers, both being published in 1911. "Shop Management" was an instant success and assured Taylor's place as the "Father of Scientific Management." Henry Towne said the "paper is the most valuable contribution to this subject which has yet been made, and includes so complete a review as to constitute almost a history."[51] Harrington Emerson added, "I regard the paper presented at this meeting by Mr. Taylor as the most important contribution ever presented to the society, and one of the most important papers ever published in the United States."[52] Towne and Emerson may be correct, but Nelson is accurate; the book is quite disjointed.

THE PRINCIPLES
OF SCIENTIFIC MANAGEMENT

In 1903, Taylor became acquainted with Morris L. Cooke (1872–1960) through a series of letters. Cooke had sought Taylor's advice concerning the use of Taylor's management methods in the printing industry. Cooke, who lived in the Chestnut Hill section of Germantown, finally met Taylor at the home of James Mapes Dodge and the two became friends. Taylor was elected president of the ASME in December 1905, and discovered he was expected to reorganize its operations. To facilitate this task, Taylor hired Cooke (at his own expense) to help in the reorganization. By 1907, Cooke was a close associate of Taylor.

During this period, interest in Taylor's ideas had grown tremendously and Taylor was presenting talks on his system of management at his estate, "Boxly." These talks were a recounting of his experiences in industry and as such became a standardized presentation.

Lillian Gilbreth, with her husband Frank, was often invited to these "Boxly" talks. She wrote of them:

Taylor had started holding meetings at his house. These took the form not of conferences but rather of lectures by Taylor himself, followed by questions. . . . The company assembled in the early morning, in the beautiful large living room at "Boxly" to be greeted by Taylor and after by his two young sons. Pads of paper and pencils were distributed, as Taylor very much objected to interruption. The lecture lasted from two hours on, then followed the time of questions, then luncheon, usually downtown, and a visit to one of the plants where scientific management in its perfected form had been installed, usually the Tabor Manufacturing Company.

Practically the same lecture seemed to be given each time, and it was also the lecture that Taylor gave when he spoke away from home, varying only in the illustrations chosen. This is the material that was expanded into "Principles of Scientific Management," but no matter how often it was heard, it was always interesting and stimulating and showed a progressive viewpoint.[53]

From 1907 to Taylor's death in 1915, Taylor relied on Cooke to analyze and improve the talks at "Boxly" and to make suggestions, corrections, and alterations of his writings. Cooke, like Sanford Thompson, was virtually Taylor's "right arm" and an important part of Taylor's team of associates, which included Carl Barth and Henry Gantt.

Taylor's and Cooke's personalities were fundamentally opposite. Cooke, on the one hand, was quick to grasp a new idea and apply it, and due to his early life as a reporter, he was adept at outlining and writing on any subject. Taylor, on the other hand, attempted to solve important problems with the aid of others, conducted experiments, and was able to discover principles important to the solution of everyday management problems. Unlike Cooke, he found organizing and writing a paper a difficult task.

While Taylor's life has been studied by several writers, his friendship with Cooke and its importance has been neglected. To understand Taylor's writings, we must examine their personal relationship. Cooke received his mechanical engineering degree from Lehigh University in June 1895. Later the same month he obtained a job as an apprentice machinist in the machine shop of Cramp's Shipyard in Philadelphia.[54] Cooke arrived at Cramp's shortly after Taylor had left, and it is possible that he first heard of Taylor's work while talking with the men at the yard.[55] During the next two years, Cooke worked in two other factories, but in 1897, turned to the printing and publishing field, where he remained until 1906. Cooke became interested in Taylor's concepts, and he applied them to the printing and publishing business from 1903 to 1906.

In May 1907, as his work for Taylor was drawing to a close, Cooke decided to turn his attention to both improving and utilizing Taylor's talks as the basis for future papers by Taylor and as the foundation for a book on management. To aid this work, Cooke had a stenographic record made of the Taylor "Boxly" talk made on June 4, 1907.[56]

On June 23, 1907, Cooke informed Taylor that he was writing a manuscript for a book on the Taylor system, tentatively titled *Industrial Management.* Cooke wrote to Taylor:

> The balance of the summer I want to utilize in finding out how near I can come to being able to edit "Industrial Management." I will be glad to devote this time . . . because I think to write a popular exposition of the Taylor System will be a thing worthwhile. I am going on the assumption that this book is to be a personal venture . . . (and) if the book is any good I can get it published—the thing is to get the book.[57]

As Cooke worked on the manuscript and studied the stenographic notes of Taylor's talk, he became convinced that Taylor was making an error in insisting that "the introduction of the Taylor system meant all of it or none of it."[58] Cooke told Taylor that although people saw the value of his ideas, they refused to have them introduced into their business in the dictatorial manner advocated by Taylor. Cooke felt the origin of this problem was the way Taylor presented his talks and that:

> absolutely nothing will be lost in softening the presentation to those who are not ready for it and they will be made thereby much more efficient missionaries.[59]

As part of his plan of softening the presentation, Cooke made a second analysis of the manuscript in October and November 1907. This analysis provides us with important clues about the content of "Industrial Management" and "Principles of Scientific Management." Cooke told Taylor that although the end of his talk was more convincing, it was weak because "you take an hour and a half telling about handling pig iron and shoveling with which everybody is familiar," and then "fifteen minutes on slide rules, etc., and the visitor . . . leaves you in a muddled frame of mind."[60] This letter is significant since it demonstrated the 1½ hours Taylor devoted to pig-iron handling and shoveling in his oral talk, which was translated into writing, and these topics cover 31 pages of the manuscript of "Industrial Management" and 32 pages of Taylor's book, *The Principles of Scientific Management* (1911).

By November 11, 1907, Cooke completed a considerable portion of manuscript and wrote to Taylor, describing the book and asking for aid in publishing it overseas. To facilitate this, Cooke included a rough draft of a letter to be sent abroad. In it, Taylor and Cooke were listed as the co-authors and the book described as follows:

> With the assistance of Mr. M. L. Cooke, I am planning to publish some time in the Spring a book entitled "Industrial Management" which is intended to be a more or less popular presentation of the principles of management which I advocate. The chapter headings which follow may give you an idea of the scope of the book.
>
> Chapter 1. Introduction
> 2. The Task Idea in Management
> 3. Functional Management
> 4. Time Study and Task Setting
> 5. Classification, Symbolization & Standardization
> 6. The Compensation of Employees
> 7. The Purchase and Handling of Stores
> 8. The Planning Department
> 9. Accounting
> 10. Conclusion
>
> I also enclose a rough draft of the preface which may give you a further idea of our object in writing this book and the lines it will follow.[61]

The preface, dated December 1907, outlined the "task system" of Taylor, saying it was designed for laymen, with illustrations chosen from the everyday experience of the average reader.

Taylor's reply, dated November 15, was a negative one, stating that Cooke should not publish abroad until it was successful in America and that *Shop Management* was already translated into French; thus, it would be better for Cooke to wait until more French and German companies adopted the Taylor system. Taylor concluded by suggesting that since they both were going to New York on the same train the following day (November 16), they could discuss the entire matter on the way.[62] We do not know what Taylor and Cooke decided or discussed on that train. One thing is evident, Cooke did not publish the book.

The first few months of 1908 were busy ones for Cooke, due to his work to install the Taylor system at the Williams, Wilkins & Company plant in Baltimore and his efforts to have Taylor present a paper to the American Society of Mechanical Engineers, In connection with the latter, Cooke wrote Taylor in March requesting they meet to discuss both the paper and manuscripts; we do not know if this meeting occurred, since Taylor's reply (if there was one) is missing.[63]

In Summer 1908, Cooke once again worked on the manuscript, writing Taylor of his progress:

> I am trying to put in as much work as possible this summer on "Industrial Management" in the hope I can get it in shape to submit it to you some time this Fall.[64]

Three events that occurred in 1909 were destined to cause the emergence of "Principles of Scientific Management," and the virtual disappearance of "Industrial Management" as a published book, and they provide us with evidence of a virtually complete manuscript of Cooke's book. The events are: (a) Cooke's work at Williams, Wilkins & Company; (b) plans for a course in Organization and Management at the University of Pennsylvania; and (c) the mailing of the "Industrial Management" manuscript to Taylor, together with a letter describing its origin and contents.

In 1909 Cooke and Gantt installed the Taylor system at the Williams, Wilkins & Company (the Waverly Press) of Baltimore, but the company demanded that Taylor and his associates assume the cost of installing the system. The work at W. W. & Co, was important for the further growth of the Taylor system and needed Taylor's financial aid, but if Taylor would underwrite the project, Cooke informed Taylor he was willing to give him the profits from "Industrial Management" to help defray this cost:

> If you should want to make the guarantee I would want it understood that I would not receive any profits from "Industrial Management" until you had been reimbursed for any payments made to W. W. & Co.[65]

While the W. W. & Co. work was in progress, Cooke, in March 1909, began helping Professor Henry Spangler initiate a course on "Organization and Business Management" at the University of Pennsylvania, because Spangler did not like the way the subject was taught at the university's Wharton School. While discussions were held with Spangler during Spring, nothing further happened until August.

In August, Cooke and Spangler both went to Atkin's Camps (35 miles from Masardis, Maine) for a vacation and had a long discussion about the proposed course. As Cooke told Taylor, Spangler wanted to initiate the course in Fall 1909, using Horace King Hathaway as the teacher, with chapters of "Industrial Management" as the basis for a syllabus:

> I told him [Spangler] that if Hathaway agreed to do anything for him we would allow Hathaway to have one or more chapters of "Industrial Management" to use as the basis of any syllabus he wanted to prepare for the use of students.[66]

Taylor apparently replied in the affirmative (although the letter is missing), since in a letter Cooke wrote on September 13, 1909, he referred to Taylor's statements and discussed his own plans for a management textbook:

I am much interested in what you say about Spangler, and the desirability of having something approximating a text book on management. During the course of the next month I will have ready for your perusal the draft of the book about which we have conferred. I am quite sure that this book—while not written as a text book—will come nearer being of real use as a text book on the subject than anything which is likely to be written for some time to come.[67]

Cooke apparently rewrote portions of the manuscript as a textbook and forwarded the manuscript to Taylor, but its fate is unknown. A few days before sending it, he wrote a long letter about the book which, while undated, can be shown by internal evidence to have been written in October or November, 1909.[68] We analyze this letter in detail because of the light it throws on "Principles of Scientific Management."

Cooke's (October–November 1909) letter on "Industrial Management," was 10 pages long and divided into 9 parts:

1. *Reasons for Writing "Industrial Management*
   Cooke said he began writing "Industrial Management" in the Spring of 1907, to show his appreciation for all Taylor had done for him and because Taylor was so absorbed in other phases of the Taylor system there was a great likelihood that Taylor would never write such a book.

2. *Cooke's Changing Viewpoint*
   In 1909, Cooke saw the book as especially useful to those installing the Taylor System. In fact, said Cooke,

   > This is so true of those who are working with me in Boston, New York, and Baltimore, that I could feel warranted in the expense of issuing it as a handbook for the exclusive use of these men if we were not going to publish it.[69]

3. *Arguments Changing Viewpoint*
   Acknowledging that there might be opposition to publishing the book, Cooke felt obligated to discuss such arguments. First, he reminded Taylor that in the past he (Taylor) had suggested that Cooke should publish

a popular description of the Taylor System that would not describe the system in detail. Second, some people would feel that in such a book Taylor and his associates would be giving away their business. Cooke said that his own experience revealed it to be the opposite, since he was often hindered in his work of installing Taylor's system because the people he met had so little knowledge of Taylor's ideas. Cooke said the only way to meet the growing demand for Taylor's system was to train more men in its concepts, and the way to get such men was to have Taylor's ideas more generally understood. Finally, Cooke said the publishing of the book would make the Taylor system a matter of record and secure it against the claims of quacks.

4. *How Cooke Wrote the Book*
Cooke described the method he used to write the book as follows:

> I first gathered everything obtainable in the way of technical papers, clippings, letters, etc. Having gone over all this material I arranged a schedule of chapters. I then sorted under the various chapter headings all the matter I had collected. Then I wrote one chapter after another filling in the blanks.[70]

This statement demonstrates that Cooke used, besides material from Taylor's talks, a variety of other sources to prepare his manuscript.

5. *The "Scheme of Chapters and Its Relationship to Taylor's The Principles of Scientific Management"*
Cooke explained that the early chapters (including Chapter 2) covered theory, with the later chapters discussing the mechanisms used to put the theory into practice. A perusal of "Principles of Scientific Management" will reveal that it follows the same format with more emphasis upon theory than upon mechanisms.

Cooke's comments on Chapter 2 are especially important since they foreshadow its use to prepare much of the manuscript for "Principles of Scientific Management":

Chapter 2 as you will note is in very crude shape. I secured it by boiling down the notes of the stenographer who reported your talk to Mr. Winston and his friends. This is the chapter that I hoped you would have written yourself by this time. . . . you will be able to take the MS. of Chapter 2 and rewrite it, so that it can be ready as a paper to read at the Spring meeting of the ASME.[71]

While Cooke said he wrote Chapter 2 by "boiling down" the notes on Taylor's talk, a comparison of Cooke's chapter and Taylor's talk reveals Cooke extensively rewrote 31 of the 62 pages of Taylor's talk and added 43 pages more. Therefore, his use of the words "boiling down" probably meant using and rewriting 31 pages of the 62 original pages.

6. *Plans for Publishing the Book*
   Cooke outlined a choice between one of two publishing houses—a technical one or a general one—and chose the latter because he was trying to make lay readers familiar with the Taylor system.

7. *Plans for Printing the Book*
   Cooke believed that they should print the book themselves with a publisher distributing the copies. The same practice was later followed with *Principles of Scientific Management*; Plimpton Press of Norwood, Massachusetts, did the printing, with Harper and Brothers acting as the publisher. He also indicated definite evidence that "Industrial Management" was complete enough to publish:

   In the matter of printing, there are several alternatives. I am sending you two pairs of sample pages. One is set in type very similar to that used in the Journal of the A.S.M.E. and the other is a fatter face, such as Houghton, Mifflin & Co. use for practically all their publications. . . . The book should not run more than five hundred pages of the size I enclose and an effort should be made to keep it nearer four hundred.[72]

8. *Advertising Plans*
   Even if everyone who wanted information on the Taylor system purchased a copy of the book, Cooke knew

(due to his experience in the field) that from a publisher's viewpoint this would not spell success. It was necessary to create a demand from new sources. To spread word of the book, Cooke planned to have 90 percent of the 250 technical and scientific periodicals published worldwide publish a review of the book and to spend $500 the first year in display advertising in publisher's lists and technical periodicals.

9. *Cooke's Final Plans for "Bringing the Book Out"*
Cooke outlined two policies they could follow in what he described as "bringing the book out":

The first is to get it correct while still in manuscript form. This will mean that you will have to read the MS. over very carefully and note on the blank pages those sections which do not meet your approval. I, in turn, will try to make them meet your objections. . . . The other method . . . and the one which I recommend, is that you shall approve the general plan of the book and authorize me to have it set up in type.[73]

Taylor never informed Cooke whether or not he received the manuscript of "Industrial Management," so Cooke wrote him, asking if the manuscript had arrived. Two months later, on January 7, 1910, Taylor mentioned the manuscript, stating he was returning the three volumes.[74]

The most important data we gain from our study of the 1909 events concerning "Industrial Management" are: (*a*) Chapter 2 of "Industrial Management" was a greatly expanded account of Taylor's 1907 talk, based on anecdotes of his personal experiences; and (*b*) Cooke had sufficient material in "Industrial Management" to fill three volumes, with distinct plans for immediate publication. Obviously, the manuscript of "Industrial Management" offered to Taylor an important source of material that was organized and ready for immediate use, a fact important to the emergence of "Principles of Scientific Management."

When Taylor mailed the manuscript of "Industrial Management" back to Cooke in January 1910, he said he had spent the past three weeks in a third attempt to write an acceptable paper for the American Society of Mechanical Engineers on the principles of scientific management. However, he felt the Meetings Committee would probably find it:

> so much in narrative form that they will look upon it as too diffuse . . . (but Taylor said he believed he could only convince his readers) . . . through these rather diffuse illustrations.[75]

The "diffuse illustrations" were Taylor's "Boxly Talks," including stories of pig-iron handling, shoveling, and high-speed steel—the very topics found in Chapter 2 of "Industrial Management" and in "Principles of Scientific Management."

After Taylor personally delivered his partial rough draft (now titled "Philosophy of Management"), to Calvin Rice of ASME, the diffuse illustrations on pig iron and shoveling still bothered him. Upon returning to Chestnut Hill, he wrote Rice (on January 14, 1910) to explain what appeared as digressions from the paper's main theme:

> in reading this over you will notice, particularly after the narrative parts start, that there appear to be several digressions from what you may look upon as the main text, which could be cut out. One of these, for instance, goes from page TM-16 to page TM-21. Apparently this has no immediate relation to what precedes it. If, however, you will carefully consider the essence of these digressions, you will find that they contain matter which is directly illustrative of the whole idea, that is, they illustrate certain elements of the philosophy of management.[76]

Analysis of this paragraph reveals two interesting facts. First, Taylor mentions a digression covering pages TM-16 to TM-21. Use of these page numbers is significant for two reasons: (a) TM refers to "Task Management," which was the title utilized by Cooke to identify Chapter 2 in 1907. Since Cooke believed "Task Management" was the most accurate description of Taylor's system, he created designations reflecting this, i.e., TM-1, etc.; (b) in previous manuscripts Taylor used Roman numerals or alphabetical letters to number the pages. If he had created designations similar to Cooke's, he would have used

"Philosophy of Management" (since the title in January 1910 was "The Philosophy of Management"). The evidence suggests the "TM" pages referred to by Taylor were either taken from "Industrial Management" or were rewritten versions.

Second, the use of anecdotes and stories indicates that Taylor followed the format of his "Boxly Talks" when preparing the "Philosophy of Management" manuscript.

Aside from writing the letter to Rice, January 14 was obviously an important day for Taylor because a collection of fragmentary notes (in the files in the Taylor collection at the Stevens Institute of Technology) contains two pages dated January 14, and marked "miscellaneous." These pages are apparently notes Taylor made on the 14th before telephoning Cooke on the 15th at Plimpton Press in Norwood, Massachusetts, to discuss the "Philosophy of Management" manuscript. These notes reveal changes Taylor anticipated in the "Philosophy of Management" manuscript that he planned to mail to Cooke the following week. There are seven notations; five concern the contents of the introduction of "Philosophy of Management" (later Chapter 1 of "Principles of Scientific Management"), one is on Gilbreth's motion study, and one is on pig-iron handling.[77] In brief, Taylor's main changes at this time were designed for the introduction of "Philosophy of Management," not with the portion containing the anecdotes.

The phone calls, correspondence, and notes between Taylor and Cooke, during January, February, and March, however, reflect Taylor's close personal tie with Cooke, since he requested Cooke's suggestions (and those of persons Cooke selected—i.e., Alfred Barter and Henry Kendall) concerning changes in the manuscript. He phoned Cooke about it on Saturday, January 15, and on the following Monday informed him the manuscript was on the way, stating he did not anticipate any drastic changes unless Cooke believed the paper needed extensive alteration (Taylor Notes, dated February 8, 1910).

> I am not at all clear that the paper would not be most effective by plunging very close to the start right into the narrative part of it, that is, the portion in which the various statements of fact are given, possibly leaving the philosophy, that is, the part which now comes first, until after the anecdotes have been told.

Cooke's reply to Taylor has not survived, nor has any of their correspondence for the period from January 18 to February 4, 1910. The mass of miscellaneous notes on the *Principles of Scientific Management* manuscript (in Taylor's handwriting) preserved at the Stevens Institute of Technology are primarily concerned with the introduction, first chapter, and final pages of Chapter 2. Only a few scattered notes deal with the 60 main pages of Chapter 2 (TM-1 to TM-69). It is possible that notes on these pages were destroyed but it is odd that only the notes dealing with the pages similar to Chapter 2 of Cooke's "Industrial Management" are missing. These contained Taylor's anecdotes (pig-iron handling, shoveling, etc.), and they were his primary vehicle for explaining his ideas on management (as he told Rice). If Taylor would have preserved any notes at all, he would have preserved these, but they are missing.

While the final typed version of Chapter 2 of "Industrial Management" exists, the notes for this chapter are strangely missing. Careful examination of the internal evidence of the manuscript of *The Principles of Scientific Management*, however, helps us clarify this mystery. This examination provides a clue to events during this time span. On page TM-1 of Chapter 2 of the manuscript, in Taylor's handwriting we find the words, "Correct abt Jan. 24." This note refers to pages TM-1 to TM-69, because he also noted on page TM-70, "not corrected." To obtain insight into other dates when portions of the basic *Principles of Scientific Management* manuscript were completed and the role played by Cooke (and others), we can analyze the manuscript page numbers, dates written on pages, and changes in the method of identifying pages. This analysis is summarized on the next page.

This table reveals that much of the basic manuscript of "Principles of Scientific Management" was in a rough draft form by February 8, 1910. The notes in Taylor's handwriting, dated February 8, concern putting the last four pages of the manuscript into its final form by assigning continuous numbers instead of separate numbers.

By the end of 1910, "Principles of Scientific Management" was in book form, and as a book, "Industrial Management"

TABLE IV-1
Page Numbers, Dates, and Contributors to Basic
Manuscript of *The Principles of Scientific Management*

Chapter	Page Numbers (January 1910)	Page Numbers (February 1910)	Pages with Dates	Contributors
Preface	Preface to TM	1–5	None	?
Chapter 1	TM-1 to TM-XIV*	6–24	None	Cooke Barter§
Chapter 2	(a) TM-1 to TM-69†	25–93	Jan. 24 (TM-1)	Cooke Kendall?‖ Barter?
	(b) TM-70 to TM-97	94–130	None	Cooke Kendall? Barter?
	(c) "a" to "h" & 2 pp.	131–140	None	?
	(d) Feb. 8, 1–5‡	141–145	Feb. 8	?

*There are several subpages here, e.g., "15a," etc.
†There are several subpages here, e.g., "TM-36a," etc.
‡There are also Taylor's own notes on material in these pages, dated Feb. 8.
§Alfred Barter of Plimpton Press.
‖Henry P. Kendall of Plimpton Press

had disappeared. It is apparent that 69 pages of the "Industrial Management" manuscript became part of "Principles of Scientific Management." The questions arise: (a) "Why did Cooke allow Taylor to use the material from "Industrial Management" so freely? and (b) why did Cooke not insist on being listed as co-author as he did with "Industrial Management" in 1907? The answer to the second question is found in a letter from Taylor to Cooke on December 10, 1910, in which Taylor promised Cooke all the profits from "Principles of Scientific Management":

> Since this publication of the "Principles of Scientific Management" is likely to interfere more or less with the sale of "Industrial Management" when it comes out, I shall be very glad to

turn over all of the profits from the sale of "The Principles of Scientific Management" to you.[78]

During the years 1910–11, the manuscript of "Industrial Management" (and remember it was three volumes long) was returned to Taylor's hands, and plans were made to publish it after the publication of *Principles of Scientific Management*. In preparation for this, Cooke, on February 25, 1911, made some suggestions regarding changes in the manuscript of "Industrial Management":

> Under the circumstances (publication of *Principles of Scientific Management*) don't you think that we should plan to change the title so as to include the words "Scientific Management"? The further along I get in the work the more ashamed I feel about some part of the manuscript. This is especially true of the first and last chapters. I hope it will be possible for you to pass on the general scheme of the book in the near future.[79]

This statement reveals that while Cooke wanted to change the first and last chapters, he did not contemplate changes in Chapter 2. However, when he refers to "under the circumstances," Cooke apparently is referring to the publication of *Principles of Scientific Management*. Under such circumstances, anyone reading Chapter 2 would perceive its similarity to *Principles of Scientific Management* and (since Taylor and Cooke were to be joint authors) wonder if it were written by Cooke or Taylor. To provide for this possibility, Cooke added page 1B to the "Industrial Management" manuscript and printed (in his own hand) a statement claiming Taylor wrote Chapter 2:

> This chapter is very largely a recital of Mr. Taylor's personal experiences in the development of scientific management, and as such has been written by himself in the first person.[80]

As we have already learned, however, Cooke had written this chapter in 1907. Obviously, this new statement was to prevent any problems with the published version of "Industrial Management."

For the next four years Cooke was Director of Public Works

for the City of Philadelphia (1912–14). This job was difficult, and except for one letter from Horace King Hathaway mentioning the book in 1914, Cooke apparently decided to forget about the book.[81] In fact, 19 years were to pass before the book surfaced again.

In 1933, when plans were in progress for an exhibit on the 50th anniversary of Taylor's graduation from Stevens Institute of Technology (to be held on December 7, 1933), Carl Barth brought Cooke some lantern slides for identification. Cooke identified them as "illustrations for the book on Scientific Management which was never published, but of which you tell me you have a typewritten copy."[82] The manuscript of "Industrial Management" remained in the possession of the Barth family until the three binders were acquired by the first author.

Taylor submitted the manuscript to the ASME in January 1910, and it was in the hands of the publication committee in May of that year. However, the ASME publications delayed so long in accepting *The Principles of Scientific Management* that, late in 1910, Taylor withdrew the manuscript and printed it privately for ASME members, and various sections were published in a three-part series in the popular *The American Magazine* under the title "The Gospel of Efficiency: The Principles of Scientific Management."[83]

Harper and Brothers also published the complete book as companion to the *Shop Management* book. *Principles of Scientific Management* did repeat much of the material found in *Shop Management*, but offered a more complete philosophy. The underlying philosophy was to substitute a science for "rule of thumb" methods in management. There are four main duties for management: (1) development of science to replace the old rule of thumb, (2) scientifically select and train, teach, and develop workmen, (3) cooperate with men to ensure work is being performed in accordance to the principles of science, and (4) have an equal division of the responsibility between management and workers.[84] Although there is shallow evidence, mainly autobiographical vignettes, to support these four principles, the book did offer philosophic support to the growing numbers of progressive or reform-minded individuals.

MENTAL REVOLUTION

The first chapter in Taylor's *Principles of Scientific Management* opens with the sentence, "The principal object of management should be to secure the maximum prosperity for the employer, coupled with the maximum prosperity for each employee."[85] Therefore, Taylor believed that the most important aspect of his entire management philosophy and the underpinning of scientific management was what he termed the "Mental Revolution." In his testimony in 1912 before the House Special Committee to investigate "The Taylor and Other Systems of Shop Management," he said:

> Scientific management is not any efficiency device, not a device of any kind for securing efficiency; nor is it any bunch or group of efficiency devices. It is not a new system of figuring cost; it is not a new scheme of paying men; it is not a piecework system; it is not a bonus system; it is not a premium system; it is not a scheme for paying men; it is not holding a stopwatch on a man and writing things down about him; it is not time study; it is not motion study nor an analysis of the movements of men; it is not the printing and ruling and unloading of a ton or two of blanks on a set of men and saying, "here's your system; go use it." It is not divided foremanship or functional foremanship; it is not any of the devices which the average man calls to his mind when scientific management is spoken of. . . . Now, in its essence, scientific management involves a complete mental revolution on the part of the working men engaged in any particular establishment or industry—a complete mental revolution on the part of the men as to their duties toward their work, toward their fellowmen, and toward their employers. And it involves the equally complete mental revolution on the part of those on the management's side—the foreman, the superintendent, the owner of the business, the board of directors—a complete mental revolution of their part as to their duties toward their fellow workers in the management, toward their workmen, and toward all their daily problems. And without this complete mental revolution of both sides scientific management does not exist. That is the essence of scientific management, this great mental revolution.[86]

Taylor was talking about his belief that with scientific management the productivity of the workers could increase manyfold as was shown in his pig-iron and shoveling experiments. Taylor believed that workers traditionally want a larger piece of the economic pie, but management and their owners would not want to give workers a larger share because they wanted to keep it for themselves. However, if the pie is growing 10, 20, or 300 percent, as in the pig-iron handling, then the pie, the ever growing pie, is growing for each, and the traditional labor–management conflict will be resolved.

It was Taylor's belief that if the workers would listen to scientific management in their organization and do as they were told, they, too, would have an ever improving standard of living. Taylor continued his testimony:

> I think I am safe in saying in the past it has been in the division of the surplus that the great labor trouble has come between employers and employees. . . . Gradually the two sides have come to look upon one another as antagonists, and at times even as enemies—pulling apart matching the strength of the one against the strength of the other.
>
> The great revolution that takes place in mental attitude of the two parties under scientific management is that both sides take their eyes off of the division of the surplus as the all-important matter, together turn their attention toward increasing the size of the surplus until this surplus becomes so large that it is unnecessary to quarrel over how it shall be divided. They come to see that when they stop pulling against one another, and instead both turn and push shoulder to shoulder in the same direction, the size of the surplus created by their joint efforts is truly astonishing. They both realize that when they substitute friendly cooperation and mutual helpfulness for antagonism and strife they are together able to make this surplus so enormously greater than what it was in the past that there is ample room for a large increase in wages for the workman and equally great increase in profits for the manufacturer. This, gentlemen, is the beginning of the great mental revolution which constitutes the first step toward scientific management. . . . Scientific management can not be said to exist . . . until after this change has taken place in the mental attitude of both the management of the men, both as to their duty to cooper-

ate in producing the largest possible surplus and as to the necessity for substituting exact scientific knowledge for opinions or the old rule of thumb or individual knowledge.[87]

Two years later, Taylor offered similar testimony to the Commission on Industrial Relations when he reported:

> Scientific management can not exist, and does not exist, until there has been a complete and entire mental revolution on the part of the workmen as to their duties toward themselves and toward their employers, and an equally great mental revolution on the part of employers toward their duties to their workmen. Until this great mental change takes place I say there can be no such thing as scientific management. That is an absolute necessity. You may have all the mechanism, all the forms of it, you may have your bonus system and your time study, but you have not got scientific management until that change has taken place.[88]

Taylor, according to Copley:

> wished to make it plain that the main difficulties he had encountered and was encountering in getting his system of management installed lay not in the attitude of workers as a class but in the attitude of employers as a class. . . . What mainly made the labor problem difficult of solution was the accursed myopic greed of those who commonly were found on the side of management. . . . Therefore the indispensable prerequisite for bringing in an era of industrial peace was a radical change of heart on the part of employers as a class. . . . Over and over again he said that employers must undergo a change of heart like unto that of a religious conversion. They must abandon once and for all the idea that human beings can be regarded in the same light as machines.[89]

"FIRST-CLASS MEN"

Scientific Management, as Taylor developed it, was more than time and motion study as so many of his contemporaries and even more current writers understand it. Taylor was developing a science of work and managing. There were four major foundations on which managers were to base their system, as presented in *Principles of Scientific Management*:

> *First.* They develop a science for each element of a man's work, which replaces the old rule-of-thumb method.
>
> *Second.* They scientifically select and then train, teach, and develop the workman, whereas in the past he chose his own work and trained himself as best he could.
>
> *Third.* They heartily cooperate with the men so as to insure all of the work being done in accordance with the principles of the science which has been developed.
>
> *Fourth.* There is an almost equal division of the work and responsibility between the management and the workmen. The management take over all work for which they are better fitted than the workmen, while in the past almost all of the work and the greater part of the responsibility were thrown upon the men.[90]

With respect to scientific selection of workers, Taylor sought to cull out workers who were not fit for particular jobs and replace them with better-qualified people. Taylor was trying to match workers with work. A scientifically matched worker was called a "first-class man." "I have tried," said Taylor, "to make it clear that for each type of workman some job can be found at which he is 'first class,' with the exception of those men who were perfectly well able to do the job, but won't do it."[91]

It was in 1897 at the Simonds Rolling Machine Company with female ball-bearing inspectors that Taylor instituted this concept, and in "Shop Management," he reported that:

> thirty-five girls were able to do the work which formerly required about one hundred and twenty is due, not only to the improvement in the work of each girl, owing to better methods, but to the weeding out of the lazy and unpromising candidates, and the substitution of more ambitious individuals.[92]

These 35 women not only improved production, but found that their daily earnings rose from $3.50–$4.50 to $6.50–$9.00 and their work day reduced from 10½ hours in June to 8½ hours in September. Taylor also introduced a five-minute rest break in both the morning and afternoon on August 1. A month later he expanded the rest breaks to 10 minutes.[93] Taylor said:

> Each girl was made to feel that she was the object of especial care and interest on the part of the management, and that if anything went wrong with her she could always have a helper and teacher in the management to lean upon.[94]

THE ART OF CUTTING METALS

The December 4, 1906, meeting of the ASME had such a large attendance (1,352) that the meeting was held, not in the usual 12 West 31st Street, New York headquarters, but in the auditorium of the New York Edison Company. It was at this meeting that Taylor presented his presidential address on "The Art of Cutting Metals," which consisted, in the printed proceedings, of almost 250 pages of text and another 56 pages of discussion and another 15 pages of reply by Taylor. This is a summary of 26 years of work and experiments by Taylor and others. The experiments in metal cutting were undertaken to foster scientific management. The information was needed, according to Taylor:

> To give each workman each day in advance a definite task, with detailed written instructions, and an exact time allowance for each element of the work.
> To pay extraordinary high wages to those who perform their tasks in the allotted time, and ordinary wages to those who take more than their time allowance.[95]

Properly planned work would answer in advance the questions which a machinist running metal-cutting equipment normally asks, "What tool shall I use? What cutting speed shall I use? and What feed shall I use?" Rule-of-thumb methods meant that the machinist, based on personal experience would answer the question without scientifically based research and therefore often come up with the wrong answers. Therefore, unusual time might be spent grinding cutting tools, picking the wrong tool, running the machine too slowly or too fast. Such mistakes cost money and wasted time.

It is of interest that during this 26-year-study various laws of metal cutting were discovered. Taylor claimed:

> we have succeeded in keeping almost all of these laws secret, and in fact since 1889, this has been our means of obtaining the money needed to carry on the work. We never sold any information connected with this art for cash, but we have given to one company after another all of the data and conclusions arrived at through our experiments in consideration for the opportunity of still further continuing our work. In one shop after another machines have been fitted up for our use, workmen furnished us to run them, and especially prepared tools, forgings, and castings supplied in exchange for the data which we had obtained to date. . . . During this period of time all of the companies who were given this information, and all of the men who worked upon the experiments, were bound by promises to the writer not to give any of this information away nor to allow it to be published. Most of the promises were verbal. . . . it is a notable fact that through a period of 26 years it has not come to our knowledge that any one of the many men or companies connected with this work has broken a promise.[96]

Taylor decided to publish, because, in his words,

> It seems to us that the time has now come for the engineering fraternity to have the results of our work, in spite of the fact that this will cut off our former means of financing the experiments.[97]

Professor E. G. Thomsen of the University of California, reflecting on these experiments, concludes that:

> . . . the principal objective of his experiments was to determine the shortest time possible for finishing the work and to determine the effect of size of cut, rigidity of work and of machine tool, and driving power of the machine tool, in the performance of a roughing cut. He hoped for and succeeded in determining what needed to be done to existing machine tools in order to bring them up to proper conditions for taking satisfactory cuts. Taylor, along with Barth and Gantt, also developed a "slide

rule" for each machine in order to help the machinist or the planning department in making a decision on the selection of the best cutting conditions.[98]

The slide rule is important to the Taylor philosophy because it takes rules of thumb and replaces them with scientifically determined methods, and therefore takes the control out of the hands of the worker and puts it in the hands of management, the planning department.[99] Taylor wrote:

> The slide rules cannot be left at the lathe to be banged about by the machinist. They must be used by a man with reasonably clean hands, and at a table or desk, and this man must write his instructions as to speed, feed, depth of cut, etc., and send them to the machinist well in advance of the time that the work is to be done. Even if these written instructions are sent to the machinist, however, little attention will be paid to them unless rigid standards have been not only adopted, but ENFORCED, throughout the shop for every detail, large and small, of the shop equipment, as well as for all shop methods. And, further, but little can be accomplished with these laws unless the old-style foreman and shop superintendent have been done away with and functional foremanship has been substituted.[100]

Taylor, Gantt, and Barth determined that 12 variables entered into determining the most economical way of cutting metal. The list Taylor uses in his paper is similar to the one used by Barth in his 1903 paper on "Slide Rules":

The quality of the metal which is to be cut.

The diameter of the work.

The depth of the cut.

The thickness of the shaving.

The elasticity of the work and of the tool.

The shape or contour of the cutting edge of the tool, together with its clearance and lip angles.

The chemical composition of the steel from which the tool is made, and the heat treatment of the tool.

Whether a copious stream of water, or other cooling medium, is used on the tool.

The duration of the cut; i.e., the time which a tool must last under pressure of the shaving without being reground.
The pressure of the chip or shaving upon the tool.
The change of speed and feed possible in the lathe.
The pulling and feeding of the lathe.[101]

Barth's list is slightly different and includes "the number of tools to be used at the same time," "the cutting pressure on the tool," and lastly "the stiffness of the work." Barth says:

> All of these variables, except the last one, are incorporated in the slide rule, which, when the work is stiff enough to permit of any cut being taken that is within both the pulling power of the lathe and strength of the tool, may be manipulated by a person who has not the slightest practical judgment to bear on the matter.[102]

Barth says that by using a slide rule for three weeks on two lathes:

> the output of these was increased to such an extent that they quite unexpectedly ran out of work on two different occasions.[103]

Taylor's art of cutting metals so transformed the trade that Henry Towne claimed Taylor had "made a greater advance than during the previous ages since the days of Tubal Cain."[104]

NOTES

1. House Hearings, 1912, p. 1699.
2. Taylor, 1903, p. 1408.
3. Day, n.d., p. 1.
4. Day, n.d., p. 1.
5. Day, 1903, p.1304.
6. Day, 1903, p. 1314.
7. Day, 1903, p. 1315.
8. Simon, 1960, p. 4.
9. Drury, 1916, p. 4.
10. Hearings, 1912, p. 1547.
11. Tabor Notes, March 9, 1911, Howard C. Meyers Jr., papers.

12. Drury, 1918, p. 160.
13. Gilson, 1940, p. 211.
14. Feiss, 1916, B. p. 29.
15. Augustine, 1924, p. 4.
16. Gilson, 1940, p. 81.
17. Feiss, 1918.
18. Feiss to Taylor, March 21, 1914.
19. Feiss to Taylor, March 13, 1914.
20. Drury, 1918, p. 160.
21. Feiss, 1916, A, p. 14.
22. Feiss, 1919, p. 5.
23. Feiss, 1919.
24. Feiss, 1919.
25. Feiss, 1916, C, p. 4.
26. Feiss, 1916, B, p. 36.
27. Welfare Work, 1919, p. 8.
28. Feiss, 1916, B, pp. 34–35.
29. Feiss, 1916, B, p. 54.
30. Feiss, 1916, B, p. 36.
31. Gilson, 1918, p. 83.
32. Gilson, 1917, p. 141.
33. Feiss, 1916, A, p. 23.
34. Gilson, 1916, p. 278.
35. Gilson, 1917, pp. 145–46.
36. Gilson, 1917, p. 150.
37. Feiss, 1916, B, p. 54.
38. A paper on open-hearth furnaces in 1886; "Notes on Belting," in 1893; and "A Piece Rate System," in 1895.
39. Thompson to Taylor, November 25, 1901.
40. Taylor to Thompson, January 6, 1902.
41. Taylor to Thompson, January 23, 1902.
42. Thompson to Taylor, August 29, 1902.
43. Taylor to Thompson, October 29, 1902.
44. Nelson, 1980, p. 116.
45. Nelson, 1980, p. 116.
46. Nelson, 1980, p. 116.
47. Thompson to Taylor, February 9, 1903.
48. Thompson to Taylor, February 26, 1903.
49. Thompson to Taylor, April 7, 1903.
50. Thompson to Taylor, July 22, 1902.
51. Taylor, 1903, p. 1456.

52. Taylor, 1903, p. 1463.
53. Gilbreth, 1925, p. 34.
54. Cooke, Record.
55. Taylor, March 12, 1895.
56. Cooke to Barth, October 23, 1933.
57. Cooke to Taylor, June 23, 1907.
58. Cooke to Taylor, June 23, 1907.
59. Cooke to Taylor, October 7, 1907.
60. Cooke to Taylor, October 7, 1907.
61. Cooke to Taylor, November 11, 1907.
62. Taylor to Cooke, November 15, 1907.
63. Cooke to Taylor, March 26, 1908.
64. Cooke to Taylor, August 9, 1908.
65. Cooke to Taylor, March 1, 1909.
66. Cooke to Taylor, September 1, 1909.
67. Cooke to Taylor, September 13, 1909.
68. Cooke to Taylor, October–November, 1909.
69. Cooke to Taylor, October–November, 1909.
70. Cooke to Taylor, October–November, 1909.
71. Cooke to Taylor, October–November, 1909.
72. Cooke to Taylor, October–November, 1909.
73. Cooke to Taylor, October–November, 1909.
74. Taylor to Cooke, January 7, 1910.
75. Taylor to Cooke, January 7, 1910.
76. Taylor "Notes," February 8, 1910.
77. Taylor, "Miscellaneous" notes, dated January 14, 1910.
78. Taylor to Cooke, December 10, 1910.
79. Cooke to Taylor, February 25, 1911.
80. Cooke, "Industrial Management," unpublished manuscript.
81. Hathaway to Cooke, January 21, 1914.
82. Cooke to Barth, October 23, 1933.
83. Taylor, *Principles*, 1911, and Special Edition, 1911.
84. Taylor, 1911, pp. 36–37.
85. Taylor, *Principles*, 1911, p. 9.
86. House Resolution, 1912, p. 1387.
87. House Resolution, 1912, pp. 1388–89.
88. Industrial Relations Commission, 1914, p. 773.
89. Copley, 1916, p. 7.
90. Taylor, *Principles*, 1911, pp. 36–37.
91. House Resolution, 1912, p. 1456.
92. Taylor, 1903, p. 1385.

93. Nelson, 1980, p. 73.
94. Taylor, *Principles*, 1911, p. 96.
95. Taylor, 1907, p. 31.
96. Taylor, 1907, p. 36.
97. Taylor, 1907, p. 36.
98. Thomsen, 1982, p. 3.
99. Taylor, 1907, pp. 39–40.
100. Taylor, 1907, pp. 53–54.
101. Taylor, 1907, p. 32.
102. Barth, 1903, p. 50.
103. Barth, 1903, p. 61.
104. Quoted in Copley, 1916, p. 10.

PART V

THE LATER YEARS

ASME PRESIDENCY

The American Society of Mechanical Engineers was the organization that spawned the American scientific management movement, and all of the American management pioneers were members of this society. It was Henry Towne's May 26, 1886, paper, "The Engineer as an Economist" that pleaded for the study of "executive duties of organizing and superintending the operations of the industrial establishments, and of directing the labor of the artisans whose organized efforts yield the fruition of his work."[1] Towne, who was president of Yale & Towne and had been employed by William Sellers & Co. in 1867–68, went on to say that:

> The management of works has known a matter of such great and far-reaching importance as perhaps to justify its classification also as one of the modern acts. (But) is almost without literature, has no organ or medium for the interchange of experience, and is without association or organization of any kind.[2]

Towne's paper was followed by two other papers on management topics, Oberlin Smith's "Inventory Valuation of Machinery Plant" and Henry Metcalfe's "The Shop-Order System of Accounts." Taylor was in the audience for these papers and, although the Towne paper is more famous today, it was the Metcalfe paper on which Taylor's comments in the discussion were published:

> We at the Midvale Steel Co. have the experience during the past 10 years, of organizing a system very similar to that of Mr. Metcalfe. The chief idea in our system, as in his, is, that the authority for doing all kinds of work should proceed from one central office to the various departments, and that the proper records should be kept of the work and reports made daily to the central office, so that the superintending department should be kept thoroughly informed so as to what is taking place throughout the works, and at the same time no work could be done in the works without proper authority.[3]

Later in the discussion Taylor again claimed that the Midvale system had been in place for about 10 years.[4] This means that Midvale was using a central planning department concept as early as 1876, about two years before Taylor joined the firm, and was therefore most likely developed under Charles Brinley.

Picking up the gauntlet issued by Towne for the study of management were other ASME members. Beyond Taylor were Gantt, Barth, Cooke, Gilbreth, Emerson, Dodge, Church, etc. Although somewhat of a maverick, the management group in the first few years grew in stature and importance in the ASME.

The ASME, founded in 1880, itself was a very prestigious organization, but its administration was in need of some overhaul by the turn of the century. Taylor had been elected vice president in 1904, and in 1905 Henry Towne's nominating committee selected him for president. He held office for the 1906 year. It was during his term as president of the ASME that the University of Pennsylvania conferred upon him the degree of Sc.D., and in 1912 he also received an honorary LL.D. from Hobart College.[5]

Taylor, as president, immediately began his overhaul of the organization by building up the various committees with hardworking members and by developing a more efficient office routine. Taylor actually was wresting the power away from

Frederick Hutton, secretary since the founding of the organization who was effectively the manager of the society. Bruce Sinclair, ASME's excellent historian, believes that "applying the principles of scientific management to the society that prided itself for having spawned the new science was probably the most famous of Taylor's reforms. . . . "[6] In his efforts to simplify and standardize the ASME office, Taylor personally hired and paid the salary of Morris Cooke to study the operations. Cooke overhauled the society's printing and publications practices and claimed a 32 percent savings in cost.[7] Secretary Hutton resigned his post (later he would serve as president) and was replaced by Calvin Rice of the General Electric Company, who was instrumental in persuading Andrew Carnegie to donate the money to erect the new Engineering Society building, which opened in 1906. Rice was paid a $6,000 salary as ASME secretary in that year.

Most of the society's income was spent on its publications. And it was here that Cooke, whose experience was in the printing industry, made his great successes. Taylor's presidential address, "The Art of Cutting Metal," was published in a two-volume issue of *Transactions* of 1906 (published in 1907).

Taylor assigned Carl Barth to devise accounting procedures that would give ASME greater control over its financial affairs. The reforms under Taylor appeared to be well-directed. The society's annual meeting drew a large attendance; the organization was no longer under the control of one person, but run through a functional structure with each function under the leadership of a good manager. Yet, Taylor was not completely successful in overhauling the society. The accounting procedures required extra bookkeepers, and Barth's special forms cost money. The elaborate new office system required almost twice the office staff of the old. The cost of printing Taylor's presidential address "ate up all the savings Cooke had achieved in the publication department!" notes Sinclair.[8]

Although Taylor's reform movement did make the society more efficient, it added a permanent staff that grew into a bureaucracy of sizable proportions in later years. Many members opposed Taylor as an individual. (Taylor did pack the important committees with "his people" and therefore could manipulate nominations and changes.) Eventually, Jesse Smith was elected president (1910–11); he was an outspoken opponent of Taylor and of some of the reforms. Others, teaming with Smith, refused to publish, in 1910, *Principles of Scientific Management.*

At the annual meeting in 1912 the society issued a report on "The Present State of the Art of Industrial Management," which did show Taylor's work as being very important and his "Shop Management" paper as the "first complete presentation of the subject" of management.[9] But the report, in an obvious attempt to belittle Taylor, spent much space on the historical development of the field, mentioning Charles Babbage and the Frenchman Coulomb as being interested in time study long before Taylor.

In answer to this time-study claim, Taylor replied that the report was far:

> from the truth . . . Time Study was begun in the machine shop of the Midvale Steel Company in 1881, and was used during the next two years sufficiently to prove its success. In 1883, Mr. Emlen Hare Miller was employed to devote his whole time to "time study," and he . . . was the first man to make "time study" his profession.[10]

ORGANIZED LABOR

The impetus behind the House of Representatives investigation of "the Taylor and Other Systems of Stopwatch Management" was a strike in 1911, at the Watertown Arsenal when scientific management was being introduced by a Taylor protégé and Barth's time-study assistant, Dwight Merrick. Although Iowa's Representative Irwin Pepper had introduced a bill asking for an investigation of the Taylor System of Shop Management in April 1911, little happened until August when the molders at the arsenal struck in refusal to their being time-studied. As a result, it has been the position of many people that Taylor was against unions. This may or may not be the case. It appears the issue was quite complex. In his 1895 paper "A Piece Rate System," Taylor defended unions as having "rendered a great service not only to their members, but to the world, in shortening the hours of labor and in modifying the hardships and improving the conditions of wage-workers."[11]

It was management's attitude toward workers which forced unionization, according to Taylor. He wrote:

> When employers herd their men together in classes, pay all of each class the same wages, and offer none of them any inducements to work harder or do better work than the average, the only remedy for the men lies in combinations; and frequently the only possible answer to encroachments on the part of their employers is a strike.[12]

Taylor's position on unions, as clearly understood by Copley, was "as a superfluous and irritating interference with the process of *sound* industrial management. . . . "[13]

In a letter to his follower C. Bertrand Thompson, Taylor wrote:

> It is truly a difficult matter to introduce scientific management into any establishment, even where a union does not exist and that the difficulties are increased many fold when a union does exist. . . . As you know, I am heartily in favor of unions where a hog employer or an employer careless of his workmen's rights is up against the old fashioned type of organization, but that my contention has been and still remains, that the union is absolutely unnecessary and only a hindrance to the quick and successful organization of any manufacturing establishment; and I am sure that an establishment running under the principles of scientific management will confer far greater blessings upon the working people than can be brought through any form of collective bargaining.[14]

For all his public statements claiming non-opposition to unions other than for possible hindrance to his system, Taylor was unhappy when Link Belt allowed the introduction of a union to the company.[15] He also suggested to David Van Alstyne, Vice President of the American Locomotive Company, whose foundry was unionized, that Van Alstyne establish an independent foundry to compete with the company foundry. The new foundry should use the Taylor system and underbid the union foundry, which would allow the American Locomotive Company to slowly close down its union shop, eventually shutting down the foundry in favor of the new nonunionized foundry—which would be secretly owned by American Locomotive.[16] It is unknown if Van Alstyne heeded the advice, but the plot illustrates Taylor's bias.

Taylor was technically correct when he testified before Congress that:

> during the 30 years that scientific management has been gradually developed . . . there has never been a single strike of employees working under scientific management—never one in all the 30 years in which it has been used.[17]

Although there were no strikes at Midvale, Simonds, or Bethlehem while Taylor was there, Nadworny claims that "union men did leave every plant where Taylor was employed,"[18] and at American Locomotive, where Harrington Emerson was assisting Van Alstyne in implementing a "Standard Time Card Dispatching and Time Study System," a strike was called in the Pittsburgh plant in October of 1908, and in December the Schenectady and Richmond plants also struck. The strike ended with the removal of both the "Standard Time" system and Van Alstyne.[19] Frank Gilbreth, normally very successful in dealing with unions as he usually sought their cooperation before initiating key work, suffered a strike in 1911, when he placed a scientific management system with Union Paper and Bag Company. In these cases, Taylor was able to blame Van Alstyne, and particularly Emerson, for mistakes at American Locomotive. Gilbreth probably had drifted from the Taylor system, hence it was not the system, but the Gilbreth approach—at least in Taylor's mind—which could be blamed.

Actually Gilbreth may have been the victim of the American Federation of Labor's (AFL) campaign against scientific management. For early in 1911, the AFL Executive Council adopted a resolution denouncing the system. Samuel Gompers,

AFL president, spoke of driving the workers beyond what was healthy, of making workers mere appendages to machines and that "science would thus get the most out of you before you are sent to the junk pile."[20]

Of course, Taylor would make no such public claim. His 1912 House testimony, quoted above, was echoed in his letter to C. Bertrand Thompson and in his public testimony to Congress' Commission on Industrial Relations in April of 1914. He tried to placate unionists in his response to Commissioner O'Connell's question about efficiency systems putting unions out of existence by claiming:

> No, I never look for unions to go out. I am heartily in favor of combinations of men. I do not look for a great modification in the principles of unions as they now exist; they are of necessity largely now fighting organizations; . . . I look for great modifications, but never for the abolition of them. I simply look for a change, that the union shall conform itself to this new idea, the idea of a standard that is over all of us, and a set of laws that will be over all sides.[21]

It is unclear whether Taylor looked for "great modifications" or did "not look for great modification"—both were included in the above quotation.

Taylor was never able to satisfy labor with such statements. Although the hearings on "The Taylor System and Other Stop Watch Management Systems" did not support the need for legislation, labor continued its attack. Various riders to appropriation bills restricted the use of the Taylor system, or at least time study and premium-bonus payment systems, in most U.S. government agencies. The time study and premium-bonus payment restrictions were finally removed in August 1949 through the efforts of Senators Taft and Flanders.[22]

It took many years for labor to drop its vendetta against scientific management. In time, Samuel Gompers actually addressed the Taylor Society,[23] and William Green, Gompers' successor, addressed the society three times, first in 1925, and again in 1927 and 1929.[24] And ultimately Morris Cooke would co-author a book in 1940, with the chairman of the CIO, Philip

Murray, entitled, *Organized Labor and Production*. They claimed, and we think history has proved them to be inaccurate, "Taylor defined scientific management as development in the direction of truly scientific method . . . and the intimate friendly cooperation between the management and the men. This latter has logically developed—largely since Taylor's time—into the union-management cooperative movement."[25] When this claim was made, the country was in the midst of the 20-year great unionization movement beginning in the 1930s and only interrupted by World War II before the movement abated in the 1950s.

THE GILBRETHS

Taylor had a number of strong followers who helped spread "the word." Barth, Cooke, and Hathaway were true disciples. Gantt was early on a member of this close-knit group, but later was to have a falling out and became independent. Emerson was never inside the Taylor group, but gained fame in helping to popularize the system. The outsiders who are most frequently mentioned when scientific management is discussed are Frank and Lillian Gilbreth. Frank, 11 years Taylor's junior, and Lillian 10 years younger than that, are luminaries in scientific management, whose impact in developing scientific management was considerable. Frank, the motion study developer, and Lillian, who earned a doctorate in psychology (Brown University), were strong supporters of the Taylor system, at least in the beginning.

Before meeting Taylor or even before reading "Shop Management," Frank Gilbreth had developed motion study and its closely related fatigue study. His most famous work was in bricklaying analysis, where he was able to reduce the number of motions to lay a brick from about 18 to 6 and increase output from approximately 1,000 to 2,700 bricks laid per day, and with less effort (less fatigue). The Gilbreths were also the originators of ergonomics and numerous other management tools, which

Frederick W. Taylor about age 17 (probably Exeter days). *(Photo courtesy of Stevens Institute of Technology, Taylor collection, Hoboken, N.J.)*

Frederick W. Taylor from Midvale Days, circa 1886. *(Photo courtesy of Stevens Institute of Technology, Taylor collection, Hoboken, N.J.)*

Taylor wearing derby. *(Photo taken by Frank B. Gilbreth.)*

Taylor wearing glasses. *(Photo courtesy of Stevens Institute of Technology, Taylor collection, Hoboken, N.J.)*

Frederick W. Taylor family picture. From left to right: Louise M. Taylor, Elizabeth
P. A. Taylor, Kempton P. A. Taylor, Frederick W. Taylor, Robert P. A. Taylor. *(Photo
courtesy of Stevens Institute of Technology, Taylor collection, Hoboken, N.J.)*

Mrs. Taylor hosting the Japanese-
American factory inspection tour in
1930. *(Photo courtesy of Tekeuori Saito.)*

Boxly. *(Photo courtesy of Stevens
Institute of Technology, Taylor collection,
Hoboken, N.J.)*

William Sellers, September 19, 1824–
January 24, 1905. *(Photo courtesy of
Stevens Institute of Technology, Taylor
Collection, Hoboken, N.J.*

James A. Wright, September 3,
1815–June 7, 1894. Taylor's uncle and
Midvale Steel Company investor. *(Photo
courtesy of the Myers, Smyth, Keely
Library.)*

Philip S. Justice, June 20, 1819–July 1,
1901. *(Photo courtesy of the Myers,
Smyth, Keely Library.)*

Charles J. Harrah, January 1, 1815–
February 18, 1890.

Henry L. Gantt, May 18, 1861–
November 23, 1919. *(Photo courtesy of
Peter B. Peterson, The Johns Hopkins
University.)*

Carl G. L. Barth, February 28, 1860–
October 28, 1939.

Morris Llewellyn Cooke, May 11,
1872–March 5, 1960.

Sanford Eleazer Thompson, February
13, 1867–February 25, 1949.

Russell Wheeler Davenport, November 26, 1849–March 2, 1905.

Charles A. Brinley, August 23, 1847–March 2, 1919.

Midvale Steel Company executives, circa Fall 1887. In the middle of second row from back, on the left, possibly Frederick W. Taylor (with cap) and Henry L. Gantt (with derby).

Taylor's Machine Shop No. 1. *(Photo courtesy of Mrs. William L. Hearne, private collection.)*

Locomotive hauling from Taylor's Machine Shop No. 1. *(Photo courtesy of Mrs. William L. Hearne, private collection.)*

General views of Midvale Steel Company, circa 1887. Top: looking west toward Germantown; bottom: looking east. *(Photo courtesy of Mrs. William L. Hearne, private collection.)*

Machine shop designed by Taylor in 1883 (photo circa 1884). *(Photo courtesy of Mrs. William L. Hearne, private collection.)*

Midvale Steel Company main office building, circa 1887. *(Photo courtesy of Mrs. William L. Hearne, private collection.)*

Inside Midvale Steel Company machine shop showing a water hose going to lathe to cool cutting tool as claimed by Taylor, circa 1887. *(Photo courtesy of Mrs. William L. Hearne, private collection.)*

Frederick W. Taylor's famous "steam hammer" (Hammer No. 10). The man under the hammer may be Taylor, circa 1888. *(Photo courtesy of Mrs. William L. Hearne, private collection.)*

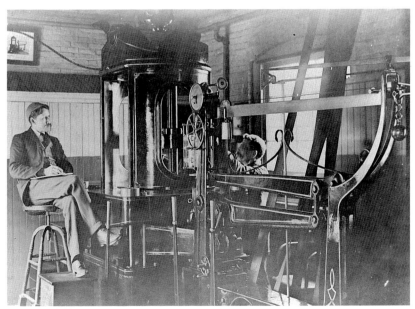

Testing engineer at work at Midvale Steel Company, circa 1885. Taylor may be in this photograph. *(Photo courtesy of Mrs. William L. Hearne, private collection.)*

Clarence Munroe Clark, August 17, 1895–June 29, 1937. Taylor's brother-in-law and best friend. *(Photo from National Cyclopaedia of American Biography, Vol. 34, p. 503.)*

Henry Knolle, May 9, 1871–February 25, 1925. The man known as "Schmidt" in Taylor's Pig Iron Story, 1899.

Mansel White, March 15, 1856–October 22, 1912. *(Photo courtesy of Arthur Bedeian and John T. White.)*

William D. Basley, February 26, 1845–February 17, 1918, accountant who greatly influenced the Taylor system.

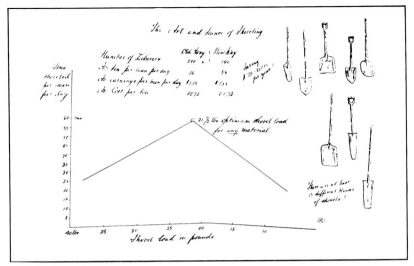

The art and science of shoveling chart drawn by Taylor indicating the optimum shovel load at 21.5 lbs. *(Photo courtesy of Stevens Institute of Technology, Taylor collection, Hoboken, N.J.)*

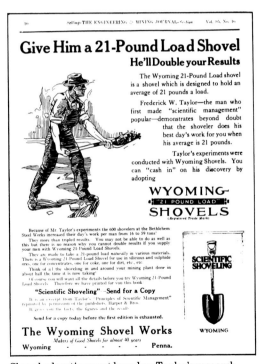

Shovel advertisement based on Taylor's research (from the *Engineering & Mining Journal*, Vol. 95, No. 16.). *(Photo courtesy of Stevens Institute of Technology, Taylor collection, Hoboken, N.J.)*

Engineers' building cornerstone laying ceremony, May 6, 1906. People in photo include: Margaret Carnegie, flower girl; Frederick W. Taylor (left of flower girl), Andrew Carnegie (back of flower girl), James Mapes Dodge (between Taylor and Carnegie). *(Photo courtesy of IEEE Center for the History of Electrical Engineering.)*

The men who influenced Taylor (1903): James Mapes Dodge (seated, far left), Henry R. Towne (seated, fourth from left—with hat), and Oberlin Smith (seated, fifth from left). *(Photo courtesy of the IEEE Center for the History of Electrical Engineering.)*

Frank (July 7, 1868–June 14, 1924) and Lillian (May 24, 1878–January 1, 1972) Gilbreth. *(Photo courtesy of National Museum of History and Technology, Smithsonian Institution.)*

Harlow S. Person, February 16, 1875–November 7, 1955, oversaw Taylor biography.

Yoichi Ueno, October 28, 1883–October 15, 1957 and Harrington Emerson, August 2, 1853–September 2, 1931, circa 1928–1930. Ueno translated Taylor's work in Japan and was Japan's pioneer scientific manager theorist. *(Photo courtesy of William Muhs.)*

Mr. Taylor discusses the principles of scientific management (*The World*, May 14, 1911).

Taylor as "Miss Lillian Gray." *(Photo courtesy of Stevens Institute of Technology, Taylor collection, Hoboken, N.J.)*

Manufacturing Investment Company, Madison, Maine.

Barth-Gulowsen Belt Bench. *(Photo courtesy of Stevens Institute of Technology, Taylor collection, Hoboken, N.J.)*

Morris L. Cooke with Charles D. Wrege, 1960. *(Photo courtesy of Bea Wrege.)*

they introduced not only to businesses, but to hospitals and educational institutions.

The first meeting of Frank Gilbreth and Frederick Taylor, arranged by Conrad Lauer, took place in December of 1907, in the lobby of the Engineering Societies Building in New York City. Gilbreth had read "Shop Management" and called it "a work of genius."[26] Taylor was aware of Gilbreth's work, having described it, although not by name, in his book *Concrete Plain and Reinforced* of 1906.[27] Sanford Thompson had been watching Gilbreth's operations since at least 1896.[28]

After the initial Taylor-Gilbreth meeting, Taylor wrote to Thompson:

> I had two or three hours talk with our friend Mr. Gilbreth, the contractor. . . . He is very much interested in our work, particularly the study of unit costs, and I think is prepared to adopt piecework, if possible, in his business. I am to have another talk with him later this month.
>
> I got what appears to me to be one very valuable piece of information out of him. I made the statement that owing to the lack of cohesion between cement and cement, and between cement and other materials, that it was impracticable to successfully plaster the outside of the concrete structure with a mixture of cement, or cement and sand. He stated that I was entirely mistaken in this, and that he had put up miles of plaster on the outside of cement buildings, which was thoroughly successful. . . .
>
> This seems to me a very valuable piece of information for us to get. I did not ask him whether we could use it in our book (on bricklaying). I have no doubt that if you set about doing so you can get next to him in some of his reinforced concrete buildings, and study form construction. . . .
>
> Perhaps you had better not tackle Gilbreth until after I see him the next time which will be about the 19th of this month (December 19, 1907).[29]

Beyond his awareness of Gilbreth's work, Taylor's view of Gilbreth also was influenced greatly by Sanford Thompson's opinion. On December 13, 1907, less than two weeks after Taylor's initial meeting with Gilbreth, Thompson sent Taylor the following letter:

when you see Gilbreth I wish you would find out the location of some of his "miles of plaster" on concrete buildings which have stood the weather for at least a year or two, as I would like to see some of them. . . . Gilbreth is one of the brightest men I know in the line of construction work, and understands details the most thoroughly. He is a great bluffer, and has the reputation of not being always "on the square." He once told me just before we got our book on "concrete" out that when it was published I would probably receive suggestions from manufacturers of mixing machines for making a test of their machines, and if I did, and if in a competitive test his (Gilbreth's) mixer came out ahead, he would give me $1,000. Before this time I had had a number of talks with Gilbreth, in fact, two or three times he dropped all his work and gave me an hour or two, criticizing some of our brick cost data and indeed he went over the manuscript on bricklaying and made a number of very pertinent corrections, at the same time complimenting it very highly. He did not, however, compliment our tables on the cost of bricklaying, saying that the method of estimating was wrong, and that it would be wrong to publish them. Whether this was his real opinion or whether he did not wish such costs to get out, I do not know. He gave me a general idea of the method he employed in estimating brickwork, but would not at that time go into details of it or tell me why he thought the tables were wrong or how they could be improved.

I ran across Gilbreth first when taking notes on bricklaying on one of the first buildings for which he was contractor, and I took a good many observations on other buildings of his with his permission. I know that he tried stopwatch methods, following out our principles on a concrete chimney without success, and I am of the opinion that this failure to get results is one reason why he did not approve of the brick tables.

I consider Gilbreth one of the most accurate estimators, but believe that when it comes to actual work on the cost-plus-fixed-sum method he plans to make a low estimate and then if the work costs more get out of it by some explanation. He built the Yale & Towne Co. concrete buildings, you remember, and on my visit there I found that he was employing about one-third more men than were necessary to do the job. This was probably done to hustle the thing along, but it was an expensive way of doing it. I have been told by an engineer who was one of the referees on a Gilbreth suit that he has a way of doctoring his accounts through one man in his employ, and makes things appear to cost sometimes double their actual cost. The statement, however, I cannot guarantee, as the apparent discrepancy may have been due to the fact that he put on too many men for the job.

With reference to form construction I have no doubt that Gilbreth has good methods, and that we could get a good many points from them. I think also he would have no objection to our studying some of the times on them, and that it will be an excellent plan if you can get permission for us to do so as soon as work opens up in the spring. We can readily eliminate his lost time due to a surplus of men.[30]

Taylor met Gilbreth a second time that December in Gilbreth's office in New York, Gilbreth explaining his eliminating of needless motion in bricklaying and showing him how the "movable scaffold" worked. Taylor suggested that Gilbreth, Sanford Thompson, and he should collaborate on a book on bricklaying.

In writing to Sanford Thompson in January of 1908, Taylor said he:

should be entirely willing to withdraw and let Gilbreth and you write the book, providing you could couple all of Gilbreth's knowledge in bricklaying with your study of time elements. This would result in the most valuable work on bricklaying that has ever been published, and would greatly enhance your personal reputation, and I should be entirely ready to withdraw my interest for the sake of accomplishing this result. However, Gilbreth entirely refused to have anyone's name associated with him in the writing of his book. He intimated that after his book was written then he might be willing to write another book with you. This, however, is not what I had in mind, and I do not think the game in that case would be worth the candle. If, however, Gilbreth could be persuaded to go in with you and pool issues on the whole thing, then I think it would be an admirable plan.

I have no doubt that by sticking to Gilbreth and being very generous in giving him our data, you will get anything that you want from him, and further, I have no doubt that he will be entirely ready to agree not to publish any of the data which we give him, or let it get out in any way. I should not feel particularly afraid of this.[31]

Gilbreth did not accept this invitation, but did accept an invitation to visit Taylor at "Boxly." The first of many meetings took place in January of 1908.[32]

Frank Gilbreth, Jr., reports that:

Gilbreth and Taylor became great friends—or so Frank thought—but Taylor was so shy and introverted that no one ever got very close to him. By then (1907), Taylor was espousing his system almost as if it were a holy course.[33]

In April of 1908, Gilbreth installed selected parts of the Taylor system (time study with an incentive wage and a modified planning department) on a factory building construction project in Gardner, Massachusetts, a mere 10 miles from Fitchburg where Simonds Rolling Machine Company was located. Sanford Thompson made the time study and King Hathaway organized the modified planning department. The union bricklayers struck in opposition to the incentive wage and Gilbreth quickly withdrew the incentive program. In November, Gilbreth, after convincing local union leaders of the benefits of his program, introduced an incentive system on another factory construction job in Chelsea, a Boston suburb. The incentive pay was $6.50 per day if they used Gilbreth methods and accomplished expected results, and only $4.50 per day if unsuccessful.[34] On this Chelsea project, Sanford Thompson again assisted. It appears that Gilbreth asked for a free supply of Hathaway's record-keeping blanks.[35] Ultimately the Taylor group began to fear and distrust Gilbreth, believing he was out to make a reputation for himself.[36]

In *Principles of Scientific Management*, Taylor wrote "For nearly thirty years past, time-study men connected with management of machine-shop have been devoting their whole time to a scientific motion study, followed by accurate time study . . . ."[37] Taylor devoted eight pages in *Principles of Scientific Management* to Frank Gilbreth's bricklaying management, or "scientific motion study, as Mr. Gilbreth calls his analysis, time study, as the writer (Taylor) has called similar work," and he called Sanford Thompson "the most experienced man in motion and time study in this country."[38] Whether or not this reference to motion study was considered a slap in the face to the Gilbreths is not known, but Frank Gilbreth, Jr., writing more than a half century later, believed these statements were intended to belittle his parents and misplace credit toward Taylor. Taylor's dating of motion study would put it to a time when Frank was 13 and Lillian three. As to Sanford Thompson as the motion study expert, Thompson is quoted by Gilbreth, Jr., as saying, "as to motion study per se, in my opinion it was original with Mr. Gilbreth."[39]

Gilbreth, himself, not only considered he was the developer of motion study, but was sure Taylor did not understand the true significance of this tool. In a long letter dated December 13, 1920, to his German representative Irene Witte, which his daughter Ernestine G. Cary has so generously shared with us, Gilbreth asserted, "So far as we are concerned we learned stopwatch method of time study from Taylor but it did not satisfy us, and consequently we had to learn from our own experience." Gilbreth continues:

> we claim that no time study can be scientific or of any permanent value unless the motions used and the method by which the work is done are recorded, and they cannot be recorded by any method that Taylor has ever used. . . . Taylor . . . did not understand motion study. In most of our cases the micro-motion process is completely separated from time study, and the time of the motions are the byproduct of the motion process of finding the easiest and newest therbligs (motions).

Continuing, Gilbreth adds, in discussing Taylor's *Principles of Scientific Management*, "Perhaps we should infer that he (Taylor) did not wish to recognize any difference between motion study and time study because it makes all different existing time study obsolete." Later in the letter he adds, "It must also be borne in mind that motion study was an entirely new idea to Mr. Taylor when it was presented to him in December 1907." Taylor did not mention motion study in his 1903

"Shop Management" paper and first writes of it in his 1911 *Principles of Scientific Management.* Frank Gilbreth's letter continues, "If a man does not decide 'How and with what it is done he cannot record the method in the least degree and therefore there will always be a question regarding the changing of the rate.' " In the Gilbreth system, he writes, "The first consideration is to find the best and easiest method and the time will be a byproduct of this investigation, as the time will be seen on the film" (Gilbreth used motion pictures to study work as early as 1911).[40]

Gilbreth continued to be a leading spokesman for Taylor's ideas through books, articles, speeches, and his summer school for college professors. In 1911, Taylor selected Gilbreth to represent him and the Taylor system at the New York Civic Forum and again in 1913, at the Western Economic Society.[41] In 1911, Taylor asked Gilbreth to write the response to all the letters which he received after the publication of "The Principles of Scientific Management," which was serialized in the *American Magazine* in March, April, and May of that year. Gilbreth's answers, instead of being issued individually, were published in book form, *Primer of Scientific Management*, in 1912.[42] By March of 1912, Gilbreth had informed Taylor of his development of micromotion study with motion pictures, which he later refined and termed "chronocyclegraph." This would, Gilbreth told Taylor, revolutionize time study. In 1912, Gilbreth left the construction field to become a management consultant full time. This of course would make Gilbreth a competitor to Taylor and his followers.

In June 1910, future Supreme Court Justice Louis D. Brandeis, a lawyer representing Eastern Railroad shippers known as the Trade Association of the Atlantic Seaboard, asked the Taylor group and those others who were close followers to assist in a rate hearing before the Interstate Commerce Commission with hopes of rolling back a railroad rate increase. It was Brandeis's contention that railroads were inefficient and that using the Taylor system could increase their profits without a shipping rate increase.[43] Assisting Brandeis in his preparation were James Dodge, H. King Hathaway, Henry Towne, Harrington Emerson, Henry Gantt, Morris Cooke, and Frank Gilbreth. In October and November, 1910, Gantt, Gilbreth, and Emerson testified and changed both the character of the hearings and also the reputation of the Taylor system. It was Gilbreth, Dodge, Kent, Gantt, and Brandeis who met in Gantt's New York City hotel room and decided to describe the Taylor system of efficiency changes as "scientific management." It was at these hearings, popularly called "The Eastern Rate Case," which Brandeis eventually won, that Emerson claimed with the use of scientific management, railroads could save one million dollars a day.[44] Such a claim caught the ear of the interested public and helped push scientific management and Taylor to center stage with the management community. The scientific management movement was also making waves in the popular press. Robert Kent remembers Frank Gilbreth saying:

> This thing is going to put scientific management on the map. There must be some organization to conserve the ground that will be won. There must be some outfit that will perpetuate Fred Taylor's work. Let us form a society to do it.[45]

Shortly thereafter, on November 9, 1910, Frank Gilbreth, Morris Cooke, Robert Kent, Wilfred Lewis, and Conrad Lauer met at the New York Athletic Club to lay the foundation for such a society. This as yet unnamed group, met once a month at Keen's Chop House in New York to discuss scientific management.[46] The group quickly grew to 30 to 40 per meeting. Luminaries such as Charles Day, Henry Towne, James Dodge, Carl Barth, and even Taylor himself, although rarely, met. To be admitted to the group, one had to qualify for membership to the ASME. In December 1911, the society was officially formed and Gilbreth wanted to call the group the "Taylor Society," but was outvoted and the name "Society to Promote the Science of Management" was chosen. The society included management consultants and businessmen who believed in Taylor's work. Gantt and Hathaway became members and Taylor was made an honorary member in 1914. The papers presented before the society originally were narrow in scope and devoted entirely to scientific management. After Taylor's death in 1915, it was changed to the "Taylor Society: A Society to Promote the Science of Management" and ultimately was folded into the American Management Association.

Gilbreth continued to experiment with various aspects of scientific management, but the *New York Times*, on March 29, 1911, reported that Gilbreth's system of paying bonuses to workers building a paper mill for the Union Bay and Paper Company had caused a strike.

At this mill, Gilbreth had paid carpenters a minimum wage of 38 cents (compared to a former rate of 35 cents an hour). Those workers whose measured output increased as they "adapted themselves to Mr. Gilbreth's methods are earning up to 50 cents per hour."[47] When Gilbreth attempted to have the bricklayers work under the same system which the carpenters did for a few weeks, the work of some of the men was not up to standard and they were paid only 50 cents an hour, compared to 75 cents an hour for the more efficient workers. These few less productive workers succeeded in passing a resolution and declaring a strike in the local union in Glen Falls "condemning Mr. Gilbreth's practice of paying bonuses and demanding that he no longer keep a tally of each man's output."[48]

The few bricklayers who struck against Gilbreth claimed that if he measured the output several incompetent members of their union would be dismissed. Other union men, however, were against the strike since under Gilbreth's system:

> . . . they were receiving the highest wages ever paid bricklayers in this section of the state, receiving bonuses of 10 and 29 percent per hour, according to the number of bricks laid.[49]

Gilbreth's first major consulting job after he left his construction business was with the New England Butt Company of Providence, Rhode Island. It began on May 13, 1912, and he was assisted by Hathaway and Hathaway aides Royal R. Keely and Albert R. Shipley. Gilbreth was eminently successful and completed the work in 13 months—not the two to five years the Taylor group expected.[50] Gilbreth thought he was greatly admired by Taylor for this success; Taylor saw the success as a threat.

In August of 1912, Hermann Aukam Company, a handkerchief manufacturer, hired Gilbreth to introduce scientific management. In March of 1914, Milton Hermann visited Taylor to complain that Gilbreth had overcharged, did poor work, and used inferior assistants to do the job. Taylor met with the Gilbreths in Providence and Frank claimed that he had, with the use of micromotion studies, reduced the number of motions required to fold handkerchiefs from 150 to 16 and that Gilbreth and Hermann violently disagreed over the pay for increased production. Frank contended that Hermann had hogged all of the profits due to his work.[51]

Taylor came away unconvinced that Gilbreth was in the right. He had Hathaway assume the work with Hermann Aukam. Hathaway was under the impression that Gilbreth had canceled his contract with the company. Gilbreth denied he had canceled the contract.[52] Once at Hermann Aukam, Hathaway reported that Gilbreth's work had brought about a confused state of affairs there and that Gilbreth was "either raving crazy or a . . . fakir."[53] Gilbreth was very bitter over the statements by Taylor and Hathaway, and because his contract was not due to expire until May 1917, he became a strong critic of Taylor and his associates.

K. H. Condit, writing in the *American Machinist* in 1923, noted that when:

> Gilbreth and Mr. Taylor first met and each discovered what the other was doing, they formed a mutual admiration society which lasted until Mr. Taylor's passion for recognition as the originator of most of the discoveries of scientific management started a controversy which lasted until his death.[54]

Daniel Nelson, who has written extensively on Taylor, and who has such perceptive insights on the man, writes:

> Taylor's break with Gilbreth, like his unhappiness with Gantt, his hostility toward Emerson, and his disapproval of other lesser figures, was as predictable as the "movement toward the door" that often followed the Boxly lectures. He had

been attracted to Gilbreth because of the latter's technical expertise, only to find that Gilbreth associated scientific management with innovative labor measures and personal advancement rather than with the highly disciplined, often hazardous "systematizing" process. Taylor's disillusionment turned to outright hostility when he became familiar with Gilbreth's flexible approach to many matters. Belatedly, Taylor realized that Gilbreth, for all his ability and enthusiasm, was no different from the other "fakirs."[55]

Taylor sought to discredit Gilbreth, even writing Professor Lionel S. Marks at Harvard not to "lay too great stress on the work that is being done by . . . Frank Gilbreth," because Gilbreth was solely interested in money, and is "likely to do great harm to our cause."[56]

Of course, with the death of Taylor in 1915, and World War I erupting in Europe, the controversy subsided. At least until the December 1920 meeting of the Taylor Society in New York, at which time Frank delivered a paper that Lillian co-authored titled, "An Indictment of Stop-Watch Time Study."[57] In this paper Taylor's much-honored time study is attacked as having:

> been proved absolutely worthless and also misleading so far as assisting in skill study is concerned. It is unethical because it does not clearly define the subject matter of an implied contract in which wage payment is based, and it is economically wasteful because it does not preserve the best that has been done.[58]

Namely using his micromotion study, Gilbreth was claiming the superiority of his micromotion to Taylor's time study. His remarks solidified this controversy which continued until Frank's death on June 14, 1924.

AT HOME

Very little of the person that was Frederick Taylor can be ascertained by reading the various biographies. Certainly he appears dogmatic, autocratic, and self-assured. There is very lit-

tle of the personality in the two-volume biography written by
Frank Copley, who was hired by Mrs. Taylor. In an earlier
piece on Taylor, published shortly after his death, Copley wrote
that Taylor "did not reveal himself to be the possessor of a
nature that ordinarily would be called lovable." He termed
him:

> domineering and imperious, he was not arrogant or arbitrary.
> He did not want you to bow down to him; he simply thought it
> behooves every man to make obeisance to superior knowledge,
> no matter in whom it might be lodged. . . . If he was egoistic, his
> was the egoism of a Richard Wagner—the egoism of a man who
> knows when he knows, and, of stout heart and inflexible will,
> has head ego enlarged and hardened by years of combat with
> little people who, from his advanced point of view, must appear
> as dunderheads and fools.[59]

The Taylor family heritage was Quaker, and that of Fred's
wife, Puritan. Although Fred Taylor was not deeply committed
to any particular religious dogma, his family were members of
the Unitarian Church.

During the early period of his life, Taylor was a very dedi-
cated, hardworking, driving individual. He did not drink, he
would not permit anything alcoholic to be served in his home,
he did not take such stimulants as tea or coffee, and he did
not use tobacco in any form. He did join the Germantown and
Young American Cricket Clubs, he sang as a tenor in the choral
society, played cricket, and was frequently found in amateur
theatricals. His biographer claims that he was good enough
that he could have earned a good living on the professional
stage.[60] But Copley said

> what this virile young man was most celebrated for was his
> female impersonations, those being made necessary by the fact
> that only members of the club, who were all young men, took
> part in the performances.[61]

One personality trait which was to distinguish him for the rest
of his life, which he picked up while serving his apprenticeship,
was a habit of swearing, which Taylor deliberately cultivated.
His biographer claims "that you often have to resort to violence

of language, if only to keep your men from doing things that impair their limbs and life."[62]

Copley first met Taylor in July 1912 and had but two long meetings. He later wrote that Taylor:

> himself regretted that the language of the mill had become with him so ingrained a habit that whenever he was excited out it was likely to speak . . . at the same time unmistakably appeared in him the gentleman and the scholar.[63]

His swearing was indeed unique. He did not swear when most men would, and he did swear when most men would not dream of it. As far as we have heard, he never swore on the golf course.[64] But he did swear when lecturing at Harvard, though, as was the case when he was in his own home, it was practically all done in telling stories and in quoting other men. The famous muckraker Miss Ida M. Tarbell once said, "Mr. Taylor never seems to be to me more of a gentleman than when he was swearing."[65]

As an indication of Taylor's fairness to humanity, his biographer points out that when a very young man in school:

> Before going to a dance he used to list, as systematically as he could, the attractive girls on the one hand and the wallflowers on the other hand, with the object of dividing his time equally between them.[66]

"He loved making fun." Robert Taylor, his adopted son, remembers one incident:

> My mother was great on antiques but he, father, only wanted antiques if they were useful . . . there was a difference. She was going into some things which he thought were a little foolish. She bought a pewter platter which was supposed to be very old and she had someone from the place come and hang it carefully in the dining room to show it off. She was proud of her new possession. Well, I guess we all have a lot of kid in us, so he spotted it and thought he would have some fun. He put some old golf shoes, good dirty ones, and hung them up so they were framed in the platter. When her guests came in for dinner, you can imagine the laughter. It was a laugh at her expense. He was really kidding her about

it—he had his jokes, no question about it . . . he played hard and he worked hard, it's true. He enjoyed life. Even eating was part of it. Of course, he was handicapped in eating from the spill in the lake, because he did have his problems from that. As for drinking, he just said that was out. He said that no man had any business fooling with the stuff. A lot of doctors may not disagree, but this was his standard.[67]

Frederick Taylor was not a large man, perhaps 5′8″ or 5′ 9″, but an athlete. He and his brother-in-law, Clarence M. Clark, who was the first secretary treasurer of the U.S. Lawn Tennis Association, were its first U.S. doubles champions at Newport in 1881. Fred played golf frequently each week, and in the winter was an accomplished ice skater. Fred even patented a scooped-handled tennis racquet and a two-handed putter. The Philadelphia Cricket Club's golf course was either right next to "Boxly" or actually partially on the Taylor estate. Frederick spent much time and money researching grass for putting greens. He was quite wealthy, leaving an estate of about a million dollars at the time of his death. Franklin, Fred's father, had left an estate of almost a million dollars at his death in 1910, but Frederick refused to accept any of it. Robert remembers that, "It went to Mary Taylor and Edward Winslow Taylor—his sister and brother. My father refused it. He didn't need it."[68]

Three maids kept the house in immmaculate order, and the estate superintendent, Robert Bender, with his wife, managed the estate grounds which included a tennis court. Another servant, most likely a cook, a coachman, and a laborer rounded out the staff for "Boxly." The house was run by the type of routine one would expect from the "Father of Scientific Management." The family income was about $60,000 a year—no taxes in those days. The maids were paid well, about $5 a week. There were three adopted children in the household. These children were distantly related through Mrs. Taylor's side of the family. William and Anna Aiken died in what appears to be a murder-suicide in 1901 and left four children. The oldest, Conrad Aiken, not adopted by the Taylors, eventually became a poet and literary critic of great renown. The three youngest children, Elizabeth, Kempton, and Robert, were adopted and quickly sent off to boarding school for their educations. Frederick Taylor's family ate well, but perhaps cautiously—due to his stomach problems, caused by falling into a very cold lake in an attempt to dock a canoe. The children were fed differently from the grownups. Robert remembers that:

> We got prunes, cereal and a glass of milk and bread if you wanted it. That was breakfast. For dinner it was reversed. You had cereal, a glass of milk and then you had prunes . . . . On Sunday we had roast beef and ice cream. Because of Frederick's stomach problems, his breakfast usually consisted of orange (sliced into six parts), two shredded wheat and milk and instead of sugar, it was some sort of glycerine he was required to use . . . (his supper) I think he ate more. He usually had some meat at night, usually with some potato and one green vegetable at least.
>
> You were supposed to talk at the table, you weren't supposed to play hi-jinks. You answered questions if you were asked, but you didn't volunteer too much because it was supposed to be high-level conversation. And it was. I mean the things of the day . . . he wanted to know how baseball practice was going. . . . But after dinner we'd always have a half-hour of reading.
>
> He read out loud, and when I was very small, I would sit on the chair with him. As I got bigger, I didn't. I sat across from him. Putmut . . . the famous cat . . . always on the Old Man's left shoulder. My mother didn't particularly care about that because he clawed the shoulder of his suit. The Old Man always wore the same colored blue serge suits. They were well made and good looking.
>
> He read for half an hour. . . . He read some Dickens and one of his great favorites was Hopalong Cassidy (the historical Wild West hero). . . . There were rules set down for that too. It was cheating to read ahead, even if he stopped at a very exciting place. Nobody was allowed to read ahead. That was a "no-no." Also, once begun, a book must be finished. . . .
>
> On our allowance there was an accountability. We early learned how to keep books. . . . Usually, the allowance was in arrears and you had to ask the Old Man. And we had to bring

the books down. There were your receivables, expenditures that had to be itemized, and the date and it had to be filled out.

He did teach us the proper strokes in tennis . . . he would take us up to the tennis courts. We would practice shots and he'd play games with us. He was always willing to play catch (baseball). The Old Man was Father and Mother to us. I mean if we were in trouble we went to him.[69]

When the kids were ill, Robert remembers, "It was the Old Man who came in and sat on the edge of your bed and asked you how you were doing." He didn't want his kids to take up either smoking or drinking. He did catch on to the fact that the two boys were sneaking smoking in the shed behind the house. Robert remembers his father saying:

I hate bribery. I don't like to do it and I don't like to ask anyone to do things that they don't want to do . . . but . . . I am going to ask you . . . don't spoil it (athletics) by smoking or getting into booze or something like that. Now if you boys go until you're twenty-one, well, you can each have a car—an automobile.[70]

Kempton, the oldest boy, didn't earn the car and he didn't get one. Robert made it to twenty-one, but his father was dead by that time. Edward Clark III, the executor of the estate, gave him the money to buy a car.

"BOXLY," AN EDUCATIONAL CENTER FOR SCIENTIFIC MANAGEMENT

During the last 15 years of his life, Taylor worked as a consultant spreading the gospel of scientific management. Lillian Gilbreth remembers:

He struck one at first glance as a powerful and directing influence, working through other men as well as himself. He was looked up to unquestioningly as leader by those of his staff—Barth, Cooke, Hathaway and others—who came to feel that, when he had spoken, the last word on any possible matter had been said. His was a face that reflected many moods. The eyes, keen and penetrating; the lips, thin and tightly closed when he was presenting an argument or meeting opposition. The most genial conversationalist in a sympathetic audience.[71]

The educational center of Taylor's campaign to spread knowledge of scientific management to the business world was his estate, called "Boxly." It was advantageously located next to the Highland Avenue station of the Chestnut Hill branch of the Reading Railroad, offering easy access from Philadelphia. Despite this close proximity to downtown Philadelphia, the physical location of "Boxly" made it virtually a country estate. Copley described the estate as follows:

> The property purchased by Mr. and Mrs. Taylor for their permanent home in the Fall of 1901 . . . was one of about 11 acres situated in Chestnut Hill at the extreme northwest limit of the city of Philadelphia. It overlooked the treetops of that most charming section of Philadelphia's park system known as the Wissahickon Valley and had formed part of a place long known as the Sheridan farm.[72]

The key elements of Copley's statement that we should examine are his claims that the property was purchased by Taylor and his wife in the Fall of 1901, and that the land "had formed part of a place long known as the Sheridan farm."

"Boxly" actually covered 11.094 acres. The entire Sheridan farm originally consisted of 22½ acres. This farm was purchased by Joseph Sill Clark (Clarence Clark's brother), on January 22, 1902, for $30,500 from the estate of Elizabeth Sheridan (who had died in 1886), which was being managed by the Commonwealth Title Insurance and Trust Company of Philadelphia.[73] On September 10, 1902, Clark purchased an additional five acres to the east of the Sheridan farm site from Sallie S. Houston for $28,500, thereby increasing the size to 27½ acres with the east side of the land ending directly at the Highland Avenue railroad station.[74]

On November 20, 1902, one month after purchasing the five acres from the Houston family, Clark sold 11.094 acres of the 27½ acres (including the land to the railroad station) to Taylor's wife, Louise M. Taylor, for the sum of $1.00! In this manner, the Taylors acquired the land for their new home for virtually nothing. Although Clark retained 16½ acres to the south of "Boxly," Mrs. Taylor acquired (according to the deed), the "stone mansion house, stone dwelling house, barn, coachhouse, stable and greenhouse."[75]

Upon securing the land from Clark, Taylor began the task of restoring the neglected gardens and making plans for a new house. The former mansion was close to the lane entering the property from the south (now Saint Martins Lane) and, due to Taylor's reclusive nature and certain restrictions in the Houston deed, inappropriate for his plans. Taylor decided to make it a home for his new gardener, Robert H. Bender, whom Taylor employed in February 1902, to restore the gardens.

The original deed from Sallie Houston to Joseph Clark, forbid the construction of any new home within 60 feet of the Houston property line. Taylor had to build his home on the western side of the property, beyond the old boxwood garden. Unfortunately, this location was dominated by a large hill that blocked any view of the beautiful Wissahickon Valley. Taylor wanted his home to have an unobstructed view of the valley so the hill was removed. Taylor believed this was necessary if "Boxly" were to be impressive enough to help sell the ideas of scientific management.

When completed, the home stood at the end of a long, wide brick walk extending through the old boxwood garden. It was an impressive looking building of Southern Colonial design with huge three-story-high pillars in front. A curving driveway extending from Saint Martins Lane, with a high wall on the north side and rising terraces on the south side, were impressive to Taylor's businessmen visitors.

In describing the Taylor Scientific Management talks at "Boxly," Lillian Gilbreth remembers:

> These took the form not of conferences but rather of lectures by Taylor himself, followed by questions. The guests at the meetings were of all types—foreigners anxious to gain knowledge of this new science of management; teachers in the colleges; men engaged in industry desirous of adapting the principles to their work; installers of systems, old men and young men, with an

occasional woman. Each one with his own problem, many attempting to translate an unfamiliar vocabulary into his own language to meet his own needs.

"Boxly" remained an educational center for Taylor's talks on management (talks which were continually rephrased by Morris L. Cooke to make Taylor's arguments more convincing) until his death in 1915. Mrs. Taylor continued to live at "Boxly" until her death on October 31, 1949. From 1943 to 1948, Mrs. Taylor discussed with C. Canby Balderston, Dean of the Wharton School of the University of Pennsylvania, and Thomas S. Gates, President of the University of Pennsylvania, the possibility of using "Boxly" (or the proceeds from the sale of "Boxly") to further Taylor's ideas. Mrs. Taylor's friendship with Dean Balderston was the result of a long friendship with the Balderston family. We should recall that the Taylor family owned many farms and other properties in Bucks County. A study of the atlases of Bucks County for the 19th Century reveals that the Taylor properties were close to those owned by E. Balderston, L. Balderston, and M. Balderston.[76] Gates had a home on Rex Avenue, just north of "Boxly" and the discussions between him and Mrs. Taylor were probably conducted in person prior to Gates' death in 1948, so no written record of their conversations apparently exists. Mrs. Taylor's will, prepared June 24, 1949, left "Boxly" to the Trustees of the University of Pennsylvania.[77]

An interesting account of the reasons behind Mrs. Taylor's decision to leave "Boxly" to the University of Pennsylvania was given by C. Canby Balderston on August 2, 1950, in a letter to Richard A. Feiss:

> From 1943 to her death Mrs. Taylor discussed with Mr. Gates, late president of our university, and myself, the use of Boxly or the proceeds from the sale of Boxly for continuous research and education for advancing and improving the knowledge and techniques in the field and for bringing the total Scientific Management approach into industry and government and institutions of all types.
>
> According to her will, she provided $10,000 for the equipping

of the laboratory of the Wharton School known as the Frederick Winslow Taylor Laboratory and directed that the balance of the proceeds from her real property in Philadelphia County be used to establish and maintain the Frederick Winslow Taylor Management Laboratory Fund.[78]

The laboratory existed at Wharton until the early 1960s when it was dismantled. A portion of the "Boxly" estate was sold in 1951 to Frederick W. G. Peck for $11,000.[79] The presidents of the University of Pennsylvania continued to live at the main house of "Boxly" until the early 1970s. At this time, the university purchased a house in downtown Philadelphia, and the remainder of "Boxly" was sold.

TAYLOR'S FINAL YEARS: 1911–1915

Simultaneous to the difficulties with his manuscript for "Principles of Scientific Management," Taylor experienced two important changes in his life. The first change was the result of the Eastern Rate Case, which increased interest in Taylor's work by a number of magazine editors, and the eventual publication of "The Principles of Scientific Management" in the popular progressive magazine, *The American Magazine*.[80] The *American Magazine* had the talented Ida Tarbell on the staff and she soon became a strong supporter of the Taylor philosophy. She wrote in her autobiography:

> Nothing was more exciting to me than the principles by which Taylor had developed his science. . . . They make the best code I know for progress in human undertakings.[81]

Taylor had purpose in choosing the *American Magazine* for his first and only popular writing. He wrote a friend:

> I have no doubt that the *Atlantic Monthly* would give us a better audience from a literary point of view than we could get from the *American Magazine*. But the readers of the *Atlantic Monthly* consist probably very largely of professors and literary men, who would be interested more in the abstract theory than

in the actual good which would come from the introduction of scientific management.

On the other hand, I feel that the readers of the *American Magazine* consist largely of those who are actually doing the practical work of the world. The people I want to reach with the article are principally those men who are doing the . . . work of our country . . . and I have an idea that many more persons of that kind would be reached through the *American Magazine* than through the *Atlantic Monthly*.[82]

A second important change in Taylor's life was the illness of his wife, Louise (not mentioned in Taylor's biography by Copley, due to Mrs. Taylor's direct control over the content of the biography). Starting in the Fall of 1910, she exhibited the first symptoms of involutional depression that incapacitated her for the remainder of Taylor's life. Her illness was cyclical in nature with periods of physical and emotional distress, alternating with periods of recuperation. During the years 1911–15 his wife's illness severely changed Taylor's life. He ceased producing any important writings, and became abrupt and antagonistic. He kept his close association with Barth and Hathaway, but had less contact with Cooke, Gantt, Thompson, and others.

At the same time Taylor's increasing fame had other results. Although there were growing problems within the ASME since Taylor's presidency, these became more acute. While Taylor's followers at first attempted to bring more discussion about management into the meetings and publications, by 1912 the social responsibility ideas of Cooke began to become a problem to the ASME, whose membership seemed to be more concerned with engineering than with management.

In 1910, Gilbreth created the idea of forming a society to "perpetuate the work begun by Fred W. Taylor."[83] Taylor viewed this new society as a way to win concessions from the ASME. This society, which in December 1911 was formalized and in 1915 was called the "Taylor Society," was independent of the ASME (although originally entrance requirements were the same for both organizations). It did not, however, force concessions from the ASME because it created a new outlet for management issues to be discussed and enabled the ASME to focus on engineering.

By 1914, Taylor was emotionally and physically exhausted. His wife had a relapse in October and in November he wrote Scudder Klyce that he was unable to work "for the lack of time and also for lack of heart."[84] In February and early March 1915, Taylor made two lecture tours in Cleveland and Youngstown, Ohio, and caught a cold that continued until his return to Atlantic City. His cold grew worse and on March 11, he wrote Richard Feiss in Cleveland that he "was so hoarse with a bronchial cough that I was almost unable to speak and the fever and grippe still continue."[85] Taylor went to the hospital in Philadelphia on March 12 and on March 21, 1915, one day after his 59th birthday, he suddenly died.

Taylor's funeral was held at "Cedron," the home of Clarence M. Clark, on March 24, 1915. He was buried at West Laurel Hill Cemetery, Philadelphia, in his father's plot at 124 River, on a hill overlooking the Schuylkill River. The epitaph on his gravestone reads, "Frederick Winslow Taylor 1856–1915 'Father of Scientific Management'."

NOTES

1. Towne, 1886, p. 428.
2. Towne, 1886, p. 429.
3. Metcalfe, 1886, p. 475.
4. Metcalfe, 1886, p. 485.
5. Urwick, 1984, p. 85.
6. Sinclair, 1980, p. 86.
7. Sinclair, 1980.
8. Sinclair, 1980, p. 92.
9. Present State, 1912, p. 1140.
10. Present State, 1912, pp. 1197–98.
11. Taylor, 1895, p. 882.
12. Taylor, 1895, p. 882.
13. Copley, 1925.
14. Taylor to C. Bertrand Thompson, December 30, 1914.
15. Taylor to Dodge, February 25, 1915.

16. Taylor to Van Alstyne, December 27, 1906.
17. House Resolution, 1912, p. 1390.
18. Nadworny, 1955, p. 23.
19. Nadworny, 1955, p. 28.
20. Nadworny, 1955, p. 51.
21. Industrial Relations Commission, 1914, p. 810.
22. Nadworny, 1955, p. 103.
23. Gilson, 1940, p. 55.
24. Del Mar, 1976.
25. Cooke and Murray, 1940, p. 137.
26. Gilbreth, Jr., 1970, p. 114.
27. Taylor and Thompson, 1906.
28. Gilbreth to S. E. Thompson, January 18, 1897.
29. FWT to Sanford Thompson, December 9, 1907.
30. Sanford Thompson to Taylor, December 13, 1907.
31. Taylor to Sanford Thompson, January 13, 1908.
32. Yost, p. 156, and Gilbreth, 1925, p. 35.
33. Gilbreth, Jr., 1970, p. 115.
34. Yost, p. 164.
35. Nadworny, 1957.
36. Nadworny, 1957, p. 25.
37. Taylor, *Principles*, 1911, p. 113.
38. Taylor, *Principles,* 1911, pp. 77–85, 88–89.
39. Gilbreth, Jr., 1970, p. 119.
40. Ernestine G. Cary, December 18, 1989.
41. Nadworny, 1957, p. 25.
42. Gilbreth, 1912.
43. Gilbreth, 1925, p. 35.
44. Brandeis, 1911.
45. Kent, 1932, p. 39.
46. Kent, 1932.
47. *New York Times*, March 29, 1911, p. 1:3.
48. *New York Times*, March 29, 1911, p. 1:3.
49. *New York Times*, March 29, 1911, p. 1:3.
50. Yost, p. 217.
51. Gilbreth, Jr., 1970, p. 140.
52. Nadworny, 1957, pp. 28–29.
53. Hathaway to Taylor, May 16, 1914.
54. Condit, 1923, p. 39.
55. Nelson, 1980, p. 135.
56. FWT to Lionel S. Marks, August 29, 1914.

57. Gilbreth, 1921.

58. Gilbreth, 1921, p. 100.

59. Copley, 1916, pp. 1, 10, 11.

60. Copley, I, p. 88.

61. Copley, I, p. 88.

62. Copley, I, p. 89.

63. Copley, 1916, p. 2.

64. Robert P. A. Taylor, 1976.

65. Copley, I, p. 91.

66. Copley, I, p. 88.

67. Robert Taylor, 1976.

68. Robert Taylor, 1976.

69. Robert Taylor, 1976.

70. Robert Taylor, 1976.

71. Gilbreth, 1925, pp. 42–43.

72. Copley, II, p. 186.

73. Elizabeth Sheridan to Joseph S. Clark, Philadelphia Department of Records, Deed Book W.S.V., no. 25, p. 47.

74. Sallie S. Houston to Joseph S. Clark, Philadelphia Department of Records, Deed Book, W.S.V., no. 233, p. 273.

75. Joseph S. Clark to Louise M. Taylor, Philadelphia Department of Records, Deed Book, W.S.V., no. 176, p. 235.

76. Atlas of Bucks County, 1870, Bucks County Historical Society, Doylestown, Pennsylvania.

77. Will of Louise M. S. Taylor, Philadelphia, Department of Records, Will Book, F. S., no. 542, p. 258.

78. C. Balderston to Richard A. Feiss, August 2, 1950, History of Management Theory Collections, Cornell University, Richard A. Feiss papers.

79. Trustees of the University of Pennsylvania to Frederick W. G. Peck, Philadelphia Department of Records, Deed Book C.J.P., no. 3127, p. 368.

80. Taylor, *Principles,* 1911.

81. Tarbell, 1985, p. 294.

82. Tarbell, 1985, pp. 292–93.

83. Kent, 1932.

84. Taylor to Klyce, November 1914.

85. Taylor to Feiss, March 11, 1915, dictated March 9, 1915.

PART VI

COPLEY'S BIOGRAPHY OF TAYLOR

The primary source of information on Taylor for the majority of management scholars has been Frank Barkley Copley's biography of Taylor. This two-volume work was published in 1923, after Copley had spent seven years in researching and writing the manuscript. The story of Copley's efforts to prepare this biography, his struggles with Mrs. Taylor and Taylor's disciples over the content, the influence of an outside editor, and his eventual death in 1941, are an important finale to any story of Taylor's life.

Shortly after Taylor's funeral on March 24, 1915, the *Frederick W. Taylor Cooperators* were formed to preserve Taylor's accomplishments and prevent the decline of the Scientific Management movement. Simultaneous with the formation of the Cooperators was the probate of Taylor's will, dated January 18, 1910. Under this will, Taylor said he was giving to his

> nephew Edward W. Clark III all the rest of my property to hold the same in trust for the benefit of my wife, Louise M. S. Taylor, to collect the income from said estate with the authority to change the investments from time to time.[1]

The will empowered Edward W. Clark III to establish *The Frederick W. Taylor Estate*. Toward this end a memorial service for Taylor was held at "Boxly" on October 13, 1915. Immediately after this service, the Cooperators and others met at the Adelphia Hotel in Philadelphia to make plans for the biography. It was decided to commission a professional writer to prepare the biography (Minutes of Cooperators, October 16, 1915). A committee of three individuals, Morris L. Cooke, Sanford Thompson, and Clarence M. Clark, was formed to find a suitable author.

According to Harlow Person, the committee selected Frank Barkley Copley to write the biography because Copley had written articles on scientific management that were praised by Taylor as excellent accounts of the subject. After Taylor's death Copley wrote a special article on Taylor's work for the *Outlook* in which he called Taylor a "Revolutionist":

> a great pioneer and discoverer in the world of industry, but a man whose heart was aflame with missionary zeal, a man who was an industrial revolutionist.[2]

Copley had asserted that the Taylor system of management was built on "the spirit of brotherly love" and that Taylor:

> was no prophet, he was no poet; he was simply a man of science, a straight-seeing, straight-thinking, straight-talking, and straight-acting engineer.[3]

Person remembered:

> This article reminded the committee that was appointed to arrange for a biography of the Father of Scientific Management of Taylor's appraisal of the earlier *American Magazine* article. Thus developed the circumstances that led to the selection of Frank B. Copley as the biographer of Taylor.[4]

In addition to the *Outlook* article, the selection of Copley as the biographer occurred through the suggestion of Cooke, who, beyond his many other activities was also a former newspaper reporter and had known Copley when he was reporter for the *New York Sun*.[5]

The money to prepare the biography came from the Frederick W. Taylor estate. All final decisions regarding the content were initially in the hands of Clark and Mrs. Taylor, but as events progressed Cooke, Thompson, Clark, and later Harlow Person, made most of the decisions concerning the organization and content of the book.

Copley began his research in Germantown in 1916. Initially he found the work relatively easy. He had the opportunity to talk with Mrs. Taylor, discuss Taylor's career with Carl Barth and, according to Person, interviewed others who worked with Taylor. Finally, with the aid of the Taylor Cooperators, he corresponded with many others who knew Taylor.

Copley was also given access to Taylor's personal papers that were stored on the third floor of "Boxly." We can only imagine the wealth of material found in this collection. The present collection of Taylor's records at Stevens Institute of Technology, while extensive, probably represents only half of the total number of papers Copley found there in 1916. In the 73 years since Copley used these records, the original collection of papers has been handled (as far as we know) by at least five different individuals.

In 1933, when the Taylor Society drew up plans for a celebration of the 50th anniversary of Taylor's graduation from Stevens, Carl Barth was asked to examine the papers at "Boxly" and select material suitable for the exhibition. In sorting through the documents, Barth unfortunately adopted the procedure of discarding any items that he could not identify.[6] We do not know how many documents Barth may have destroyed in this manner, but at least some were thrown away.

After the death of Mrs. Taylor in 1949, and before "Boxly" was turned over to the University of Pennsylvania under the terms of Mrs. Taylor's will, Taylor's two sons, Kempton and Robert, visited "Boxly." They spent three hours removing papers from the third floor and burning them in the driveway.[7] What they destroyed in this process will probably never be known.

After the destruction of these papers, Taylor's sons apparently decided to donate the remaining material to Stevens. A few days later, Professor George Barnwell of Stevens arrived at

"Boxly" and, like Barth, proceeded to discard items he believed should not go to Stevens. What exactly Barnwell discarded still remains a mystery.

The remaining Taylor papers were finally examined by Elizabeth Hayward of Stevens and J. Christian Barth, Carl's son, and then moved to Stevens where they are presently available to scholars and have been of enormous help in writing this book.

During 1916, Copley performed his research among Taylor's papers at Boxly and interviewed former Taylor associates in Philadelphia. In 1917, he returned to New York City to begin writing the manuscript. Copley worked full time on the manuscript until August 1917, and part time from September 1917 to June 1919. During this period, he forwarded sections of the manuscript, as he completed them, to members of the committee.

During World War I, the involvement of members of the committee in the war effort delayed any deep consideration of Copley's manuscript. In addition, changes were being made in the minds of Taylor's disciples about how to view his life and contributions. Morris Cooke, Harlow Person, and Sanford Thompson saw the necessity of reinterpreting his contributions and recasting of the structure of the Taylor Society. The reaction of Carl Barth, Taylor's most devoted disciple, to these changes was significant because while the committee wanted to create an image of a Taylor that never really existed, Barth wanted to preserve what actually happened in Taylor's life.

There is no existing evidence that Barth communicated his feelings to the members of the committee, but he did write to Richard A. Feiss expressing his feelings about Taylor and the Taylor Society:

> I too feel that the Taylor Society is rapidly getting de-Taylorized, the way things are tending. In fact, I have never seen much else in the Society than an agency for the gradual degeneration of the technical and managerial perfection Mr. Taylor stood for, and which he felt convinced would never be mastered except by a comparatively small percentage of the great number of men who feel called upon to manage others, but who do not have

the capacity to hold in their minds the enormous number of intricately interrelated details that form the tissues of the managerial muscles, without which the finest managerial brain in all its wisdom, cannot secure proper executive action.

The efforts to secure a large membership, even if these efforts were confined to the lower grades only, must inevitably lead to a degeneration of the membership as a whole; and as such efforts to increase the membership is a necessity under the present reorganization of the Society which calls for a considerable income, I fear that reorganization "carries along with it the germ of its own destruction." However, I may be entirely wrong about this, and I do not mean to underestimate what the Society has done, and is now attempting to do even more intensively, namely to give to a larger group a knowledge, more or less intimate according to the varying capacities of the individual recipients, of the fundamental Taylor principles, and some of the details already in successful use for carrying the principles into effect.[8]

Barth's remark that the Society was an "agency for the gradual degeneration of the technical and managerial perfection Mr. Taylor stood for" is a revolutionary statement. Even a casual reading of Copley's book demonstrates that he never stressed the intricate details of the Taylor System so desired by Barth and Taylor.

Considering the image of Taylor the committee had in mind, and while they appreciated Copley's efforts, they apparently were unsure of their ability to criticize his writing and began to wonder if they should not call in another person to review Copley's work. Early in July 1919, Copley and Edward W. Clark III met in New York City to discuss the fears of the biography committee. On July 11, 1919, Copley wrote to Clark expressing his feelings concerning the plan to bring in an outside individual to review, criticize, and aid Copley in preparing the manuscript. Copley said:

> The more I think over your plan to get an outside man to read the manuscript of Mr. Taylor's biography, the more I feel that it is susceptible of modification.
>
> The manuscript now going to you is not the final one. In passing this ms. to you I am *not* saying, Here are the goods. There

are only two reasons why this ms. is going to you as I write it (1) that you may have some tangible evidence that a return is being made for the money you are called on to keep putting out; (2) that you who knew Mr. Taylor intimately may have your work facilitated of giving me the benefit of whatever criticisms and corrections you may have to offer before I proceed to go over the ms. and put it into the shape that I am willing to stand by.

Frankly it is objectionable to me that an outsider should be called in to sit in judgment on my work before it is complete. It is quite likely that when I am in a position to go over what I have written and view it as a whole, I shall anticipate many, if not all, of the criticisms you will have to offer. That's all right in your case; but I haven't the least idea of what kind of a man you will bring in from the outside—his selection is being made entirely by you—and I certainly don't want him placed in a position where he, with some show of right, can demand that his name appear on the title page as the editor of the work, or say later on that he had to tell me what, in the main, I had to do.[9]

At the very time that Copley was writing to Clark, Cooke and Thompson already had begun a search for an editor. Cooke sought the aid of an old friend, Winthrop S. Scudder, art editor of the Houghton Mifflin Company in Boston. Scudder told Cooke he had four people in mind, "all of whom had had wide experience in similar work" in editing biographies.[10] These individuals were: Florence Converse (on the staff of *The Atlantic Monthly*), Herbert R. Gibbs (with the Literary Department of the Houghton Mifflin Company), Mark Anthony De Wolfe Howe (vice president of The Atlantic Monthly Company), and William Roscoe Thayer (editor of the *Harvard Graduate Magazine*). Of these four individuals, only Gibbs reviewed Copley's manuscript.[11]

While Cooke was consulting with Scudder, Thompson had already contacted Dr. Henry G. Pearson, Professor of English at Massachusetts Institute of Technology. On July 15, 1919, Thompson wrote Edward Clark III that Henry Pearson could undertake the job.[12]

Henry G. Pearson was a professional ghost writer who rewrote book manuscripts. According to Pearson's son, Harold, his father spent virtually every summer rewriting some book. He believes his father did rewrite portions of the Taylor manuscript during the years 1920–22.[13]

Copley's manuscript was forwarded to Pearson and on October 1, 1919, he prepared an outline of how the book could be divided. Five months later, on March 19, 1920, Pearson prepared a detailed report which included an analysis of various portions of what he considered the primary chapters of the book: those on Midvale and Bethlehem. Pearson's report was divided into several sections: "Basis and Scope of This Report," "Length of Book," "Style," "Treatment," and "General Considerations."[14]

Pearson said the report was based on:

> a study of the manuscript presented by Mr. Copley, of the detailed criticism of it made by members of the committee in a page by page analysis, and of their general criticisms as made in writing and in conference with me.[15]

The report's purpose, Pearson said, was:

> to present a plan which interprets the desires of the committee as expressed in their individual notes, and in joint session, and by the guidance of which Mr. Copley may successfully complete his work.[16]

For our purpose there were two other items in this report that deserve consideration.

1. Pearson suggested the book was too long (approximately 350,000 words). Therefore, he said:

> In order to produce a book which shall carry the message of Taylor's work most effectively to the men to whom it will be of most value, Mr. Copley should aim to bring his treatment within the compass of one volume.[17]

2. To bring Copley's large manuscript down to a length suitable for inclusion in one volume, Pearson said he attached an outline to achieve this goal:

> I append an outline based on his manuscript which suggests a scheme for carrying out these ideas. For the two periods covering

the years 1880–90 and 1890–1905, I give topics which may serve for the arrangement of material in chapters.[18]

Copley's reaction to Henry Pearson's report was predictable. He immediately informed Dr. Harlow Person that if he were forced to follow Pearson's suggestions he would quit the project. He asked for copies of the general criticisms which Pearson claimed were "made by members of the committee in a page by page analysis."[19] Despite meetings with Pearson on April 10 and 11, 1920, one meeting with the committee on April 14, 1920, and a meeting with Person and Pearson in New York on April 24, 1920, Copley was unable to obtain any copies of the written criticisms.[20] Copley finally concluded that the criticisms cited by Pearson were "mostly his own personal views."[21]

At the April 24, 1920, meeting it was decided Copley should attend the annual Taylor Society meeting at Rochester, New York, on May 6–7, 1920, supposedly to confer with Thompson, Barth, and Hathaway. The committee, however, failed to tell Copley that Pearson was also invited to attend.

On May 7, 1920, Thompson, Barth, Pearson, W. H. Hemmerly (who worked for Thompson-Lichtner), and later Harlow Person, met with Copley in his hotel room. Cooke, who also attended the Taylor meeting, however, did not attend the committee's meeting. Cooke, at the time, was not pleased with the selection of Henry Pearson over one of the Scudder candidates, so boycotted the conference with Copley.

The meeting in Copley's room, according to Copley in a letter written several days later, consisted primarily of Barth testifying on important events in Taylor's life:

> It was interesting to see Mr. Thompson question Mr. Barth and take notes. It was still more interesting to see Mr. Pearson also question Mr. Barth, and also take notes.[22]

The next afternoon, on May 8, 1920, the committee, along with Pearson, had a meeting at the Rochester Chamber of Commerce. At this meeting, Pearson gave orders to Copley concerning what had to be in the biography and what had to be removed. Of the meeting, Copley wrote to Clark:

he advised me that, in order to understand Mr. Taylor's character, I would better "spend two or three months reading Mr. Taylor's works." This remark was permitted to stand. Mr. Pearson and Mr. Thompson then discussed in my presence what could and could not be permitted to remain in Book V. It was proposed by Mr. Thompson that he reduce to writing such things as I could do and such principles as I must follow in preparing the final manuscript.[23]

The information Barth provided during the interview at Rochester was so new and important to Thompson, that although he had been associated with Taylor from 1895 to 1915, he took four pages of notes. Some of the more important statements he recorded appear below:

(At Midvale) Rough methods of pushing things through were introduced:

The first effort was to find out how long it took to do the work by overall times. The stopwatch was concealed and this was the mere beginning of time. Time to remove metal on the lathe was the big problem.

The first thing was what the machine would do, and then what the men would do.

The work at Midvale was chiefly axle-turning and locomotive tires. The problems were simple so that little planning and routing was required.

Mr. Thorne, at William Sellers Co. gave the first idea of the route sheet but did not develop it. Functional foremanship was developed at Midvale, but secretly because of the natural opposition of the management to so radical a change.

Even at Bethlehem they were very circumspect in referring to this.

Real work in metal cutting (according to Barth) was done at Sellers by Barth after leaving Bethlehem.[24]

Copley's reaction to these curious events was to demand justice for the devotion he had exhibited toward the project for the past four years. To achieve this justice, Copley made four proposals:

First, that "Henry G. Pearson now disappear from the job completely and permanently."

Second, that "there be a response to my repeated request that the members of the committee and all to do with this project take me completely into their confidence as to their views."

Third, that "After I have been put in possession of the views of all concerned, I be permitted to proceed with the work of outlining to you the course I propose to take in preparing the final manuscript. But I must make it absolutely plain that if Mr. Pearson is to be the judge of the merits of this outline, I cannot undertake to prepare it."

Fourth, that "if, after I submit to you the aforesaid outline, I am to proceed with the work of preparing the final manuscript, I be not hampered by anyone standing over me and attempting to tell me what to do."[25]

We do not know the reaction of the members of the committee to Copley's letter since any reactions to his letter have apparently not been preserved. The only indication we have of their reactions are three final analyses of Copley's manuscript by Mrs. Taylor, Sanford Thompson, and Harlow Person a few days after Copley's letter to Edward Clark III.

In her analysis, Mrs. Taylor said there was a large amount of material that was not related to Taylor and that it should be eliminated. This was data on the history of the Quakers, Puritans, chapters on Autocracy and Democracy. In addition, there was excessive sarcasm and sneering, which she wished eliminated.

Mrs. Taylor believed that Copley's manuscript failed to present a clear idea of Taylor's life and his devotion to the study of management:

A true account of his life could not possibly be told without describing the development of scientific management. Everything in his life was subordinated to this subject.

I want to feel in reading the book that I am following the development of the man, as he struggled with the various problems as they daily faced him, so that one will fully realize the heroic efforts he made to try and make clear to the world the need of science and of a better understanding of human relations.[26]

An important feature of Mrs. Taylor's criticism was that she concluded by stating she approved of the rearrangement of the manuscript outlined by Harlow Person. The Person analysis is discussed after that of several others.

Because the present location of Copley's original manuscript is unknown, we do not know the final influence of Mrs. Taylor's criticisms (outside of the chapters on Quakers, Puritans, Autocracy, and Democracy, and the removal of all sarcasm and sneering remarks) on Copley's final manuscript. It appears she relied primarily on Harlow Person's suggestions for the final manuscript.

A slightly different attitude toward her influence was expressed by Taylor's adopted son, Robert P. A. Taylor, who in discussing the manuscript said:

> Oh yes, nobody knows how much was deleted out of the thing because anything she didn't like . . . she didn't like any swear words or anything in it or something of the sort, so she would just strike them out and so forth, because after all she was boss . . . she was hiring him to do the job.[27]

He added:

> Oh, I'm sure there was much more personal about him that was deleted, which was unfortunate for the next biographer . . . . I never heard him swear around the house. He was a different man at home. . . . His enthusiasm at work and the drive to work is obvious in Copley, but you don't get any of the fun of the man at all. He was a good mimic and a good storyteller, with a dialect. It was his makeup because he used to do some acting as a kid, I know, with a small group. It wasn't anything special but this was unusual in a Quaker family. It was okay with the Unitarians. It wouldn't have been allowed in a Quaker family.[28]

The second analysis, by Thompson, dated May 16, 1920, contained a number of criticisms of the biography:

> The chief criticism, in my opinion, is in the lack of clear and graphic presentation of the development of his life and work.

Second criticism is the necessity for a more philosophical treatment of the development of scientific management in the shop.

Third point criticized, which really is covered in the points already given, is the extraneous matter in many of the books.

Fourth general criticism is the lack of a clear statement of the growth of scientific management, and the development of its technique.[29]

The third and probably most influential analysis was prepared by Person. He made a careful study of the five books comprising Copley's manuscript at this time and said his "recommended omissions, additions, and a new emphasis resulting from interpretation would make a book somewhat as follows as to content, balance and length":

Book I.   A popular essay on Taylor's characteristics and on scientific management, featuring him as a genius embodying a passion for the scientific method in simple as well as big things.

(10,000 to 15,000 words)

Book II.   Ancestry and Early Life—say, to 1878.

(15,000 to 20,000 words)

Book III.   At Midvale—the big period in Taylor's life— giving the story of the development of the mechanisms, step by step—full of human interest and of vital scientific interest.

(70,000 to 75,000 words)

Book IV.   The period 1890 to 1912; the smoothing and coordinating of the mechanisms; the first half featuring Bethlehem, the circumstances surrounding presentation of "Notes on Belting," "A Piece Rate System," and "Shop Management," and the second half of the book presenting a studied exposition of the nature and purpose of scientific management.

(100,000 to 125,000 words)

Book V.   Activities from 1912 to 1915, including chapter on Taylor in his family and nonprofessional life.

(10,000 to 15,000 words)

Total   120,000 to 150,000 words.[30]

In his general criticism of each of the books of the manuscript, Person said the manuscript was entirely too long and should be cut in half. He said there was a necessity to correct Copley's style which tended to impair the entire book. For example, he said the profanity was bad and Copley made too many cynical and sneering references to people who opposed Taylor and his ideas.

Harlow Person also indicated particular material in the manuscript that should be eliminated. Like Mrs. Taylor, he said the chapters on Puritanism, Hegelianism, and Quakerism were not relevant. Further, he suggested Copley's discussion of Taylor's ancestry was too long and the implied principles of heredity unscientific. A very strange suggestion by Person was the elimination or reduction of any references to Barth, Hathaway, Whitney, and others: "The chapter on Barth should be eliminated and the treatment of him reduced to a paragraph; likewise with respect to Hathaway, Whitney, etc."[31]

By far the most important statements by Person were contained in his sixth point regarding Taylor's early life, because these suggestions apparently led Copley to severely revise this portion of his manuscript. Person wrote:

> There are some vital facts of Taylor's life lacking, especially with respect to the periods 1878–89 and 1889–1900. Taylor lived his life, *so far as posterity is concerned*—made his great contribution to society—chiefly in the period 1878–89. That period should be given from a third to a half of the book. Scientific management was developed during that period and the story of its development step by step is the story of Taylor—the *essence* of Taylor. The author should make a more profound study of scientific management in its details, or he will never grasp the soul of Taylor; then he should rewrite the decade 1878–89. The

success of the book depends upon the treatment of that period. The decade 1889–1900 is given enough space, but not the right emphasis. There is too much about the Maine, Wisconsin, and Fitchburg life—which is relatively unimportant—and too little about Bethlehem and its significance. The period 1878–89 is the period of the development of mechanisms of scientific management; 1889–1900 the period of coordinating and smoothing out the mechanisms and of the formulation of a philosophy.[32]

Several portions of this statement deserve further discussion because of their influence on Copley's final work: "Taylor lived his life, *so far as posterity is concerned*—made his great contribution to society—chiefly in the period 1878–89. This period should be given from a third to half of the book." An analysis of Volume I of Copley's book reveals that 236 pages (more than half) of the 467 pages are devoted to Taylor's life at Midvale from 1878–89.

In regard to the decade 1889–1900 that "there is too much about the Maine, Wisconsin, and Fitchburg life—which is relatively unimportant—and too little about Bethlehem and its significance," we find that in Volume I only 125 pages are devoted to a discussion of Taylor's work at the Manufacturing Investment Company, despite the fact that this period led to Taylor's accounting system. Similarly, the story of the work at Simonds Rolling Machine Company is also underreported, although Taylor's espionage work was prominent at this time. In brief, Harlow Person's comments apparently made Copley reduce his presentation of the 1889–1900 period.

As suggested by Harlow Person, Copley increased his coverage of the developments at Bethlehem, which covers 164 pages of Volume II. As of May 14, 1920, only Mrs. Taylor, Thompson, and Person had prepared criticisms of the biography. Thompson wrote Cooke and Edward W. Clark III asking for their criticisms, but we have no evidence that they ever answered his request.[33]

We do not know what occurred regarding the manuscript during the year 1921, but in 1922 the manuscript was finally forwarded to Scudder's friend Herbert R. Gibbs at Houghton Mifflin. In a letter dated March 8, 1922, Gibbs said the proposed length of the book, 300,000 words, was too long and should be reduced to 150,000 words. To reduce the size of the book, Gibbs suggested three main changes, two of which already had been suggested by Person:

> To illustrate what we mean by saying that the book as it stands seems to us amplified in unnecessary ways, we suggest three points. Is it important to devote so much attention to the remote ancestry? particularly because this seems to involve a second questionable point, namely, a good deal about the Puritans and the Quakers in both old England and New England. We are not questioning the interest of what is said, but only wondering whether, for the purposes of this book, those matters might not wisely be reduced to very brief terms. A third point is the amplification of particular periods of Mr. Taylor's life, the special connections with industries that do not have the largest bearing upon his engineering and scientific management development. One case of this sort, it seems to us, is that of the Bethlehem Steel Company. We speak of these matters in entire frankness, assuming, of course, that the author of the book is always the final arbiter of such questions.[34]

Clark forwarded a copy of Gibbs's letter to Cooke, observing that the suggestions would be a shock to Copley:

> You will remember his objections to cutting the book down to 250,000 from 350,000 words and that he always claimed that he could not specify any particular number of words . . . so that the suggestion of 150,000 words from one of the best publishers in the country will be quite a surprise to him.[35]

Clark also told Cooke he would not send Gibbs's letter to Copley until he and Cooke had a chance to discuss its contents.

Gibbs had also said that the size of the book (two good-sized volumes) would reduce sales. This fact led him to ask about the financial arrangements:

> Nothing has been definitely said in our correspondence with you about the financing of this book, and we do not know whether it is the expectation of Mr. Taylor's family to be responsible for the expense; but our present feeling about the probable sale of the book is such that it does not seem likely that we should wish to undertake the issue at our own risk.[36]

The biography committee after March 1922 remains a mystery. Apparently no further negotiations were made with Houghton and Mifflin, and in April 1922, Leon Pratt Alford of the Ronald Press offered to be the publisher.[37] The Ronald Press offer never materialized, and in 1923, Harper and Brothers became the publisher.

Just before Harper published Copley's final manuscript, Edward W. Clark III wrote Cooke a letter on the subject. Clark said Copley's final revision reduced the manuscript to 296,000 words and, more important, that Copley adopted Person's revisions. Clark said, "Dr. Person was very active in the revision and secured from Mr. Copley practically all the major changes and most of the minor changes which he thought necessary."[38]

In Copley's acknowledgments in the published book he wrote that he "in fact is indebted to Dr. Person for far more in the way of valuable suggestion than can here be well stated."[39] This appears to be an admission by Copley that Person's suggestions regarding the 1878–98 and 1898–1900 periods were incorporated in the book.

The relationship with Harlow Person apparently continued until Copley's death in 1941. It was Person who prepared Copley's only known obituary and in it Person gave his readers a curious bit of information on Copley's life after publication of Taylor's biography:

> At one time or another he served New York City newspapers, the *World, Evening World, Sun* and *Journal*. Eventually he became a special writer for newspapers and monthly magazines, a field of work *to which he did not return after completing the biography of Taylor*. At the time of his death he had several manuscripts for books underway.[40]

Unfortunately, we do not know why Copley did not return to being a special writer after the Taylor biography was published. In 1936, Copley informed Cooke that he had lost his home in Dobbs Ferry and was forced to move to a walk-up tenement in the Bronx.[41] Copley moved to St. Petersburg, Florida, in 1939, and died there on January 14, 1941.[42]

NOTES

1. F. W. Taylor will W-1717–1915, dated June 18, 1910.
2. Copley, 1916, p. 10.
3. Copley, 1916, pp. 13, 22.
4. Person, 1941, p. 117.
5. Cooke to Wrege, October 18, 1959.
6. J. Christian Barth, interviewed by C. D. Wrege, November 10, 1960.
7. Nartowitz to C. D. Wrege, 1978.
8. Barth to R. A. Feiss, October 17, 1919, p. 1.
9. Copley to E. W. Clark III, May 13, 1920.
10. Scudder to Cooke, July 14, 1919.
11. Herbert R. Gibbs to E. W. Clark III, March 8, 1922.
12. Thompson to Clark, July 15, 1919.
13. Harold Pearson to C. D. Wrege, October 16, 1985.
14. Pearson, March 19, 1920, p. 1.
15. Pearson, March 19, 1920, p. 1.
16. Pearson, March 19, 1920, p. 1.
17. Pearson, March 19, 1920, p. 1.
18. Pearson, March 19, 1920, p. 3.
19. Pearson, March 19, 1920.
20. Copley to E. W. Clark III, May 13, 1920, p. 5.
21. Copley to E. W. Clark III, May 13, 1920, p. 5.
22. Copley to E. W. Clark III, May 13, 1920, p. 6.
23. Copley to E. W. Clark III, May 13, 1920, p. 6.
24. Thompson, "Notes on Conference at Rochester," 1920, pp. 1–3.
25. Copley to E. W. Clark III, May 13, 1920, pp. 7–9.
26. Mrs. Taylor, General Criticism, n.d., p. 1.
27. Robert Taylor, 1976.
28. Robert Taylor, 1976.
29. Thompson comments, May 16, 1920, pp. 1–2.
30. Person, Final Memorandum, pp. 3–4.
31. Person, Final Memorandum, p. 2.
32. Person, Final Memorandum, p. 2.
33. Thompson to Cooke and Edward W. Clark III, May 24, 1920.
34. Gibbs to E. W. Clark III, March 8, 1922.
35. E. W. Clark III to Cooke, March 9, 1922.
36. Gibbs to E. W. Clark III, March 8, 1922.
37. Alford to E. W. Clark III, April 22, 1922.
38. E. W. Clark III to Cooke, September 17, 1923.

39. Copley, I, p. v.

40. Person, "Frank Barkley Copley," *Advanced Management*, 1941, p. 117 (emphasis added).

41. Cooke interview with C. D. Wrege, December 27, 1959.

42. *St. Petersburg Times*, January 16, 1941, p. 2.

PART VII

TAYLOR'S LEGACY

Our heroes are often larger than life; Frederick Winslow Taylor is an American hero. The fact that he was human, that he had feet of clay, should not detract from the ultimate contribution of this remarkable hero. This account of Frederick Taylor is a detailed one, one filled with specifics. The details of his life should not obliterate the overall contribution when viewed as a total picture, for he left us a great legacy. Frederick Taylor advanced a total system of management, one which he built from pieces taken from numerous others—whom he rarely would credit, and in some cases perhaps did not know the origin of the idea. His system was never totally installed, by him or any other person, although Link Belt, Tabor, and Clothcraft came close. His genius lies in formulating a philosophy, of being a missionary, where none had previously existed.

Frank Gilbreth's classic book *Motion Study* written in 1911, before the Taylor–Gilbreth feud, praised Taylor. He wrote:

> Much toward standardizing the trades has already been done. In this, as in almost countless other lines of activity, the investigator turns oftenest with admiration of the work of Frederick W. Taylor. It is the never-ceasing marvel concerning this man that age cannot wither nor custom stale his work. After many a weary day's study the investigator awakes from a dream of

greatness to find that he has only worked out a new proof for a problem that Taylor has already solved.

Time study, the instruction card, functional foremanship, the differential rate piece method of compensation, and numerous other scientifically derived methods of decreasing costs and increasing output and wages—these are by no means his only contributions toward standardizing the trades whose value it would be difficult to overestimate; they are but a few of the means toward attaining standards which have been placed by Taylor, their discoverer, within the hands of any man willing to use them.[1]

Daniel Nelson is correct in describing Taylor's innovations as a "synthesis of old and new techniques that acted as a catalyst on the late 19th-century movement."[2] But the phrase above understates the contribution of Taylor, as Nelson's book so ably demonstrates. Taylor may not have invented, but contributed to the use and synthesis in management of time study, motion study, functional foreman, cost control systems, written instructions for workers, the planning department, matrix management, etc. His work was early translated into many languages—most of the European languages as well as Japanese. *Pravda*, in 1918, reports Lenin as saying, "We should try out every scientific and progressive suggestion of the Taylor system" (quoted in Chambers, 1973, p.64).

The frequently criticized and equally praised Frederick Taylor was a champion of the ideas which form the basis for many of today's management practices. He experienced success, criticism, failure, and even fame in his lifetime. He had the ego and the determination to advance his ideas and ideals in the face of substantial opposition. His characteristics did not endear him to the critics or help him successfully promote those thoughts. Nonetheless, those ideas have survived because of his personal strength, the power of his followers whom he inspired, and because his concepts were fundamentally sound. As business consultant Robert Wood so clearly points out:

> When people today think of Taylor (if they think of him at all), they tend to think of dehumanizing time-motion studies. . . . This does an enormous disservice to Taylor and to . . . scientific management. . . . What Taylor principally urged was what came to be known

as the systems approach to manufacturing: The idea that every part of a factory or a whole organization should be scientifically analyzed and redesigned to achieve the most efficient output. Managers should look at every aspect of a manufacturing operation as a piece of an integrated system, and should think through the consequences for the entire system of fiddling with any of its parts. Unfortunately, as the power of the human relations movement grew in the 1950s and 1960s, this eminently sensible systems approach to running a business came to be considered insufficiently sensitive to human needs and wants, too mechanical.[3]

Peter Drucker once wrote that, "Whenever anything is being accomplished, it is being done, I have learned, by a monomaniac with a mission."[4] And so Taylor was a "monomaniac with a mission." He was the epitome of a fanatic, champion, zealot. He believed in his cause and he accomplished much. His published accounts of his experiences seemed more directed to impress specific audiences than to being accurate. His publications, patents, and other pursuits led him to be financially secure and enabled him to direct his attentions to the mission of spreading the gospel of scientific management. Yet his philosophy was poorly understood by many and as highly controversial in his day as it is today. He seems to have attracted more enemies than followers.

The basic Taylor management philosophy was every bit as dynamic as was the business development of his time—that incredible 1880–1915 period. A major concern of the Taylor philosophy was the need to develop a cooperation and mutual respect between labor and management. Without mutual respect and benefit, the system would be unacceptable to either side, yet it was the system which offered both great benefits. As he wrote:

> . . . the fundamental interests of employees and employers are necessarily antagonistic. Scientific management, on the contrary, has for its very foundation the firm conviction that the true interests of the two are one and the same.[5]

The system's base was research and experimentation to replace the old "rule-of-thumb." It was a philosophy based on knowledge, on science. Taylor wrote:

Scientific management does not necessarily involve any great invention, not the discovery of new startling facts. It does, however, involve a certain COMBINATION of elements which have not existed in the past, namely, old knowledge so collected, analyzed, grouped, and classified into laws and rules that it constitutes a science.[6]

Farhana Siddiqi in her doctoral dissertation, written under Peter Drucker's direction, wrote:

Taylor was occupied with the task of the individual worker and with organizational factors impeding performances, such as poor planning, uneven flow of jobs and materials, incorrect speed and cut, and so on. Gilbreth, coming from the construction industry and influenced by his wife's interest in education and psychology, was less preoccupied with organizational handicaps to production, and more concerned with those due to defects in the worker's own method. . . . Taylor sought to achieve his goal of raising the productivity of manual work by rationalizing the system of management in the productive unit as a whole.[7]

It was this whole, this industrial organization, that

is governed by definite regularities, by principles which can be discovered through observation and analysis. Once these principles are known, they can be applied in the working situation to regulate the various activities and other functions of production as to insure maximum productivity. Thus scientific knowledge replaces intuition and rule of thumb methods in organizational behavior.[8]

Siddiqi has correctly interpreted Taylor, and she continues:

management must bear the main responsibility for this radical transformation. Instead of leaving the worker alone to solve the operational problems by which he is confronted in his work, management should train him to perform his task in the best way.[9]

In Taylor's testimony before the Special Committee of the House of Representatives in January of 1912, he said, "scientific management is a scheme for greatly increasing the output of the man without materially increasing his effort."[10] Drucker said that:

people laughed—yet this is, of course, exactly what has come to pass in the developed countries, and primarily as a result of the application of Taylor's principles. It has come to pass precisely the way Taylor predicted. . . . It has come about because we have learned to study tasks, to organize them, to plan them, to provide the right tools and the right information—though no one would claim that we have reached perfection.[11]

Many attack Taylor and the philosophy of scientific management, particularly for its supposed insensitivity to human needs. Drucker, a strong supporter of scientific management, notes two glaring "blind spots" in the philosophy. His attack comes from understanding the original writings and understanding the social setting of America at the turn of the 20th century. The first "blind spot" and one which affected the Gilbreth Motion Study more than the Taylor Time Study was:

the belief that because we must analyze work into its simplest constituent motions we must also organize it as a series of individual motions, each if possible carried out by an individual worker. This is false logic. . . . Scientific Management purports to organize human work. But it assumes—without any attempt to test or to verify the assumption—that the human being is a machine tool (although a poorly designed one). . . . The human being does individual motions poorly; viewed as a machine tool, he is badly designed.[12]

Drucker sees Taylor as laying aside the personality, emotions, appetites, and soul issues which make up the human psyche. As to Taylor being attacked for "dehumanization" of the worker, especially by today's organizational behavioralists and psychologists, is, in Drucker's words, "unfair and unjust."[13] It is unfair and unjust because Taylor at the turn of the century did not know of post-Freudian psychology.

The second major "blind spot" addressed by Drucker is the "divorce of planning from doing." And this is a Taylor philosophical problem. Taylor did discover that planning work and doing work are different, and that is a significant insight. Writes Drucker:

But, it does not follow from the separation of planning and doing in the analysis of work that the planner and the doer should be two different people. . . . Planning and doing are separate parts of the same job; they are not separate jobs. There is no work that can be performed effectively unless it contains elements of both.[14]

But the central theme of the Taylor philosophy and one he repeated in his writings and in the House Testimony was to substitute industrial harmony and trust for industrial warfare and fear. To do that required changes from traditional practices. The first was to pay high wages to employees. His *Shop Management* book clearly states, "This book is written mainly with the object of advocating HIGH WAGES and LOW LABOR COST as the foundation of the best management. . . . "[15] This requirement for high wages has led some to see Taylor as viewing the employee as one-dimensional, concerned only with money. Taylor did not believe that higher wages by themselves would motivate. Although the word "motivate" was not commonly used until the 1920s, Taylor understood that the worker is driven by more than material rewards. In *Shop Management*, he writes in anticipation of Barnard, Adams, Porter-Lawler, etc.:

> Fixing two prices (payments) for the same piece of work . . . always causes the greatest feeling of injustice and dissatisfaction in the man who is discriminated against. . . . We may say the difference is one of sentiment, yet sentiment plays an important part in all our lives; and sentiment is particularly strong in the workman when he believes a direct injustice is being done him.[16]

Near the conclusion of *The Principles of Scientific Management*, he says that scientific management may be summarized as:

Science, not rule of thumb.

Harmony, not discord.

Cooperation, not individualism.

Maximum output, in place of restricted output.

The development of each man to his greatest efficiency and prosperity.[17]

Before Taylor, it was commonly believed, and axiomatic

to economists, that more production could be obtained only through harder work. Taylor proved otherwise. It was, as Drucker notes:

> Frederick W. Taylor did what no one had even thought of before: he treated manual work as something deserving study and analysis. Taylor showed that the real potential for increased output was to "work smarter." It was Taylor who defeated Marx and Marxism. Taylor's *Principles of Scientific Management* not only tremendously increased output. It made possible increasing workers' wages while at the same time cutting the product's prices and thereby increasing the demand for it. . . . Without Taylor, the number of industrial workers would still have grown fast, but they would have been Marx's exploited proletarians. Instead, the larger the number of blue-collar workers who went into the plants, the more they became "middle class" and "bourgeois" in their incomes and their standard of living. And the more they turned conservative in their lifestyles and their values rather than becoming Marx's revolutionaries.[18]

Taylor offered the world a better way to live through improved productivity, but he presented his ideas to the industrial world as a medicine instead of a candy—he may not have been the best salesperson for the philosophy. He was often arrogant, somewhat caustic, and inflexible in how his system should be implemented. A more reserved approach may have brought better results. It may have been style not substance which held back the Taylor philosophy. Taylor was cerebral; like a machine he was polished and he was also intellectual. The world, however, is emotional, and intellect and emotion do not often mix well. Taylor's brilliant reasoning was marred when he attempted to articulate it, for his delivery was often demeaning, even derogatory at times.

Despite the facts and myths which surround Taylor, it is important to recognize the benefits of the philosophy of scientific management for current problem solving and the potential it still offers the future. Edwin Locke in an evaluation of Taylor's work concludes:

> with respect to the uses of a scientific approach to management . . . Taylor's views not only were essentially correct but they

have been well accepted by management. . . . (His) track record is remarkable. The point is not, as is often claimed, that he was "right in the context of his time" but is now outdated, but that most of his insights are still valid today.[19]

Taylor's work is valid today, even in knowledge work, which also requires task study and task management. We agree with Peter Drucker's conclusion:

> The need today is neither to bury Taylor nor to praise him. It is to learn from him. The need is to do for knowledge work and knowledge worker what Taylor, beginning almost a century ago, did for manual work and manual worker.[20]

NOTES

1. Gilbreth, 1911, p. 94.
2. Nelson, 1975, p. 460.
3. Wood, 1989, pp. 71–72.
4. Drucker, 1979, p. 255.
5. Taylor, 1911, p. 10.
6. Taylor, 1911, p. 139.
7. Siddiqi, 1980, pp. 5, 6, 8.
8. Siddiqi, 1980, p. 23.
9. Siddiqi, 1980, pp. 23–24.
10. Testimony, p. 1461.
11. Drucker, 1976, p. 26.
12. Drucker, 1954, pp. 282–83.
13. Drucker, 1974, p. 202.
14. Drucker, 1954, p. 284.
15. Taylor, *Shop Management*, 1911, p. 22.
16. Taylor, 1911, pp. 79–80.
17. Taylor, 1911, *Principles*, p. 140.
18. Drucker, *The New Realities*, 1989, pp. 188–89.
19. Locke, 1982, pp. 22–23.
20. Drucker, 1976, p. 27.

REFERENCES

Alford, Leon Pratt. *Henry Laurence Gantt: Leader in Industry*. New York: American Society of Mechanical Engineers, 1934.

American Cricketeer. Philadelphia, Germantown Cricket Club and Young American Cricket Club, 1877–1902.

Atlas of the County of Montgomery, State of Pennsylvania, 1871.

Augustine, S. "As We Were." *Clothcraft* IV, no. 4 (March 1924), p. 4.

Baker, Ray Stannard. "Frederick W. Taylor—Scientist in Business Management." *American Magazine* 71, (March 1911), pp. 564–70.

Barth, Carl G. "Report on the Fixing of Rates for Loading Pig-Iron by Half Pigs on Buggies in the Yards." South Bethlehem, Pennsylvania, May 29, 1900, Taylor Bethlehem Book #1, pp. 82–84.

Barth, Carl G. "Report on Time Observations on a Cycle of Observations." South Bethlehem, Pennsylvania, May 31, 1900, Taylor Book #1, pp. 90–91.

Barth, Carl G. "Slide Rules for the Machine Shop as Part of the Taylor System of Management." *ASME Transactions* 25, (1903).

Barth, Carl G. "First Comprehensive Diagram of a Taylor System of Organization, About 1908." Chart 179A, Barth Collection, Harvard University Graduate School of Business Administration.

Barth, J. Christian. Interview by C. D. Wrege, November 10, 1960.

Bethlehem Steel v. *Niles-Bement-Pond Company*, United States Circuit Court, District of New Jersey, Case 4641, 1906–09, United States Army Records Center, Bayonne, New Jersey.

Bethlehem Steel Company v. *Niles-Bement-Pond Company, Federal Reporter*, 166, 1909, pp.880–99. Testimony from this case filed under witnesses Frederick W. Taylor (1906), Maunsel White (1906), John Hay (1906), F. Warfield (1907), George Keim (1907), Oliver Kenyun (1907), and Charles Halcomb (1908).

Bjork, Kenneth. *SAGA in Steel and Concrete: Norwegian Engineers in America*. Northfield, Minnesota: Norwegian-American Historical Association, 1947.

The Bolt. Stevens Institute of Technology, 1883.

Brandeis, Louis D. *Scientific Management and the Railroads*. New York: Engineering Magazine Company, 1911.

Brinley, C. A. *Russell W. Davenport*. New York: G. P. Putnam's Sons, 1905.

Brinley, C. A. Letters 1873–80, Howard G. Meyers, Jr. papers.

Bromer, John A.; J. Myron Johnson; and Richard P. Widdicombe. "A Conversation with Robert P. A. Taylor." Hoboken, New Jersey: The Stevens Institute of Technology, 1978 (unpublished manuscript).

Bulletin of the Phillips Exeter Academy XI, no. 1 (April 1915).

Butcher, William, Jr., and Annie Butcher to the William Butcher Steel Works, August 20, 1867, *JTO Deed Book 146*, pp. 305–08, City of Philadelphia.

Califf, Joseph M. "The Development of the Modern High-Powered Rifled Cannon." *The Railroad and Engineering Journal* LXII no. 4 (April 1889), pp.159–61; no. 5 (May 1889), pp.207–08; no. 6 (June 1889), pp.257–59; no. 7 (July 1889), pp. 320–22; no. 8 (August 1889), pp. 360–63; no. 9 (September 1889), pp 401–3; no. 10 (October 1889), pp.453–55.

Combination Atlas Map of Montgomery County, Pennsylvania. Published by J. D. Scott in 1877.

Cary, Ernestine Gilbreth. Personal correspondence to R. Greenwood, December 18, 1989.

Chambers, Peter. "Frederick Winslow Taylor: A Much-Maligned Management Pioneer." *Management Review*, February 1973, pp. 62–64.

Chen, Rita S., and Sheng-Der Pan. "Frederick Winslow Taylor's Contributions to Accounting." *Accounting Historian's Journal* 7, no. 1 (Spring 1980), pp. 17–35.

Chomienne, C. "Notes on Steam Hammers. *The Railroad and Engineering Journal* LXII, no. 6 (June 1888), pp.254–57; no. 7 (July 1888), pp. 301–7; no. 8 (August 1888), pp. 350–56; no. 9 (September

1888), pp .403–7; no. 10 (October 1888), pp .455–58; no. 11 (November 1888), pp. 500–4; no. 12 (December 1888), pp. 546–50. Volume LXIII, no. 1 (January 1889), pp. 26–31; no. 2 (February 1889), pp. 60–66; no. 3 (March 1889), pp. 124–27; no. 4 (April 1889), pp. 162–67; no. 5 (May 1889), pp. 219–22; no. 6 (June 1889), pp. 261–65; no. 7 (July 1889), pp. 323–25; no. 8 (August 1889), pp. 353–57; no. 9 (September 1889), pp. 406–7.

"Clarence Munroe Clark." *National Cyclopaedia of American Biography*. vol. 34, p. 502.

Cleveland Plain Dealer, May 25, 1921.

Condit, K. H. "Management Methods and Principles of Frank B. Gilbreth, Inc." *American Machinist* 38, no. 1 (January 4, 1923), pp. 33–35.

Cooke, Morris L., and Philip Murray. *Organized Labor and Production: Next Steps in Industrial Democracy*. New York: Harper & Brothers, 1940.

Copley, Frank Barkley. "Frederick W. Taylor Revolutionist." privately printed 1916, Philadelphia: Frederick W. Taylor Cooperators, reprinted from *Outlook*, September 1, 1915.

Copley, Frank B. *Frederick W. Taylor: Father of Scientific Management* (2 vols.). New York: Harper and Brothers, 1923.

Copley, Frank B. "Taylor and Trade Unions," in *Bulletin of The Taylor Society*, August 1925.

Correspondence and Reports Concerning Frederick W. Taylor, arranged chronologically. This material is found in five collections: The Frederick W. Taylor Collection at Stevens Institute of Technology, Hoboken, New Jersey; the History of Management Theory Collections at The Labor-Management Documentation Center, Cornell University; The Morris L. Cooke papers at Franklin D. Roosevelt Library; The Manufacturing Investment Company papers at The Consolidated Papers Company, Appleton, Wisconsin; and the William C. Whitney papers in The Library of Congress. Frederick W. Taylor is cited as *FWT* in this listing.

   1. *The Frederick W. Taylor Collection at Stevens Institute of Technology, Hoboken, New Jersey*:
     a. Correspondence:
      George Simonds to FWT, August 16, 1889.
      Edward Sawyer to FWT, April 25, 1890.
      George Simonds to FWT, August 16, 1890.
      George Simonds to FWT, August 20, 1890.
      FWT to George Simonds, September 2, 1890.

FWT to Edward Sawyer, June 30, 1891.
Chauncey Smith to FWT, November 9, 1892.
FWT to Chauncey Smith, December 28, 1892.
Edward Sawyer to FWT, February 27, 1893.
FWT to Chauncey Smith, May 1, 1893.
FWT to George Hammond, May 18, 1893.
Chauncey Smith to FWT, June 6, 1893.
William D. Basley to FWT, July 12, 1893.
FWT to George Hammond, August 4, 1893.
FWT to Chauncey Smith, August 4, 1893.
FWT to Edward Sawyer, August 4, 1893.
FWT to Chauncey Smith, August 18, 1893.
FWT to Edward Sawyer, August 18, 1893.
FWT to George Hammond, August 25, 1893.
FWT to George Weymouth, April 20, 1895.
H. Shadbolt to FWT, September 22, 1895.
H. Shadbolt to FWT, November 13, 1895.
Newcomb Carlton to FWT, November 22, 1895.
FWT to Arthur Moxham, February 21, 1896.
Alfred Bowditch to FWT, February 25, 1896.
FWT to Alfred Bowditch, March 2, 1896.
FWT to Herbert Pratt, March 12, 1896.
FWT to Alfred Bowditch, March 24, 1896.
FWT to Casper Goodrich, June 3, 1896.
FWT to O. A. Fox, October 22, 1896.
Alfred Bowditch to FWT, December 11, 1896.
George Weymouth to FWT, March 18, 1897.
George Hathorn to FWT, April 19, 1897.
Russell W. Davenport to FWT, November 22, 1897.
FWT to George Hathorn, December 18, 1897.
FWT to Robert Linderman, January 3, 1898.
FWT to Robert Linderman, January 7, 1898.
FWT to Robert Linderman, January 8, 1898.
FWT to Robert Linderman, May 1898.
Sanford Thompson to FWT, June 8, 1898.
Sanford Thompson to FWT, June 24–27, 1898.
FWT to Sanford Thompson, April 3, 1899.
R. R. Haydock to FWT, June 23, 1903.
Horace King Hathaway to FWT, January 20, 1906.
FWT to David Van Alstyne, December 27, 1906.

Morris L. Cooke to FWT, June 23, 1907.

Morris L. Cooke to FWT, October 7, 1907.

Morris L. Cooke to FWT, November 11, 1907.

FWT to Morris L. Cooke, November 15, 1907.

Morris L. Cooke to FWT, March 26, 1908.

Morris L. Cooke to FWT, August 9, 1908.

Morris L. Cooke to FWT, March 1, 1909.

Morris L. Cooke to FWT, September 1, 1909.

Morris L. Cooke to FWT, September 13, 1909.

Morris L. Cooke to FWT (undated), internal evidence indicates it was written in October–November, 1909.

FWT to Morris L. Cooke, January 7, 1910.

FWT to Calvin Rice, January 14, 1910.

FWT to Morris L. Cooke, January 17, 1910.

FWT to Morris L. Cooke, December 2, 1910.

FWT to Morris L. Cooke, December 10, 1910.

Morris L. Cooke to FWT, February 25, 1911.

Horace King Hathaway to Morris L. Cooke, January 21, 1914.

Richard A. Feiss to FWT, March 13, 1914.

Richard A. Feiss to FWT, March 21, 1914.

H. K. Hathaway to FWT, May 16, 1914.

FWT to Lionel S. Marks, August 29, 1914.

FWT to C. Bertrand Thompson, December 30, 1914.

FWT to James Mapes Dodge, February 25, 1915.

William Fannon to F. Mitchell, April 21, 1916.

b. Reports and Papers:

"Bookkeeping under the Taylor System," n.d., Scrapbook 3, pp. 28–67.

"Bookkeeping under the Taylor System," n.d. (carbon copy), 40 pp.

"Miscellaneous Bookkeeping Forms," F. W. Taylor, n.d., Scrapbook 3.

"Cost of Emptying and Filling a Digester," November 7, 1892.

Taylor–Thompson Contract, 1895.

"Affidavit," E. A. Kendall, December 4, 1895.

"Report to William Cramp & Sons, Ship and Engine Building Co., Philadelphia, March 12, 1895, filed under "Clients."

"Miscellaneous" notes, January 14, 1910, filed under "Books and Papers: Original Works" for Principles of Scientific Management.

"Notes" dated "February 8" (1910), under "Books and Papers."

"Report of conversation by and questions put to Mr. F. W. Taylor, Chestnut Hill, June 4, 1907.

"Report on Progress Made in Manufacture of the Simonds Rolling Machine Company, July 1, 1907.

"Memorial Papers, Casper Goodrich," 1915.

"Robert P. A. Taylor, A Conversation with," interviewed by John A. Bromer, J. Myron Johnson, and Richard P. Widdicombe, October 14, 15, 1976 (copy dated July 1978).

2. *History of Management Theory Collections at the Labor-Management Documentation Center, Cornell University, Ithaca, New York*:

a. Frederick W. Taylor Correspondence:

Carl Barth, "Introduction," Notebook No. 1.

FWT to Sanford Thompson, August 3, 1893.

FWT to Sanford Thompson, January 8, 1896.

FWT to Sanford Thompson, January 9, 1896.

FWT to Sanford Thompson, January 12, 1896.

FWT to Sanford Thompson, January 13, 1896.

Sanford Thompson to FWT, February 10, 1896.

Sanford Thompson to FWT, February 14, 1896.

FWT to Sanford Thompson, February 15, 1896.

Sanford Thompson to FWT, February 21, 1896.

FWT to Arthur Moxham, February 21, 1896.

FWT to Sanford Thompson, March 2, 1896.

FWT to Sanford Thompson, March 6, 1896.

Sanford Thompson to FWT, March 19, 1896.

FWT to Sanford Thompson, March 24, 1896.

FWT to Sanford Thompson, October 16, 1896.

FWT to Sanford Thompson, April 3, 1899.

Sanford Thompson to FWT, November 25, 1901.

FWT to Sanford Thompson, January 6, 1902.

FWT to Sanford Thompson, January 12, 1902.

FWT to Sanford Thompson, January 23, 1902.

Sanford Thompson to FWT April 22, 1902.

Sanford Thompson to FWT July 22, 1902.

Sanford Thompson to FWT, August 29, 1902.

FWT to Sanford Thompson, October 29, 1902.

Sanford Thompson to FWT, December 22, 1902.

Sanford Thompson to FWT, February 9, 1903.

FWT to Sanford Thompson, February 16, 1903.

Sanford Thompson to FWT February 26, 1903.

Sanford Thompson to FWT April 7, 1903.

Sanford Thompson to FWT April 9, 1903.

Morris L. Cooke to FWT, June 23, 1907.

Morris L. Cooke to FWT, October 7, 1907.

FWT to Sanford Thompson, December 9, 1907.

FWT to Sanford Thompson, January 13, 1908.

FWT to Scudder Klyce, November 1914.

FWT to Richard Feiss, March 11, 1915, dictated March 9, 1915.

Carl Barth to Sanford Thompson, September 29, 1933.

C. C. Balderston to Richard Feiss, August 2, 1950.

Morris L. Cooke, "Industrial Management," unpublished manuscript, 1907–10.

b. Midvale Steel Company Records:

United States Patent No. 65,339, Thomas Shaw and William Butcher, Jr., for "Improved Machine for Shoting Metals," June 4, 1867. Assignment of Patent No. 65,339 to William Butcher Steel Works, June 25, 1868.

Personnel Chronologies, Midvale Company, 1937.

Comments on Frederick W. Taylor, Midvale Company, 1925.

B. F. Fulky to Charles M. Parker, July 15, 1948.

c. Charles Jefferson Harrah Photographs:

Forty-eight photographs of the Midvale Steel Company, 1880–90.

Copy of Charles Harrah letter to his daughter, Florence Harrah Wood, November 22, 1922.

d. Correspondence:

Howard C. Myers, Jr., papers; Samuel Huston to Richmond, Potts, and Loring, June 24, 1871; July 26, 1871; November 27, 1871; February 20, 1872.

3. *Morris L. Cooke Papers, Franklin D. Roosevelt Library, Hyde Park, New York:*

a. Correspondence:

Winthrop S. Scudder to Morris L. Cooke, July 14, 1919.

Sanford Thompson to Edward W. Clark, July 15, 1919.

Frank B. Copley to Edward W. Clark III, May 13, 1920.

Sanford Thompson to Morris L. Cooke and E. W. Clark III, May 24, 1920.

Herbert R. Gibbs to Edward W. Clark III, March 8, 1922.

Edward W. Clark III to Morris L. Cooke, March 9, 1922.

L. P. Alford to Edward W. Clark III, April 22, 1922.

Edward W. Clark III to Morris L. Cooke, September 17, 1923

Morris L. Cooke to Carl Barth, October 23, 1933.

b. Reports and Papers:

Henry G. Pearson, "Suggestions for Revision of the Life of F. W. Taylor—General" n.d.

Henry G. Pearson, "Report of the Committee on the Biography of Frederick W. Taylor Proposing a Plan for the Completion of Mr. Copley's Work," March 19, 1920.

"General Criticism of Mr. Copley's Manuscript Made by Mrs. Taylor," n.d.

Sanford E. Thompson, "Notes on Conference at Rochester," 1920.

Sanford E. Thompson, "Comments on Taylor Biography" and "Comments on Books," May 16, 1920.

Harlow Person, "Final Memorandum on Manuscript of Copley's 'Taylor'," n.d.

4. *The Manufacturing Investment Company papers at The Consolidated Papers Company Inc., Appleton, Wisconsin*:
"Report on the Relative Cost of the Madison Mill to that of Other Similar Mills," December 19, 1892.

5. *William C. Whitney Papers, The Library of Congress. Washington. D.C.*
William Calhoun to William C. Whitney, October 7, 1885, Green Box no. 1, vol. 3.

Clipping from *Engineering News*, December 21, 1893, on the formation of the Metropolitan Street Railway, Green Box no. I, vol. 3.

Clipping from *Engineering News*, December 27, 1894, on the formation of the Wisconsin Inter-Urban Railroad, Appleton, Wisconsin, and H. D. Smith, Green Box no. 1, vol. 3.

Davis, Ralph Currier. "Frederick W. Taylor and the American Philosophy of Management." *Advanced Management*, December 1959, pp 4–7.

Day, Charles. "The Machine Shop Problem." In *Transactions*, American Society of Mechanical Engineers, vol. 24 (June 1903), pp. 1302–21.

Day, Charles. *Industrial Plants: Their Arrangement and Construction.* New York: The Engineering Magazine Company, 1911.

Day, Charles. *Betterment Reports,* Dodge and Day Company, n.d.

Del Mar, Donald., and Rodger D. Collings. *Classics in Scientific Management: A Book of Readings.* Birmingham, Alabama: University of Alabama Press, 1976.

District Reports (Philadelphia), 1915.

Drucker, Peter F. *The Practice of Management.* New York: Harper and Brothers, 1954.

Drucker, Peter F. *Management: Tasks, Responsibilities, Practices.* New York: Harper & Row, 1974.

Drucker, Peter F. "The Coming Rediscovery of Scientific Management." The *Conference Board Record,* June 1976, pp. 23–27.

Drucker, Peter F. *Adentures of a Bystander.* New York: Harper & Row, 1979.

Drucker, Peter F. "Will Unions Ever Again Be Useful Organs of Society?" *Industrial Week,* March 20, 1989, pp. 17–22.

Drucker, Peter F. *The New Realities.* New York: Harper & Row, 1989.

Drury, Horace B. "A Discussion of How Far Scientific Management Is Coping with Present-Day Industrial Problems and What Is the Outlook for the Future." *Bulletin of the Taylor Society,* November 1916.

Drury, Horace B. *Scientific Management: A History and Criticism.* New York: Columbia University, 1918.

The Eccentric. Stevens Institute of Technology, 1883.

Engineering News 42, no. 16, October 19, 1899.

Feiss, R. A. "Scientific Management Applied to the Steadying of Employment, and Its Effect in an Industrial Establishment." *Annals of the American Academy* LXI (September 1915) pp. 103–11.

Feiss, R. A. "Discussion of Valentine Paper." *Bulletin of the Taylor Society,* January 1916, pp. 14–15 (1916, A).

Feiss, R. A. "Personal Relationship as a Basis of Scientific Management." *Annals of the American Academy* LXV (May 1916), pp. 27–56 (1916, B).

Feiss, R. A. *Personal Relationship in Business Administration.* Boston: Privately printed, 1916 (1916, C).

Feiss, R. A. *A National Labor Policy.* Boston: Privately printed, 1919.

Feiss, R. A. "Price-Slip for Piecework." Patent No. 1,272,243, granted July 9, 1918.

Frederick Winslow Taylor: A Memorial Volume. New York: Taylor Society, 1920 (Hive Press reprint, 1972).

Fry, Louis W. "The Maligned F. W. Taylor: A Reply to His Many Critics." *Academy of Management Review*, July 1976, pp. 124–29.

Gallo, Daniel R., and Frederick A. Kramer. *The Putnam Division.* New York: Quandrant Press, 1981.

Gantt, H. L. *Work, Wages, and Profits.* 2nd ed. New York: Engineering Magazine Co., 1916.

Germantown Historical Society Scrapbook, n.d., 60 pp.

Germantown Independent (newspaper), January 17, 1881; June 2, 1883; August 11, 1883; October 8, 1886.

Gies, Joseph. "Automating the Worker." *Investment Technology* 6, no. 3 (Winter 1991), pp. 56–63.

Gilbreth, Frank B., to S. E. Thompson. Correspondence, January 18, 1897. Letter in possession of R. G. Greenwood.

Gilbreth, Frank B. *Bricklaying System.* New York: The Myron C. Clark Publishing Co., 1909.

Gilbreth, Frank B. *Motion Study: A Method for Increasing the Efficiency of the Workman.* New York: D. Van Nostrand Co., 1911.

Gilbreth, Frank B. *Primer of Scientific Management.* New York: D. Van Nostrand Co., 1912.

Gilbreth, Frank B., and L. M. Gilbreth. *Applied Motion Study.* New York: Sturgis and Walton, 1917.

Gilbreth, Frank B., and L. M. Gilbreth, "An Indictment of Stop-Watch Time Study." *Bulletin of the Taylor Society* VI, no. 3 (June 1921), pp. 100–108.

Gilbreth, Lillian Moller. *The Quest of the One Best Way: A Sketch of the Life of Frank Bunker Gilbreth.* New York: Society of Industrial Engineers, 1925. Note: The date is *not* listed in the book, but it is known when it was published.

Gilbreth, Frank B., Jr. *Time Out for Happiness.* New York: Thomas Y. Crowell Company, 1970.

Gillespie, James, and Harley C. Wolle. "Report on Establishment of Piece Work in Connection with Loading of Pig Iron at the Works of the Bethlehem Iron Company." June 17, 1899. Stevens Institute Collection Scrapbook #6.

Gilson, Mary Barnett. "The Relation of Home Conditions to Industrial Efficiency." *Annals of American Academy* LXV, (May 1916), pp. 277–89.

Gilson, Mary Barnett. "Work of the Employment and Service Department of the Clothcraft Shops." U. S. Bureau of Labor Statistics, Bulletin 227, Washington, D.C., 1917, pp.139–52.

Gilson, Mary Barnett. "Instruction In Garment Making In the Clothcraft Shops." *National Society for Vocational Education*, Bulletin 27, New York, May 1918, pp.81–85.

Gilson, Mary Barnett. *What's Past Is Prologue*. New York: Harper & Brothers, 1940.

Gopsill, James. *Gopsill's Philadelphia City Directory*. Philadelphia, Pennsylvania: James Gopsill, 1867–99.

Hagen, Robert P. "Taylor's Challenge to Management." *SAM Advanced Management Journal* 53, no. 2, (Spring 1988), pp .45–48.

Halsey, F. A. "The Premium of Paying for Labor." Paper CCCXLIX in *Transactions*, American Society of Mechanical Engineers, vol. XII, 1890–91, pp. 755–80.

Hanson, J. W. *Wonders of the Nineteenth Century*. Chicago: W. E. Conkey Company, 1900.

Harrison, Frank E. *The Managerial Decision-Making Process*. Boston: Houghton Mifflin Company, 1975.

"Hay, Suppes Families." *Chester Times*, May 3, 1943.

Hayward, Elizabeth Gardner. *A Classified Guide to the Frederick Winslow Taylor Collection*. Hoboken, New Jersey: Stevens Institute of Technology, 1951.

Hoagland, John H. "Management before Frederick Taylor." *Proceedings of the Academy of Management*, 1955, pp. 19–30.

House Resolution, see "The Taylor and Other Systems of Shop Management.

Hsu, Ti., and Charles D. Wrege. "New Information on Taylor's Pig-Iron Studies: A Quantitative Interpretation." Paper presented at the Annual Meeting of the Academy of Management, Boston, 1984.

Huston, Samuel, to Reverend William McCombs. Montgomery County, Deed Book 166, April 1, 1869.

Industrial Relations, Final Report and Testimony Submitted to Congress by the Commission on Industrial Relations. vol. 1, 64th Congress, 1st Session, Document No. 415 (1914).

The Iron Age, December 21, 1876; June 19, 1882; June 29, 1882; February 23, 1899; and July 2, 1903.

Johnson, J. Myron. "Fred Taylor '83: Giant of Non-Repute." *The Stevens Indicator* 97, no. 2 (Spring 1980), pp.4–8.

Kakar, S. *Frederick Taylor: A Study in Personality and Innovation*. Cambridge, Massachusetts: MIT Press, 1970.

Kent, Robert T. "The Taylor Society Twenty Years Ago." *Bulletin of the Taylor Society* XVII, no. 1, (February 1932).

Kent, Robert T. "A Taylor Society Anniversary: The Taylor Society Twenty Years Ago." *Taylor Society Bulletin* 17, (February 1932), pp. 39–41.

Klaw, Spencer. "Frederick Winslow Taylor: The Messiah of Time and Motion." *American Heritage* 30, no. 5 (August/September 1979), pp. 26–39.

Kovwenhoven, John A. "The Designing of the Eads Bridge." *Technology and Culture*, 1982, pp. 535–568.

Langolis, C. V., and C. Seignobos. *Introduction to the Study of History*. London, U.K.: Frank Cass & Co. LTD., 1966.

Lea, Francis B. *Genealogical and Memorial History of New Jersey*, vol. IV, 1923.

Lea, Francis B. *Genealogical and Memorial History of New Jersey*, vol. IV, 1923.

Lea, John A. *The Gold and Garbage in Management*. Athens, Ohio: Ohio University Press, 1980.

Litterer, Joseph A. "Systematic Management: The Search for Order and Integration." *Business History Review* 35 (Winter 1961), pp. 461–76.

Locke, Edwin A. "The Ideas of Frederick W. Taylor: An Evaluation." *The Academy of Management Review* 7, no. 1 (January 1982), pp. 14–24.

McCleod, John E. *History of the Great Northern Paper Company*. Madison, Maine: Great Northern Paper Company, 1974, unpublished manuscript, University of Maine Archives.

Metcalfe, Henry. "Report to Major S. C. Lyford." November 11, 1880, Special Collections, West Point Military Academy Library.

Metcalfe, Henry. "The Shop-Order System of Accounts." In *Transactions*. American Society of Mechanical Engineers, vol. VII (1885–86), pp. 440–68 plus discussion, pp. 469–88.

Midvale Company, c. 1971, *Midvale Steel: A Brief History of Philadelphia's Oldest Steel Mill*. 3 pp.

Midvale Company, *Midvale: 1867–1942. The Seventy-Fifth Anniversary of the Midvale Company*. 1942, 43 pp.

Midvale Safety Bulletin, January 1927.

Midvale Steel Company of Philadelphia, *Fiftieth Anniversary: 1867–1917*, Philadelphia, 1917.

Montgomery County Federated Historical Society, Montgomery

County. *The Second Hundred Years*. Published by the Montgomery County, Pennsylvania Historical Society, 1983.

Montgomery County Federated Historical Society. *Biographical Annals of Montgomery County*, vol. II, 1904.

Nadworny, Milton J. *Scientific Management and the Unions 1900–1932*. Cambridge, Massachusetts, Harvard University Press, 1955.

Nadworny, Milton J. "Frederick Taylor and Frank Gilbreth: Competition in Scientific Management." *Business History Review* 31, no. 1 (Spring 1957), pp. 23–34.

Nalle, Richard T. *Midvale and Its Pioneers*. New York: Newcomen Society of England, 1948.

Nartowitz, John, to C. D. Wrege, October 1, 1978.

Neck, Chris P., and Arthur G. Bedeian. "Maunsell White III: Louisiana Inventor and Victim of the Matthew Effect." *New Orleans Genesis* XXVII, no. 108 (October 1988), pp. 399–404.

Nelson, Daniel. "Scientific Management in Transition: Frederick W. Taylor at Johnstown, 1896." *Pennsylvania Magazine of History and Biography* XCIX (October 1975), pp. 460–75.

Nelson, Daniel. *Managers and Workers: Origins of the New Factory System in the United States 1889–1920*. Madison, Wisconsin: University of Wisconsin Press, 1975.

Nelson, Daniel. "Taylorism and the Workers at Bethlehem Steel, 1898–1901." *The Pennsylvania Magazine of History and Biography* CI no. 4 (October 1977), pp. 487–505.

Nelson, Daniel. *Frederick W. Taylor and the Rise of Scientific Management*. Madison, Wisconsin: University of Wisconsin Press, 1980.

New York Times, June 22, 1882.

New York Times, June 25, 1882.

New York Times, October 1, 1886.

New York Times, February 8, 1909.

North American, December 27, 1904.

North American, February 12, 1905.

On the Art of Cutting Metals—75 Years Later: A Tribute to F. W. Taylor. New York: The American Society of Mechanical Engineers, 1982.

Outerbridge, Alexander E., and Coleman Sellers, Jr. "William Sellers." The *Journal of the Franklin Institute* CLIX, nos. 949–54 (January–June 1905), pp. 365–81.

Person, Harlow. "The Genius of Frederick W. Taylor." *Advanced Management* X, no. 1 (1945), pp. 2–11.

Person, Harlow. "Frank Barkley Copley: April 17, 1875–January 14, 1941." *Advanced Management* 6, no. 3. (July–September 1941).

Peterson, Peter B. "The Pioneering Efforts of Major General William Crozier (1855–1942) in the Field of Management." *Journal of Management* 25, no. 3 (1989), pp.503–16.

Petersen, Peter B. "Fighting for a Better Navy: An Attempt at Scientific Management (1905–12)." *Journal of Management* 16, no. 1 (1990), pp. 151–66.

Philadelphia Department of Records:

Sarah Alden to Joseph L. Ferrell, file D.H.L., book 52, p.86.

Elizabeth Sheridan to Joseph S. Clark, file W.S.V., book 25, p.47.

Sallie S. Houston to Joseph S. Clark, file W.S.V., book 233, p.273.

Will of Louise M. S. Taylor, Will book, F.S. Number 542, p.258.

Trustees of the University of Pennsylvania to Frederick W. G. Peck, file C.J.P., box 3127, p.368.

Philadelphia & Reading Railroad. *Germantown and Chestnut Hill Branch timetables*, in effect May 24, 1885. Historical Society of Pennsylvania, Reading Company File.

"The Present State of the Art of Industrial Management." In *Transactions*. American Society of Mechanical Engineers, vol. 34 (1912), pp. 1131–1229.

Price, Brian. "Frank and Lillian Gilbreth and the Manufacture and Marketing of Motion Study, 1908–1924." *Business and Economic History*, 2nd series, vol. 18 (1989,) pp. 88–98.

Property Atlas of Montgomery County, Pennsylvania. Published by J. L. Smith in 1893.

Reece, Benjamin. "Management of Forces Engaged in Railway Track Repairs." In *Transactions*. American Society of Civil Engineers, vol. XIII (1884), pp. 396–408.

Rhode, Everett W. Consolidated Paper Inc., Appleton, Wisconsin, correspondence to Charles D. Wrege, May 18, 1981.

Rose, Joshua. (ed.), C. L. Mateaux, *The Wonderland of Work*. New York City: Cassell Publishing Company, 1884.

St. Petersburg Times, January 16, 1941, p. 2.

Schachter, Hindy Lauer. *Frederick Taylor and the Public Administration Community*. Albany, N.Y.: State University of New York Press, 1989.

Scranton, Philip, and Walter Licht. *Work Sights: Industrial Philadelphia, 1890–1950*. Philadelphia: Temple University Press, 1986.

Sears, Richard D. *Fifty Years of Lawn Tennis in the United States*. New York, United States Lawn Tennis Association, 1931.

Siddiqi, Farhana. "Management of Work: The Contribution of F. W. Taylor and other Pioneers to Scientific Management." Ph.D. dissertation, Claremont Graduate School, 1980.

Simon, Herbert A. *The New Science of Decision*. New York: Harper & Row, 1960.

Simonds, George. (Obituary), *Osage City News* and *Boston Transcript*, November 6, 1894; *Boston Globe*, November 7, 1894.

Simonds Rolling Machine Company v. *Hathorn Manufacturing Company*. Pleadings and Evidence, Circuit Court of the United States, District of Maine, No. 487, 1898 (Simonds).

Sinclair, Bruce. *A Centennial History of the American Society of Mechanical Engineers*. Toronto: University of Toronto Press, 1980.

Smith, Oberlin. "Inventory Valuation of Machinery Plant." In *Transactions*. American Society of Mechanical Engineers, vol. VII (1885–86), pp. 433–89, plus discussion, pp. 469–88.

South Bethlehem. *Pennsylvania Globe* 21, no. 125 (May 27, 1898).

Tarbell, Ida M. *All in the Day's Work: An Autobiography*. Boston: G. K. Hall & Co., 1985 (reprint of 1939 Macmillan edition).

Taylor, Frederick W. "The Relative Value of Water-gas and Gas from the Siemens Producer for Melting in Open-Hearth Furnace." In *Transactions*. American Society of Mechanical Engineers, vol. VII (1886), pp. 669–79.

Taylor, Frederick W. "Notes on Belting." Paper DLXVIII in *Transactions*. American Society of Mechanical Engineers, vol. XV (1893–94 meetings), pp. 204–38, plus discussion, pp. 238–59.

Taylor, Frederick W. "A Piece-Rate System, Being a Step Toward Partial Solution of the Labor Problem." Paper no. 647, in *Transactions*. American Society of Mechanical Engineers, vol. XVI (1895), pp. 856–903.

Taylor, Frederick W. to Maunsel White, January 14, 1902.

Taylor, Frederick W. "Shop Management." In *Transactions*. American Society of Mechanical Engineers, vol. XXIV (1903), pp. 1337–1480.

Taylor, Frederick W. "On the Art of Cutting Metals." Paper no. 1119 in *Transactions*. American Society of Mechanical Engineers, vol. 28 (1907, for 1906 meeting), pp. 31–280, plus discussion, pp. 281–350.

Taylor, Frederick W. "The Gospel of Efficiency: The Principles of Scientific Management." *The American Magazine* LXXI, no. 5 (March 1911), pp.570–81; vol. LIXI, no. 6 (April 1911), pp.785–93; vol. LXXI, no. 6 (May 1911), pp.101–13. The series of three articles and the Ray Stannard Baker article are titled as a group, "The Gospel of Efficiency."

Taylor, Frederick W. *The Principles of Scientific Management*. New York: Harper and Brothers, 1911.

Taylor, Frederick W. *The Principles of Scientific Management*. (Special edition for confidential circulation) New York: Harper & Brothers, 1911. (Noted as special edition in references.)

Taylor, Frederick W. "The Principles of Scientific Management." Manuscript, Taylor Collection, Stevens Institute of Technology.

Taylor, Frederick W. *Shop Management*. New York: Harper and Brothers, 1911.

Taylor, Frederick W., and Morris Llewllyn Cooke. *Industrial Management*. Unpublished manuscript 1909. History of Management Theory Collections, Labor-Management Documentation Center, Cornell University.

Taylor, Frederick W., and Sanford E. Thompson. *Concrete Plain and Reinforced*. New York: Wiley and Sons, 1906.

Taylor, Frederick W., and Sanford E. Thompson. *Concrete Costs*. New York: John Wiley & Sons, 1912.

"The Taylor and Other Systems of Shop Management." Hearings before Special Committee of the House of Representatives. House Resolution 90 (1912) 3 vols. (Referenced as House Resolution, 1912).

Towne, Henry R. "The Engineer as an Economist." In *Transactions*. American Society of Mechanical Engineers, vol. VII (1885–86), pp. 428–32, plus discussion, pp. 469–88.

Towne, Henry R. "Gain-Sharing." Paper CCCXLI. In *Transactions*. American Society of Mechanical Engineers, vol. X (1888–89) pp. 600–26.

Tweesdale, Geoffrey. *Sheffield Steel and America*. New York: Cambridge University Press, 1986.

United States Brewers Association Convention, 1868.

Urwick, Lyndall F. "Are the Classics Really Out of Date? A Plea for Semantic Sanity." *Advanced Management Journal*, July 1, 1959.

Urwick, Lyndall F., and William B. Wolf, eds. *The Golden Book of Management: New Expanded Edition*. New York: Amacom, 1984.

Urwick, Lyndall F. *The Life and Work of Frederick Winslow Taylor*. London: Urwick, Orr and Partners, Ltd, 1957.

Welfare Work for Employees in Industrial Establishments in the United States. U. S. Bureau of Labor Statistics, Bulletin 250, Washington, D.C., 1919.

Week, The. newspaper for McDonogh School, Maryland.

Wheelan, Thomas L. "A Forgotten Legacy." *S.A.M. Advanced Management Journal*, January 1973, pp. 60–62.

Whiting, Richard J. "Genealogical Records and Management History." Paper presented to Academy of Management annual meeting, August 15, 1983.

Whiting, Richard J. "John Richards—California Pioneer of Management Thought." *California Management Review* 6, no. 2 (Winter 1963), pp.35–38.

Whiting, Richard J. "Historical Search in Human Relations." *Academy of Management Journal* 7, no. 1 (March 1964), pp. 45–53.

Williams, C. W., to W. B. Wilson. National Archives, Record Group 151, Box 167.

Wood, Robert Chapman. "A Lesson Learned and a Lesson Forgotten." *Forbes,* February 6, 1989.

Wrege, Charles D., and Amedeo G. Perroni. "Taylor's Pig-Tale: A Historical Analysis of Frederick W. Taylor's Pig-Iron Experiments." *Academy of Management Journal* 17, no. 1 (March 1974), pp.6–27.

Wrege, Charles D. "Morris L. Cooke's Unpublished Book, *Industrial Management* (1907), Forgotten Foundation Stone of F. W. Taylor's *Principles of Scientific Management* (1911)." Paper presented at the Academy of Management Convention, New Orleans, Louisiana, 1975.

Wrege, Charles D. "The 'Search for Schmidt,' A Case Study Illustrating Research Methods Available to Management Historians." *Working Paper Series*, Management History Division, Academy of Management, October 1976.

Wrege, Charles D. "Taylor-Thompson" in *N-File Newsletter*, Management History Division, Academy of Management, no. 11, November 1977, p.3.

Wrege, Charles D., and Anne Marie Stotka. *History in Boxes: Discovering the Concealed World of Frederick W. Taylor*, unpublished manuscript.

Wrege, Charles D., and Anne Marie Stotka. "Cooke Creates a Classic: The Story behind F. W. Taylor's Principles of Scientific Management." *Academy of Management Review* 3, no. 4 (October 1978), pp. 736–49.

Wrege, Charles D., and Ronald G. Greenwood. "Discovering the Roots of Taylor's *Shop Management*; Taylor's Secret Six-Year Study at the Building Trades." Proceedings, Midwest Academy of Management, 1981, pp. 417–28.

Wrege, Charles D., and Ronald G. Greenwood. "Origins of Midvale Steel (1866–80): Birthplace of Scientific Management." *Essays in*

Economic and Business History, ed. Edwin J. Pertins, vol. VII, 1989, pp.205–19.

Wrege, Charles D. "Nineteenth Century Origins of 'Bookkeeping Under the Taylor System.' " *Academy of Management Proceedings*, 1983, pp. 100–110.

Wrege, Charles D., and Ronald G. Greenwood. "Frederick W. Taylor and Industrial Espionage: 1895–1897." *Business and Economic History*, 2nd series, vol. 15, 1986, pp.28–32.

Wren, Daniel A. *The Evaluation of Management Thought.* 3rd ed. New York: John Wiley & Sons, 1987.

Yost, Edna. *Frank and Lillian Gilbreth: Partners for Life.* New York: The American Society of Mechanical Engineers, 1949.

INDEX

Other Business One Irwin Titles of Interest to You

SUPERTECH
How America Can Win the Technology Race
Thomas G. Donlan

Insights into the technologies of tomorrow and how laws, regulations, and economic structure either foster or hinder their growth. Features the latest developments of Cray Research, IBM, Apple, Sun, INTEL, and Control Data.

ISBN: 1-55623-371-X $22.95 Published January 1991

PEROT
An Unauthorized Biography
Todd Mason

The first true portrait of the man who has been called America's last folk hero. Discover how H. Ross Perot pulled off one of the shrewdest start-ups ever . . . parlayed it into a billion dollar fortune . . . and is now competing head-to-head with his former company.

ISBN: 1-55623-236-5 $24.95 Published May 1990

VOODOO DEFICITS
Robert Ortner

The former Under Secretary for Economic Affairs and Chief Economist with the Department of Commerce dispels common economic myths about U.S. competitiveness and the true effects of the federal deficit. He offers blueprints for getting this country back on track and maintaining its lead as the world's preeminent industrial power.

ISBN: 1-55623-280-2 $24.95 Published April 1990

THE DISNEY TOUCH
How a Daring Management Team Revived an Entertainment Empire
Ron Grover

A behind-the-scenes account of one of the greatest business turnarounds of the 20th century. Grover shows how Disney mastered the success that other companies only dream about. He sheds light on how CEO Michael Eisner took the company from stagnant earnings to soaring profits.

ISBN: 1-55623-385-X $22.95 Published February 1991

MONEY MADNESS
Strange Manias and Extraordinary Schemes On and Off Wall Street
John M. Waggoner

A fascinating account of America's penchant with money and get-rich-quick schemes. Looks at the often humorous episodes from the past 300 years including The Great North Carolina Gold Rush, George Washington's Canal, and American Express' Salad Oil Daze.

ISBN: 1-55623-290-X $22.95 Published December 1990

SWEET SUCCESS
How NutraSweet Created Billion Dollar Business
Joseph E. McCann

The story of the creation of Aspertame and The NutraSweet corporation. Using exclusive interviews and previously unpublished records, McCann takes readers behind the scenes to reveal how a mature American corporation turned an accidental lab discovery into a billion dollar industry.

ISBN: 1-55623-268-3 $24.95 Published July 1990

Prices Subject to Change Without Notice
Available in bookstores and libraries everywhere.